TOWARDS A THEOLOGY OF CH

This book is a treasure store which I commend happily, and with delight at the excellent timing that has bought it into being at this point in the Church's life.

From the foreword by The Most Revd Justin Welby, Archbishop of Canterbury, UK

These essays offer a timely word of bracing encouragement to a church that has lapsed into forgetful resignation to declining membership; at the same time, they pose a stern implicit challenge to churches that seek to augment their numbers through gimmicks or marketing technologies. These authors remind us that the growth of the church was from the first driven by the explosive power of the word and the work of the Holy Spirit. Our hope for church growth lies in a deeply rooted theological account of what God has done and is doing to establish his eschatological lordship over all creation. This book summons us to remember that we are participants in the scriptural story: 'And the word of God grew, and number of the disciples in Jerusalem increased greatly ...' (Acts 6:7).

Professor Richard B. Hays, George Washington Ivey Professor of New Testament and Dean of the Divinity School, Duke University

The bold claim of this far-reaching set of essays on Church growth is that it is when our understanding of God is small and fearful that we are uneasy about the idea of Church growth. God is the creator of all things, and works towards their fulfilment, and the Church is drawn into this action of God for the world. Christian practices of prayer, sacraments and personal holiness pull us deeper into the missionary heart of God, who loves the world and claims it for himself. It is only as the Church allows itself to be shaped by the God whom we worship that Church growth can become more than pragmatism, and instead be a rejoicing at the work of the God who is the source of all life and hope.

Dr Jane Williams, St Mellitus College, UK

This wonderful collection illuminates and stimulates from many angles. In the light of a robust belief in Christian mission, this collection reflects in Biblical, historical and theological terms on the theme of church growth. Contributors represent a broad ecumenical spectrum and complement each other beautifully. I recommend the book to all theologians, pastors and Christians seeking resources for reflection on the future of the Christian community.

Professor Lewis Ayres, Bede Professor of Catholic and Historical Theology, Durham University and Distinguished Fellow at Notre Dame's Institute for Advanced Study

Concern about church growth and decline is widespread and contentious, yet theological reflection on church growth is scarce. Reflecting on the Bible, dogmatic theology and church history, this book situates the numerical growth of the church within wider Christian theology. Leading international scholars, including Alister McGrath, Benedicta Ward and C. Kavin Rowe, contribute a spectrum of voices from evangelical, charismatic, liberal and anglo-catholic perspectives. All contributors unite around the importance of seeking church growth, provided this is situated within a nuanced theological framework. This book offers a critique of 'decline theology', which has been influential amongst theologians and churches, and which assumes church growth is impossible and/or unnecessary. The contributors provide rich resources from scripture, doctrine and tradition, to underpin action to promote church growth and to stimulate further theological reflection on the subject. The Archbishop of Canterbury provides the foreword.

Ashgate Contemporary Ecclesiology

The field of ecclesiology has grown remarkably in the last decade, and most especially in relation to the study of the contemporary church. Recently, theological attention has turned once more to the nature of the church, its practices and proclivities, and to interpretative readings and understandings on its role, function and ethos in contemporary society.

This new series draws from a range of disciplines and established scholars to further the study of contemporary ecclesiology and publish an important cluster of landmark titles in this field. The Series Editors represent a range of Christian traditions and disciplines, and this reflects the breadth and depth of books developing in the Series. This Ashgate series presents a clear focus on the contemporary situation of churches worldwide, offering an invaluable resource for students, researchers, ministers and other interested readers around the world working or interested in the diverse areas of contemporary ecclesiology and the important changing shape of the church worldwide.

Other titles in this series:

The Wisdom of the Spirit
Gospel, Church and Culture
Edited by Martyn Percy and Pete Ward

Testing Fresh Expressions
Identity and Transformation
John Walker

Mothering as a Metaphor for Ministry
Emma Percy

Towards a Theology of Church Growth

Edited by

DAVID GOODHEW
Cranmer Hall, Durham, UK

ASHGATE

Published by
Ashgate Publishing Limited
Wey Court East
Union Road
Farnham
Surrey, GU9 7PT
England

Ashgate Publishing Company
110 Cherry Street
Suite 3-1
Burlington, VT 05401-3818
USA

www.ashgate.com

British Library Cataloguing in Publication Data
A catalogue record for this book is available from the British Library.

The Library of Congress has cataloged the printed edition as follows:
Towards a theology of church growth / edited by David Goodhew.
pages cm. -- (Ashgate contemporary ecclesiology)
Includes bibliographical references and index.
ISBN 978-1-4724-1399-4 (hardcover) -- ISBN 978-1-4724-1400-7 (paperback) -- ISBN 978-1-4724-1402-1 (epub) -- ISBN 978-1-4724-1401-4 (epdf) 1. Church growth. I. Goodhew, David, 1965- editor.
BV652.25.T67 2015
262--dc23

2014042811

ISBN 9781472413994 (hbk)
ISBN 9781472414007 (pbk)
ISBN 9781472414014 (ebk – PDF)
ISBN 9781472414021 (ebk – ePUB)

Printed in the United Kingdom by Henry Ling Limited,
at the Dorset Press, Dorchester, DT1 1HD

Contents

Notes on Contributors

Dr Mark Bonnington is Fellow in New Testament, St John's College, Durham and Senior Minister of Kings Church, Durham, England. His published work includes: *The Antioch Episode of Galatians in Historical and Cultural Context* (Paternoster, 2003).

Prof Ivor J. Davidson is Professor of Systematic and Historical Theology, University of St Andrews, Scotland. He has published widely in the field of patristics and wrote the widely used *The Birth of the Church: From Jesus to Constantine* (Monarch, 2005).

Dr Dominic Erdozain is Visiting Scholar at the Candler School of Theology, Emory University, Atlanta, USA and Visiting Researcher, Kings College, London. His works include: *The Problem of Pleasure: Sport, Recreation and the Crisis of Victorian Religion* (Boydell Press, 2010). He is currently writing *The Soul of Doubt: The Religious Roots of Unbelief*, for Oxford University Press.

William Glass is a PhD student in Systematic Theology at Southern Methodist University in Dallas. He wrote 'Signa Unitatis: Communion and Scriptural Exegesis in the Thought of Geoffrey Wainwright' (*Pro Ecclesia,* Fall 2013) and is co-author of the forthcoming *Least of the Apostles: Paul of Tarsus and the Shape of Early Christianity* (Pickwick Publications [Wipf and Stock]).

Revd Dr David Goodhew is Director of Ministerial Practice at Cranmer Hall, a theological college which is part of St John's College, Durham. He edited the collection *Church Growth in Britain: 1980 to the Present* (Ashgate, 2012).

Revd Dr David Marshall is Associate Professor of the Practice of Christian-Muslim Relations and Director of the Anglican Episcopal House of Studies at Duke University, North Carolina. His work centres on the relationship of Christianity and Islam. He wrote *God, Muhammad and the Unbelievers: A Qur'anic Study* (Curzon, 1999).

Revd Prof Alister McGrath is Andreas Idreos Professor of Science and Religion at the University of Oxford. He has written widely on both academic and more popular levels and is best known for his *Christian Theology: An Introduction* (5th edn, Wiley-Blackwell, 2010).

Revd Dr Ashley Null is Lecturer at Humboldt University, Berlin and visiting fellow of St Johns College, Durham. His work centres on Thomas Cranmer, notably: *Thomas Cranmer's Doctrine of Repentance* (OUP, 2006).

Prof C. Kavin Rowe is Associate Professor of New Testament at Duke University Divinity School, North Carolina. He is recognised as one of the rising stars of New Testament scholarship, especially for his work on Luke and Acts. He is author of the widely acclaimed *World Upside Down: Reading Acts in the Graeco-Roman Age* (OUP, 2009).

Revd Dr Miranda Threlfall-Holmes is Vicar of Belmont and Pittington, County Durham, England. She has published widely in the field of church history, including the study *Monks and Markets* (OUP, 2005).

Revd Dr Graham Tomlin is Dean of St Mellitus College, London. He has written a detailed study of the theology of the cross and, amongst many other works, *The Provocative Church* (4th edn, SPCK, 2014).

Sr Benedicta Ward is a member of the Anglican Order of Sisters of the Love of God and Reader in the history of early Christian Spirituality at the University of Oxford. She has written a huge range of works on Christian history and spirituality, being best known for her work on the desert fathers and mothers.

Rt Revd Martin Warner is Anglican Bishop of Chichester and has written several books, including *Known to the Senses: Five Days of the Passion* (Moorehouse, 2005).

Foreword

The Most Revd and Rt Hon Justin Welby, Archbishop of Canterbury

It has very often been true in the Church that to say one thing is automatically interpreted as meaning you are denying another. I fear that a book about church growth automatically signals, to some, that the writers are not concerned with the Kingdom of God or with spiritual depth.

David Goodhew and those who have contributed to this excellent book have started, correctly, with the understanding that any commitment to church growth must be entirely divorced from questions about the survival of the Church. This book is essentially about theology and growth, not about the continuance of the Church of England or of any other church. For far too long the very term *growth* has been resisted in some quarters. Rather like the work of cleaning sewers, it was confined to a particular section of people, who might be admired and were certainly useful, even essential, but were never to be envied or imitated. As David comments in his first chapter, the theological foundation for church growth is far more important than issues of survival.

This book is deeply embedded in church history. A long-term perspective on church history demythologises any aspect of a 'golden age' in Christendom. Instead, the reader is drawn back to the face of Christ, who alone is the reason for growing churches. Church growth begins with the fact that God reaches out to us in Jesus Christ. Having found us and captured our horizons, Jesus liberates us into a new world in which we are irresistibly drawn to imitate that reaching-out. Such imitation is defined by the historic truth that we have inherited, based in the Scriptures that testify to Jesus and his call, while it is also shaped by the context of our times.

I suggest that we live in a period that future historians may subsequently describe as 'the second phase' of the current church growth movement. Twenty to thirty years ago when the notion was coined afresh in the modern era, it focused very much on matters of technique. To this day we are too easily tempted to follow some formulae which promise that our church will grow – rather than flying in the passion of love for Christ with every sinew of our being, and noting how the slipstream draws others into relationship with him and with all who belong to him.

The people who have contributed to this volume demonstrate the importance of this second phase of the church growth movement. It focuses on the nature of God himself. Learning from its previous weaknesses, it recognises how growth is as fundamental as worship to the health of every tradition of the Church.

This book is a treasure store which I commend happily, and with delight at the excellent timing that has brought it into being at this point in the Church's life.

Justin Cantuar:
Feast of St Luke – evangelist, physician and
earliest church growth theologian
18 October 2014

Acknowledgements

There are many people who richly deserve thanks for their help in bringing the project to fruition.

First and foremost, the contributors deserve huge thanks for their insights, produced within a tight deadline in the midst of many other demands. Jo Wells contributed to the conference on which this volume was based and all the contributors are grateful to her for that input and numerous other ways in which she has helped this project reach fruition. I, the contributors and all at Ashgate are extremely grateful to Archbishops Justin Welby and John Sentamu for their encouragement and support all the way through this project.

Ant Cooper, junior research fellow of the Centre of Church Growth Research at Cranmer Hall, gave huge amounts of time and effort to organise the conference from which this volume emerged. The contributors, conference attendees and especially myself are deeply in his debt for his diligence, efficiency, IT skills and good humour. I am very grateful to Sue Hobson and Alison Bradshaw and the staff of St John's College for their hard work in bringing the conference to fruition. The Allchurches Trust provided crucial financial support for the conference and I am most grateful to the Trust for its support.

Tavis Bohlinger acted as research assistant in the final stages of production. His careful editing has been of great value. Ellie Bangay, Richard Brand, Bright Onuka, Chris Morgan, Rachel Deigh, Josh Penduck, Mark Wigglesworth and Roger Driver were members of the MA module which provided a perceptive, constructive sounding board for ideas outlined in the introduction and conclusion – although they bear no responsibility for the form which those ideas eventually took. Jenny Moberly, Medi Volpe and Josh Penduck were very helpful and stimulating conversation partners with regard to doctrinal theology.

The staff and students of Cranmer Hall and the Wesley Study Centre in Durham constitute a highly stimulating environment in which to work through the ideas propounded in this book. David Wilkinson, as Principal of St John's College, and Mark Tanner, as warden of Cranmer Hall, Durham, provided crucial support which ensured the project could be completed. I and all at Ashgate owe them a deep debt of thanks.

Sarah Lloyd, the editor from Ashgate who oversaw the production of this volume, has been unfailingly thoughtful, encouraging and wise. David Shervington, Aimée Feenan, Hattie Wilson and Barbara Spender provided crucial help in preparing the manuscript for publication. Sam Saunders, Chris Dobson, Ed Thornton and Malmesbury Abbey made possible the picture which is the cover of the paperback edition. Charlie Mackesy kindly agreed to the reproduction of a photo of his sculpture in Chapter 7. Thank you to you all.

An earlier version of Kavin Rowe's Chapter 4 was published as an article in the journal *Interpretation*. I and the staff of Ashgate are grateful to the editors of Interpretation and to Kavin for their permission to reprint this article in this volume.

My wife, Lindsey, and our children Aidan and Benjamin continued to show commendable patience with a distracted husband and dad during the preparation of this volume. I am immensely grateful to them for this – and much more besides.

David Goodhew
Cranmer Hall, St John's College, Durham

PART I:
Introductory Questions

Chapter 1
Towards a Theology of Church Growth: An Introduction

David Goodhew

Introduction

The drive to grow church congregations numerically has become common amongst denominations, clergy and local churches in recent years. Such concern is becoming ever more urgent amidst significant congregational decline, especially amongst historic churches working in the west such as the Anglican, Methodist, reformed and Roman Catholic churches.[1] However the theological justification for numerical church growth has been little explored by contemporary theologians. Alongside this silence is considerable unease at talk of 'church growth'. Churches and church leaders pondering church growth have, therefore, many questions to face and limited theological resources upon which to draw to answer them.

This volume offers reflection on the Bible, Christian doctrine and church history on the subject of numerical church growth by a range of leading scholars. The scholars come from a wide range of theological traditions – catholic and evangelical, liberal and charismatic – and do not always agree with one another. But they find unanimity in showing the importance and legitimacy of numerical church growth. The volume argues that the numerical growth of the church should be a central concern for churches and individual Christians. But it also seeks to guard against ill-thought-out justifications of church growth which draw less from theology than from pragmatic notions of what constitutes 'success'.

---

[1] A recent assessment of numerical growth and decline can be found in: T. Johnson and B. Grim, *The World's Religions in Figures: An Introduction to International Religious Demography* (Oxford: Wiley-Blackwell, 2013). It should be noted that, outside the west, many churches are seeing marked numerical growth. Within the west, there are substantial pockets of church growth as well as decline. See, for example, P. Brierley, *Capital Growth: What the 2012 London Church Census Reveals* (Tonbridge: ADBC Publishers, 2013).

This chapter introduces *Towards a Theology of Church Growth* in three ways. Its first section, 'Questioning Church Growth', explores the problems and potential of the language of 'church growth'. The second section of this chapter is a summary of the book. If readers lack time to read the whole, they can get a sense of the volume here, but all readers are strongly recommended to read the individual chapters in their entirety. The third section of this chapter is entitled 'Questioning Church Growth in the Context of Late Modernity'. It explores the context in which theology is done in the contemporary west – and how this has encouraged a 'decline theology' in which numerical church growth is seen as impossible and even undesirable. It is central to the argument of this chapter that such 'decline theology' can, and should, go.

Questioning Church Growth

'Church' is a word with a great many meanings. In this debate and in this volume it is taken as referring primarily to local congregations. A discussion of the non-congregational aspects of church growth is beyond the scope of this volume. It remains a truth almost universally acknowledged that the church, so defined, in the modern western world is in decline.[2] There is now considerable empirical evidence to show that this assertion is a serious overstatement. The church in the modern west is declining in many places, but growing in many others.[3] The church outside the west is, mostly, growing.[4] And it is not only academics and journalists who are often pessimistic as to whether churches can grow. Many theologians, church leaders and church members share a similar pessimism.[5]

---

[2] One example offers an illustration. Andrew Marr's *A History of Modern Britain* (London: Pan Macmillan, 2007) is the most widely read modern history of Britain and assumes churches are of minimal significance in contemporary history. For Marr, ecclesial marginality is a given and does not need demonstrating.

[3] T. Karnes and A. Karpathakis, *New York Glory: Religions in the City* (New York: New York University Press, 2001); B. Tah Gwanmesia, *Blessings Under Pressure: The Work of Migrant Churches in the City of Rotterdam* (Rotterdam: SKIN, 2009); D. Goodhew (ed.), *Church Growth in Britain: 1980 to the Present* (Farnham: Ashgate, 2012); Brierley, *Capital Growth*; A. Rogers, *Being Built Together: A Story of New Black majority Churches in the London Borough of Southwark* (London: University of Roehampton, 2013).

[4] See, for example: H. McLeod (ed.), *The Cambridge History of Christianity: vol. 9 World Christianities, c.1914–c.2000* (Cambridge: CUP, 2006).

[5] For examples of such thinking, see: D. Goodhew, 'Towards a Theology of Church Growth: an Introduction' in this volume: 28–32; D. Erdozain, 'New Affections: Church Growth in Britain, 1750–1970' in this volume: 217–20.

In part, this reflects an assumption about the empirical state of churches in the modern west – that their decline is 'inevitable'. But, in significant measure, wariness of numerical church growth has roots in theological assumptions about what the Bible, Christian doctrine and church tradition say.

Any discussion of numerical church growth requires such questioning. Numerical church growth – that is, the numerical growth of local congregations and the multiplication of local congregations – can be questioned as being theologically unnecessary, or even theologically suspect. Is the pursuit of numerical church growth 'arrogant' in a world of many faiths? Is the seeking of numerical church growth a dubious 'proselytism' which should be avoided? Is it Biblically justified, or is the pursuit of the 'kingdom' mainly about something else? Do the key doctrines of the Christian faith – such as the incarnation and the Trinity – primarily focus on things other than numerical growth? Looking across the key movements and figures within the Christian tradition, do they concentrate less on the numerical growth of the church than on other goals, such as societal justice, transcendent worship and mystical prayer?

Such questions have value. Growth in the Christian life is never just about 'bums on seats'. The New Testament is about God's Kingly rule, into which church has to fit – and which is not coterminous with the church. The gospel is incarnate in the small and overlooked as much as in the large and spectacular. And 'church growth' is a wide concept. One influential definition sees growth in the Christian life as a three-fold balance, entailing growth in personal holiness, growth in societal transformation and the numerical growth of church congregations.[6]

This volume assumes the validity of such a definition of church growth but focuses primarily on the issue of the numerical growth of local church congregations. Church growth is more than numerical growth. Hence questioning church growth is a necessary exercise. And the contributors to this volume ask hard questions of the pursuit of the numerical growth of the church. But that does not mean concern for numerical growth is per se illegitimate or unimportant.

Indeed, the phrase 'questioning church growth' can be taken in a different sense. In a context where Christian faith has, in much of the west, been pushed to the margins of elite discourse, this volume argues that to speak of numerical church growth is an act of creative subversion. Talking of church growth

[6] Address by the Most Revd Rowan Williams to General Synod, 23 November 2010, available at http://rowanwilliams.archbishopofcanterbury.org/articles.php/919/archbishops-presidential-address-general-synod-november-2010 accessed 30 October 2013.

creatively questions the priorities and practices of academia, government and media – and it also questions the priorities and practices of theologians, church leaders and congregations. Epistemologically, is the 'tolerance' of the west as 'tolerant' as it assumes, or can it amount to a privileging of particular forms of late modern western rationality? Biblically, does the widespread assumption that 'kingdom' is largely distinct from and superior to 'church' fit the text of the New Testament? How important in the New Testament is the numerical growth of the church? Doctrinally, might seeking the numerical growth of the church chime with key doctrines such as the incarnation, eschatology and pneumatology much more than has been assumed? And might those doctrines be stunted when the numerical growth of the church is treated as unnecessary or even theologically disreputable? Historically, did many key figures in the Christian tradition – from the Celtic saints to St Francis, from Thomas Cranmer to the Wesleys – focus much more on the numerical growth of the church than is currently recognised? So, if we mute the desire of such figures to grow congregations, do we then fail to listen attentively to the Christian traditions these figures and movements embody, imposing on them an agenda of our own?

This volume views with suspicion the suspicion about numerical church growth that is exhibited by many theologians, church leaders and others. It argues that seeking to grow the church numerically, if done responsibly, is epistemologically justified, deeply rooted in the scriptures, a natural outworking of Christian doctrine, and that it is integral to fidelity to Christian tradition across much of church history. And critiquing church growth strategies as mere 'proselytism' ignores the deep incoherence of 'proselytism' as a concept.[7]

If the above is true, seeking the numerical growth of the church is intrinsic to being faithful to Christ. Far from being a theologically disreputable 'bigging yourself up', working to grow the church numerically is good and godly. The numerical growth of local churches is not the only aspect of growth in the Christian life, but it is a central part of growth in the Christian life. Conversely, a theology which sidelines or critiques growing the church numerically needs scrutiny itself. Is such a theology genuinely rooted in Christian scriptures, doctrines and tradition as well as in wider rationality – or is it, in significant measure, conforming to the elite culture of the west which assumes that congregations 'must' shrink in the face of 'inevitable' secularisation? Speaking of

[7] 'Proselytism' when referring to attempts to impose an ideology by force or deception is routinely rejected by people of all ideological positions. But the term 'proselytism' is commonly used to criticise the attempt, *simpliciter*, to persuade anyone to think differently. Such usage is hugely problematic – see: K. Rowe, *World Upside Down; Reading Acts in the Graeco-Roman Age* (Oxford: OUP, 2009): 171, 263–4.

a theology of church growth has the corollary of raising the question of whether there has been a 'theology of decline' which, explicitly and implicitly, runs through the discourse of many modern and late modern theologians, church leaders and congregations – a theology which needs to be questioned.

The word 'towards' in the title of this book needs to be stressed. This volume tries to point towards what a theology of church growth could look like. The volume seeks to take forward a theological conversation, not to be its last word. A fully-fledged theology of church growth needs much further work and some of the questions begged by this volume are sketched in its conclusion. But, since very little theological work has been done in this area (especially in the historic denominations), this volume hopes to provide theological 'straw' to be used towards the wider task of building up church and kingdom.

There is a confessional aim to this volume. The authors come from a wide range of Christian traditions but share a desire to see the church grow – numerically and in other ways. Theology has a material effect, for good or for ill, on Christian churches at local levels. When theologians, church leaders and congregations have lacked a theology of church growth and have internalised a theology of decline, they thereby contributed to the shrinking of the local church. Conversely, if a worked-out theology of church growth can be built, that will significantly facilitate the numerical growth of local churches. Any growth worth having comes from God and is not the work of human hands. But to say that need not lead to a kind of missiological quietism, in which growing churches numerically is seen as an ineffable mystery, about which humans can do nothing. Numerical church growth is the work of God, but humans are meant to contribute to that work. And that contribution includes the work of theology.

Towards a Theology of Church Growth: A Summary

The numerical growth of the church is a subject that receives limited discussion in contemporary theology. The work of Donald McGavran stands out as an exception. It has received significant critique.[8] However it is evaluated, it has had little influence outside the evangelical constituency – and diminishing influence of any kind in recent decades.[9] This volume works through key disciplines within

[8] The objections are summarised in A. Milbank and A. Davidson, *For the Parish; A Critique of Fresh Expressions* (London: SCM Press, 2010): 64–92.

[9] McGavran is referenced briefly, and not uncritically, in recent key missiological texts: the Archbishops' Council, *Mission-Shaped Church: Church Planting and Fresh Expressions of Church in a Changing Context* (London: Church House Publishing, 2004):

theology; epistemology, Biblical studies, doctrine and church history (which might be viewed as Christian experience across time). There are, of course, other theological disciplines which have much to contribute to a theology of church growth. Their exclusion is not a statement as to their importance, but a reflection on constraints of time and space.

Epistemology

There is a widespread concern across western culture that stating that one creed is closer to the truth than another is arrogant and intolerant of other viewpoints. To assert that one creed is true and others at least not quite as true is seen as 'proselytism', the latter being viewed as a dubious activity. David Marshall, in Chapter 2 of this volume, starts with the world outside the boundaries of Christianity, noting that a wide range of ideologies – from atheism to Islam – see no problem in propagating their views and attract no opprobrium for promulgating their respective standpoints. Marshall refers to Muslims who are heavily involved in dialogue with people of other faiths, yet also seek to persuade others of the truth of Islam. This is in marked contrast to Christian circles, often characterised by reserve and anxiety over the legitimacy of proclamation of their faith.[10]

The wariness of saying one creed is 'better' than another stems, in part, from an entirely right desire to seek mutual respect between different belief-systems. However, David Marshall explores how problematic it is to go from this to the assertion that it is 'arrogant' to say that one faith is 'the truth'. The assertion that truth is plural is itself an assertion. An example is the widely influential pluralism of John Hick. Hick claims the need for a 'Copernican revolution' between Christianity and other faiths, whereby Christianity should not claim to be 'the truth' and should recognise that all the faiths are equally valid. Quoting the theologian Gavin D'Costa, Marshall comments:

> ... although Hick argues that both theistic and non-theistic religions are equally salvific in value, "he holds that our final (and therefore presumably true) relation to the 'Real' is one of eternal loving communion with a personalist, all-loving God". That is, although Hick intends to relativize traditional Christian claims about Jesus as determinative revelation of God, he at the same time implicitly maintains

108; M. Moynagh, *Church for Every Context: An Introduction to Theology and Practice* (London: SCM Press, 2012): 168–9, 172.

[10] D. Marshall, 'Dialogue, Proclamation and the Growth of the Church in Pluralist Societies', in Goodhew (ed.), *Towards a Theology*: 37–9.

> a picture of God essentially as revealed in Jesus. Yet it is not at all clear why this should be so. The religions of the world, taken on their own terms, do not all believe in a personalist God who seeks loving communion with all human beings. The Christian understanding of God looks rather unlike what some religious traditions speak of when they use the word "God". Hick at one moment tells us that we can't claim that Christianity gives us a uniquely true account of God, and at the same time he proposes a basically Christian understanding of God, placing that God as the divinity secretly at the heart of the world's religious traditions.[11]

Hick's pluralism claims to be a big tent which includes all possibilities, but, in reality, it only works by forcing diverse ideologies to conform to a distinct faith, different from and standing over all other faiths. Marshall concludes:

> ... to engage a religious tradition wisely requires attention to its own particulars: its own answers to its own questions, within its own universe of meaning. Questions of likeness and difference must not be assumed on the basis of some metaphysical *a priori*. It might be thought that Hick's pluralist theology offers the best possible basis for inter-religious dialogue, but in fact his prior convictions about what religions *are* and what they are *for*, seriously weaken the possibility of respectful and attentive engagement with another religious tradition in all its difference from one's own.[12]

Hick, who is deeply hostile to any idea of 'conversion', is seeking to convert all other faiths to his particular form of pluralism. This chimes with Kavin Rowe's critique of the term 'proselytism', used to describe seeking to persuade another to change their standpoint. Rowe comments that those hostile to 'proselytism' are themselves 'proselytising' their hostility to proselytism.[13]

Using contemporary Roman Catholic and Anglican thinking, Marshall comments that dialogue and proclamation are complementary. Humility and confidence in Christian belief are not opposites, but go together:

> ... dialogue and proclamation are equally necessary and inter-penetrating practices of a Christian engagement with other religious communities, reflecting the humility and the confidence that are both fundamental features of authentic Christianity. This approach recognises that there are salutary challenges in some of

---

[11] Marshall, 'Dialogue, Proclamation and the Growth of the Church': 41–2.

[12] Ibid: 43.

[13] Rowe, *World Upside Down*: 171, 263–4.

> Hick's points, especially where he identifies tendencies to Christian triumphalism and an inability to recognise God's presence and activity beyond the Church; but it resists his conclusion that in order to meet those challenges Christians must radically revise and relativize their understanding of the heart of their faith, the uniqueness and universal relevance of the revelation and the redemption given by God in Jesus Christ.[14]

Marshall's chapter offers a challenge to churches, especially in the west. The challenge is to show a proper humility towards those outside the church, of whatever belief-system, working hard to hear and respect their views. But the challenge is also to show a proper confidence in the Christian gospel. As Marshall shows, proclaiming Christ as Lord and encouraging others to follow Christ is at the heart of the Christian tradition. Anglican Archbishops Rowan Williams and John Sentamu comment:

> ... conversion must never become a word of which Christians fight shy ... there should be nothing embarrassed or awkward about the Church's commitment to draw others to Christ. This we do, not in order to win favour for ourselves, nor to make others more like us, but simply because we want to share God's gifts as we have received them – freely and unearned.[15]

Marshall comments that combining dialogue and proclamation in mission has proved difficult. Newer Christian denominations have, broadly speaking, been more committed to proclamation. In the historic denominations, dialogue has a marked habit of overshadowing proclamation.[16] Marshall's chapter constitutes a challenge to both groups. Those who emphasise proclamation are challenged as to whether they show humility in so doing. But those in the historic churches are challenged as to whether they have internalised the false neutrality of a Hickian 'pluralism' (which is just as much a specific standpoint as any other ideology) and refused to countenance Christianity as good news that needs to be proclaimed.

[14] Marshall, 'Dialogue, Proclamation and the Growth of the Church': 44.

[15] Ibid: 51.

[16] Ibid: 53.

The New Testament and Church Growth

Marshall points to how the New Testament stresses the importance of proclaiming the Christian faith and encouraging others to adhere to it.[17] The following two chapters by Mark Bonnington and C. Kavin Rowe focus on the New Testament.

Bonnington, in Chapter 3, surveys the question of how Jesus' emphasis on the kingdom relates to his followers' emphasis on the foundation of new communities of believers – churches. Surveying over a century of thought on the kingdom-church relationship, Bonnington stresses the centrality of the kingdom in the New Testament, its eschatological nature, the way it is a creation of God not humanity and the way it must not be seen too easily as 'of this world'. The kingdom is present yet also still to come. Jesus' actions as well as his words – and especially his actions by his death on the cross – are central to how the kingdom needs to be understood. This has crucial consequences for how the relationship between kingdom and church should be understood.

> Loisy's famous saying that "Jesus announced the kingdom, but it was the church that came" is a sharp observation but it can now be seen to exaggerate the tension between Jesus and the Church and the kingdom and the cross. Eschatology need be neither so naively imminentist nor so other-worldly that it fails to resist escapism that leaves no room for the kind of constructive engagement in mission and service so clearly evident in the New Testament.[18]

Bonnington emphasises how the kingdom and church complement one another in the New Testament and how questionable is the exegesis which sees them as in opposition. This has crucial implications for ecclesiology, since a church genuinely seeking after the kingdom is eschatological and can never have survival/mission/growth as its ultimate focus

> The discovery of a purposeful and forward thinking church – a teleological church if you like – can never merely have survival/mission/growth* (*delete as appropriate) in its sights as its final goal. To do so is to reduce teleology to missiology rather than eschatology. We may be looking up at the sky at last but we must not mistake the edge of our bunker for the horizon. To do so is to fail to

---

[17] Ibid: 48.

[18] M. Bonnington, 'The Kingdom of God and Church Growth in the New Testament', in Goodhew (ed.), *Towards a Theology*: 65.

> do justice to the bible's vision of the goal of both humanity and the cosmos which worship anticipates and towards which it points.[19]

But a right emphasis on the kingdom has *also* to come to terms with the huge enthusiasm of the first Christians for founding communities of believers, not as a by-product of 'higher' aims, but as essential to the task of following Jesus. 'It cannot be stressed enough that the early Jesus movement did not just make converts, it created communities too.'[20]

Bonnington explores the dynamics of numerical church growth in the New Testament. It was remarkably far-flung – with Christian communities sprouting across the Mediterranean world within a few decades of the ministry of Jesus. The book of Acts shows considerable attentiveness to numbers (as does the New Testament in general). Acts conveys 'a sense that the early Jesus followers felt themselves to be part of a burgeoning movement'.[21] Itinerant leaders criss-crossed the Mediterranean, seeking not merely 'to leave behind converted individuals but to establish communities with a distinct and clear new identity'.[22] The work of growing church enthusiastically adopted the wider culture where the latter facilitated this task – whether it was the good transport networks of Roman trade routes, Greek as a common language, trades that were easily conducted in a range of settings so as to facilitate church-planting or the siting of churches in tightly packed ancient cities, whose population density facilitated conversation about Christ.

Personal conversion, community formation and lifestyle change were intertwined. Proclamation and conversion led people to change their lifestyles – and such change was crucial to the growth of churches, for conversion was a high commitment activity, particularly for gentiles:

> A slave converted and wanted to go out early or late to meet other believers. He made up for it by working harder. A household converted and the household gods disappeared from the corner of the room. The master avoided the temples of the gods but instead invited people to dine with him at his own house. When he did so he omitted the traditional libation to his guild's divinity and instead thanked the God of heaven for the meal. Insider and outsider alike knew something had changed and the reasons why were freely on offer. When this was questioned or opposed, and believers still persisted, the new faith was taken more seriously and

[19] Ibid: 66.
[20] Ibid: 74.
[21] Ibid: 68.
[22] Ibid: 69.

> the reputation of the church grew. Coming up against the authorities the believers made the case for their faith respectfully, accepted protection gladly and carefully kept their theological distance from Roman divinities and power ... The fact that everyone had given up something from their past for the sake of Christ surely created communities where the sense of joint ownership of the new was universal and challenged people to change.[23]

These new communities had accountability to the apostles, but high local autonomy. They were usually small – constrained by the size of the homes in which they met. They grew as small and diverse communities – whose very diversity was itself an expression of the faith proclaimed. 'Churches like this, churches of inclusion and transformation, grew.'[24] Numerical church growth was integral to the New Testament, not some accidental, let alone mistaken, add-on.

In Chapter 4 C. Kavin Rowe explores the ecclesiology of the book of Acts with particular regard to how the new churches related to wider society.[25] He concludes that the ecclesiology of Acts is fundamentally counter-cultural. The churches of Acts are predicated on the effort to share the good news and the experience that that good news is gladly heard, at least by some. How culturally destabilising this was can be seen by looking at the disturbances in Ephesus over the attempt by the apostle Paul to plant a church, detailed in Acts, chapter 19. Opposition was led by Demetrius a silversmith, who saw the new church as a threat to the temple to the goddess Artemis. Rowe comments, regarding Demetrius' charge that Paul was subverting the state:

> Two millennia later, Demetrius' charge may appear somewhat overdone. But as abundant evidence demonstrates, it would be difficult to overestimate the importance of Artemis to Ephesian life. As a 1st-century inscription put it, the temple of Artemis was known as "the jewel of the whole province [of Asia] on account of the grandeur of the edifice, the age of its veneration of the goddess, and the abundance of its revenue". It functioned not only as a "house of worship", but also as the arbiter for regional disputes, a bank, a holding facility for important civic archives, and an asylum for debtors, runaway slaves, and other persons in dire trouble. The temple sent its own representatives to the Olympic Games, was the beneficiary of private estates, had abundant sacred herds, owned considerable real

---

[23] Ibid: 71.

[24] Ibid: 74.

[25] C. Kavin Rowe, 'Acts: Towards an Ecclesiology for Church Growth', in Goodhew (ed.), *Towards a Theology*. This chapter was originally published as 'The Ecclesiology of Acts', in *Interpretation: A Journal of Bible and Theology*, 66 (3), 2012 reproduced with permission.

> estate from which it drew its famous revenue, and so on. In short, as one scholar wrote, Artemis of the Ephesians was "an indispensable pillar in the cultural structures and life of Asia, and was therefore a crucial factor in the lives of all ... whom Christianity hoped to convert".[26]

So early churches were culturally destabilising, but these first Christian communities also sought to support the state where they could. This is apparent later in Acts, in the scene where Paul is on trial in Caesarea. Rowe sums up the episode as showing that the first Christians sought a new way of life, but not a *coup d'etat*. To say that Jesus was Lord was to challenge the existing King in key respects, but not in every respect.

> The culturally destabilising reality of the Christian mission is overlooked, and Christianity becomes a politically innocuous or even irrelevant "spiritual" movement; or the declaration of innocence of sedition is overlooked and Christianity is read as a liberating, overt frontal challenge to the Roman Empire. But, in fact, we should not be forced to choose one side or the other. Indeed, precisely because they are both parts of the same narrative, we should read them together.[27]

Rowe concludes that central to being a Christian is a readiness to adopt a different way of life and count the cost of being culturally destabilising. This is central to the question of a theology of church growth. It was of the essence of the early church to be counter-cultural and central to how it destabilised ancient culture was the way early Christianity sought the numerical growth and proliferation of churches. This was not hostility to ancient culture. It was an expression of creative subversion. Valuing and seeking numerical church growth in the present is to be similarly counter-cultural in a western world where attempting to live under the Lordship of Jesus is (always was?) to go against the grain. Conversely, redefining Christianity so that the numerical growth of the church is unnecessary, or even dubious, needs questioning. Late modern wariness of, or scepticism towards, numerical church growth has some merit, but it could simply be fitting in with the spirit of the age, which only accepts faith as long as it operates within the confines of the wider 'sacred canopy' of the secularisation theory.

---

[26] Ibid: 79.

[27] Ibid: 85.

Doctrine and Church Growth

Turning to key doctrines of the Christian faith, they have much to say with regard to the nature and value of numerical church growth. In Chapter 5 Alister McGrath stresses that doctrines provide a 'big picture', which acts as a vital frame for theological thought. That overarching narrative helps churches avoid slipping into mere pragmatism. Concern for numerical church growth has an obvious pragmatic motivation. It is no accident that the numerical decline of many churches has been the precursor to their concern for church growth. Therefore, attention to key doctrines of the Christian faith is essential for right thinking about numerical church growth. This 'big picture':

> discloses a glorious, loving and righteous God, who creates a world that goes wrong, and then acts graciously and wondrously in order to renew and redirect it, before finally bringing it to its fulfilment. And we ourselves are an integral part of this story, which discloses our true purpose, meaning and value – who we really are, what is really wrong, what God proposes to do about this, and what we must do in response.[28]

In chapters 5, 6 and 7 of this volume Alister McGrath examines eschatology, Bishop Martin Warner examines the incarnation and Graham Tomlin looks at pneumatology. Other key doctrines – such as the atonement and creation – greatly deserve examination, but constraints of space make that impossible in this volume.

McGrath starts with the 'seed' of the basic Christian gospel and stresses that the basic gospel is good. Developing that biological metaphor, 'it might reasonably be suggested that an innate capacity to grow is built into the genetic profile of the Christian faith'.[29] Since the 'seed' of the Christian gospel is good already, it doesn't need adapting in order to be made good enough to connect with 'contemporary culture'. 'The churches' task is fundamentally to exhibit and communicate the goodness of the seed, not to alter it in the light of transient cultural trends.'[30] But attention does need to be given to breaking up the ground in which that seed falls – we need 'deep church' which requires great attentiveness both to the Christian tradition in all its fullness and to the translation of the

---

[28] A. McGrath, 'Theology, Eschatology and Church Growth', in Goodhew (ed.), *Towards a Theology*: 95.

[29] Ibid: 97.

[30] Ibid: 98.

faith into the particular context of a particular community. McGrath quotes the comment of C.S. Lewis that:

> We must learn the language of our audience. And let me say at the outset that it is no use at all laying down *a priori* what the "plain man" does or does not understand. You have to find out by experience ... You must translate every bit of your Theology into the vernacular.[31]

In eschatology, that attentiveness to the present is coupled with 'the long view':

> An eschatological perspective challenges the privileging of the present, forcing us to realize the transiency of our culture. We have to take the long view – thinking in terms of centuries, not years. None of us sees the "big picture", which allows us to grasp the significance of our present moment in the greater scheme of things.[32]

Focus on eschatology paradoxically makes us focus on the small – since we cannot see the end of all things and cannot say whether what appear to us to be insuperable obstacles may, in coming decades, be overcome. The local and parochial become crucial since that is the one place we can immediately touch, 'trying to understand how to proclaim and embody the gospel in this specific place that has been entrusted to us'.[33]

McGrath critiques world denying eschatologies which assume a decaying world from which God will rescue the faithful, advocating N.T. Wright's notion of a collaborative eschatology, in which the end times have been inaugurated by God in the cross and resurrection of Christ and where Christians and churches are called to collaborate in God's transformation of the present.

> We are not to see ourselves as cogs in an impersonal machine, or as extras in a movie that has already been shot and whose outcome is predetermined. Rather, our stories are taken up within the overall story of God's purposes and intentions, so that our story thus becomes part of this greater story without ceasing to be our own story.[34]

Eschatology thus frames the work of numerical church growth. It shows that the growth of the church is God's work, that it is a work we are called to

---

31 Quoted in McGrath, 'Theology, Eschatology and Church Growth': 99.

32 Ibid: 101.

33 Ibid: 103.

34 Ibid. 106.

collaborate in, but a work whose final end is not ours to determine. Thinking eschatologically inoculates Christians against a pragmatism that assumes church growth is a matter of getting the right technique and against a defeatism that assumes that there is nothing humans can do in the matter.

A more specifically eschatological perspective enables the church to see the struggles and perplexities of the present age in a new way, enabling us to work for growth, not as an act of cultural defiance, but as an act of faithful obedience, grounded in the future hope inaugurated through the resurrection of Christ.

Martin Warner, in Chapter 6, focuses on the importance of the incarnation in thinking about church growth, the incarnation being 'the archetype of Church growth'. The incarnation ensures that any talk of church growth is 'always about Jesus. He is our constant point of reference. He is, uniquely, the way to the Father, the one to whom the Spirit leads, the revelation of our true identity'. And a focus on Christ means a focus on numbers, since Jesus calls his followers to 'make disciples of all nations'.[35] However, since Christ came out of love for the whole world and came to serve the world, such concern for numbers is kept from slipping into a desire for power. This has direct implications for Christian apologetics, which, unless they communicate love and service, are useless – whatever cognitive truth they contain.

> Our strategy for growth, inspired by Jesus Christ, is based on love ... It is well expressed by Pope Paul VI in his 1957 call to love the modern world: "Let us love and try to understand, esteem, appreciate, serve it and suffer for it. Let us love it with the heart of Christ."[36]

Warner concludes that the way forward is through an emphasis on Christian anthropology, which seeks a common humanity, out of which faith can connect with those who have no faith. Drawing on a range of patristic sources, Warner stresses that doctrines of creation and incarnation have a very high view of human potential:

> Imaging redemption in all its phases of history is what the human person is capable of by God's intent. This anthropological statement about a capacity marks the human as different from the animal species; it is a statement about our

[35] M. Warner, 'Incarnation and Church Growth', in Goodhew (ed.), *Towards a Theology*: 108.

[36] Ibid: 112.

> spiritual capacity that also gives content to how we understand the image of God within us.[37]

Human imagination is warped, but the incarnation of Christ, by making God visible and touchable, breaks through that barrier:

> When the Word is still invisible, our self-understanding of the image of God within is so weakened that it is easily lost. This is a description of a people with a pitifully weakened and impoverished imagination. But of itself, the vision of the Word made flesh reconfigures our very minds and nature so as to re-establish our identity.[38]

Consequently, the growing of the church depends in substantial part on the use of the imagination and on non-verbal as well as verbal forms of communication. This can be seen through great art and historic church buildings, but it can also be seen across culture:

> Look, for example, at the Hillsong website. The images are a profoundly anthropological meditation on the theological quality of communion, *koinonia*, in Greek. Imagery is used very provocatively as an apologetic for the self-understanding of this Church which is "about God and people".[39]

This speaks powerfully into a western world in which more and more people live alone.

The imaginative vision, at best, looks beyond the purely human and moves towards that vision which Christians call worship. For Warner, the summit of Christian worship is the eucharist.

> The work of worship is, ultimately, the work of God in which we are given the privilege of doing service. Our service is the offering of life in sacrifice, motivated by love of God ... This is the point at which we conform ourselves to the sacrifice of Jesus Christ in the great act of giving thanks, the Eucharist.[40]

---

37 Ibid: 115.
38 Ibid.
39 Ibid: 121.
40 Ibid: 122–3.

But the eucharist, in turn, 'is about the formation of the Church'.[41] The church is a worked example of Christian apologetics – an argument enfleshed. For Warner, a eucharistic vision of the growth of the church integrates church growth which is numerical with church growth which is relational (i.e., growth in relationship with God and with fellow believers and with wider society and with the earth). And all such growth is rooted in gazing upon Christ, who shows people what God wants them to become.

In Chapter 7 Graham Tomlin unlocks a different, equally crucial, area of doctrine – pneumatology. Tomlin notes how it is a Christian tradition which stresses the importance of the Holy Spirit – Pentecostalism – that has seen the most vigorous numerical growth in the modern era. In saying this, Tomlin both commends the importance of a full-blooded pneumatology, but is also alert to the ways in which Pentecostal theology is susceptible to an idolatrous assumption that the Spirit is capable of being controlled by humans.

Tomlin sees the tension in viewing the Holy Spirit as free from human control, yet given freely by God, as akin to the tension between seeing church growth as in the hands of God, yet requiring committed human effort if it is to come to pass. For Tomlin, the practice of invocation of the Holy Spirit is the key way of managing this tension. By asking continually for the Holy Spirit we have access to him, yet the fact that we have to ask reflects how we cannot ever control him.

> This practice of invocation of the Spirit has helped the church avoid two equally dangerous forms of presumption: blithely taking for granted the presence of the Spirit, or acting as if the Spirit was not necessary and that we can do it all ourselves.[42]

Tomlin stresses the 'connectional' role of the Holy Spirit in connecting people to God in Christ. But he also stresses that suffering is intrinsic to such a ministry. Any pneumatology has to be a *pneumatologia crucis*. This is the crucial underpinning for mission. Mission, including the numerical growing of the 'successful' church, is rooted in suffering and the cross, rather than in neo-liberal paradigms of what constitutes 'success'.

> Theologically speaking, mission and the consequent growth of the church begin with the begetting of the Son and the procession of the Spirit from the Father. It

[41] Ibid: 123.

[42] G. Tomlin, 'The Prodigal Spirit and Church Growth', in Goodhew (ed.), *Towards a Theology*: 131.

> starts with the Trinitarian life of God before it ever involves the creation, let alone the human part of that creation.[43]

Stress on the Holy Spirit enables a synthesis of the different ways in which the church is called to grow – since the Holy Spirit is crucial as the divine agency which grows people by maturing them and by healing them. Yet it is also the octane for numerical church growth. It is the propulsive force behind the 'third sending' (the first two being the sending of the Son and of the Holy Spirit), which is the sending of the church to bring people back to their true calling and this happens in the church.

> That is why church growth matters. Healthy well-functioning churches are places where people can be restored and become agents of change and renewal within the world beyond the church. The reason we need churches to grow is not to pay the bills, or to feel good about ourselves. It is to enable humanity, in tune with the Spirit of God, to fulfil its divine calling to care for and nurture the world which God has created.[44]

The growth of Pentecostalism (both as a denomination and as it has been absorbed by other churches) is partially linked to that tradition's frequent invocation of the Holy Spirit. And to say this is to challenge many other churches as to whether their tendency to shrink may be linked to their less frequent invocation of the Holy Spirit and general tendency to downplay the third person of the Trinity.[45] However, whilst there is much that the historic churches can learn from Pentecostalism, there are also areas where the Pentecostal and charismatic traditions need challenge – notably in the acquisition of a more cross-shaped pneumatology and a greater accent on character. All churches, of whatever flavour, need continually to invoke the Holy Spirit if they wish to grow – numerically and in other ways.

---

[43] Ibid: 136.

[44] Ibid: 141.

[45] Western Christianity in recent decades has critiqued earlier epochs for their downplaying of the Holy Spirit. However, it may be questioned whether modern western Christianity has yet arrived at a truly robust pneumatology.

Church Growth across the History of the Church

The history of Christianity is a key resource for theology, rooting theology in the lived experience of faith. As such it is a key resource for any theology of church growth and chapters eight onwards tap into diverse strands of church history.

In Chapter 8 Ivor Davidson links the New Testament and the first centuries of the church to show the commitment of early Christians to growing the church and how Christian actions and proclamation intertwined. Davidson shows how, in the common culture made possible by imperial Rome, churches proliferated across a huge area. The idea that connectedness is a modern phenomenon is a myth. And churches grew and proliferated in number because of the agency of the many rather than that of the few:

> ... there is little doubt that the Christian message had spread from the earliest not just through the work of "official" servants of the gospel: it was disseminated in great measure by the activities of ordinary people, both in their everyday social contexts and as they travelled. Ancient society was often remarkably mobile, the vast geographical expanse of imperial territory being connected by road networks of a calibre that would not be bettered until the nineteenth century, with plenty of opportunities for passengers to book passage on commercial ships. People moved around for all kinds of reasons – as traders and artisans, as soldiers and slaves, as economic migrants and refugees. Their faith travelled with them, "gossiped" in everyday forms. Christian communities came to be remarkably well connected from early on, with most believers in the first century living no more than a few days' travel from one of the church's major hubs.[46]

Growing churches numerically was integral to early Christianity: 'A desire for numerical expansion was natural to the logic of Christian confession,'[47] often fuelled by eschatological hope and persecution.

Exact numbers are hard to estimate, but appear to have been relatively small until the third century, and showed marked regional variation. There are scholarly debates about the precise boundaries of faith – about what was and was not 'church'. But to say that the precise line between, for example, 'gnosticism' and 'orthodoxy' was still being worked out is not to say that all was blurred. In the highly plural religious culture of *pax Romana* Christianity was not just 'another

---

[46] I. Davidson, 'Church Growth in the Early Church', in Goodhew (ed.), *Towards a Theology*: 147.

[47] Ibid: 148.

new god' in a culture which supported many new deities; 'the gospel brought an entirely new social and conceptual system'.[48] Christianity was markedly different from other new faiths in that it sought conversion (unlike pagan polytheism and Judaism). Such 'exclusivity' ran strongly against the grain of ancient culture that had little interest in 'conversion'. And other key aspects of Christology were profoundly 'weird' to gentile ears:

> the idea that this God *loved* human beings, willed that they should know him personally, and suffered and died in human form so as to make it possible – that would have struck many pagan hearers as simply bizarre.[49]

Charismata, such as the claim to be able to understand foreign tongues, miraculous healings and exorcisms were significant in the growth of the church across the early centuries, not just in the period immediately after Pentecost. And the wider, embodied social practices of Christians were interleaved with their proclamation and reinforced that proclamation – forgiveness, acceptance, dignity and social inclusion, regardless of background, status, gender, wealth or gift. Early churches could be fallible and feeble, but such practices were attractive in the ancient world where life was highly precarious and these qualities fed church growth. The early churches had a particular connection with those in greatest need, the vulnerable and the lowly, slaves, thieves, prostitutes and drunkards – and a particular connection with women and children, whom the wider culture looked down upon. At the same time, church growth entailed increasing response to intellectual challenges. In the fourth century, many Christians responded to dramatic growth after the conversion of Emperor Constantine with alertness to the debasing of the faith and a new stress on catechesis.[50]

In the late modern west, when many churches feel themselves to have returned to a place on the margins, akin to the period prior to Constantine's revolution, there is much to learn from the early centuries of the Christian faith. Davidson comments on the marginality of Christianity in the contemporary west, saying:

> Whether this is a threat or an opportunity for Christian faith depends greatly on perspective. Christians today may well lament their marginality, taking it as

---

[48] Ibid: 155.
[49] Ibid: 157.
[50] Ibid: 158ff.

> evidence that numerical church growth is not God's purpose in their generation. Alternatively, they may, as the early church did, consider it an opportunity to hope in God's promises, his power to transform the least likely of cultural situations, and to do so in ways which will yet in fact mean substantial, visible growth.[51]

Sr Benedicta Ward, in Chapter 9, examines a world which was, in some ways, even more precarious than that of the Roman Empire – looking at the growth of the 'Celtic' church of Saints Aidan and Cuthbert. What is striking is the way this tradition mixed proclamation, action and contemplation. The missiology of Gregory the Great deeply informed the practice of the English monks: 'For him mission was to arise out of prayer since it was to be the work of God through the preachers, not their own work'. Thus the early Saxon mission was learnt by word and example – *Verbum et exemplum docere.* The witness born by the most famous saint of northern England, Cuthbert, ended in a life devoted to prayer. What is intriguing is the way that Cuthbert had earlier to be forced from his island sanctuary to be bishop. For Cuthbert, his episcopal role was anything but 'preferment' and was instead an example of what Tomlin, earlier in this volume, called a *pneumatologia crucis.*[52] Ward stresses how all growth in the Christian life is rooted in growth of prayer, quoting Michael Ramsey's comment that: 'The supreme lesson of our fathers is that there comes first the call to prayer to God: it is the one thing needful.'[53]

In Chapter 10, Miranda Threlfall-Holmes examines a very different epoch – the high middle ages in western Europe. Crucial to this task is 'demythologising' the middle ages – often wrongly seen as a period in which 'everybody went to church'. Non-attendance varied from place to place but could be 'fairly common', embodied by the Norwich woman in 1492, of whom it was said that she 'observes an evil custom with various people from neighbouring households, who sit with her and drink during the time of service'.[54]

Threlfall-Holmes notes that many mediaeval commentators complained of how little people attended.[55] At the same time, some leading mediaeval

[51] Ibid: 167.

[52] Hence Bede says Cuthbert was 'compelled to submit his neck to the yoke of the bishopric'. Bede, *Ecclesiastical History of the English People*, B. Colgrave and R. Mynors (eds) (Oxford: OUP, 1969): 437–9.

[53] Quoted in B. Ward, '*Verbum et exemplum docere*: Bede, Cuthbert, Aidan and mission in the early English church', in Goodhew (ed.), *Towards a Theology*: 177.

[54] M. Threlfall-Homes, 'Growing the Medieval Church: Church Growth in Theory and Practice in Christendom c.1000–c.1500', in Goodhew (ed.), *Towards a Theology*: 182.

[55] Ibid: 181–2.

ecclesiastics showed great evangelistic zeal, which sits ill with the assumption of assiduous attendance. St Francis is often cited as an example of one who preferred actions to verbal proclamation, but to say this is to pass over the intensely missionary character of his movement. The aphorism attributed to St Francis, that one should preach the gospel at all times, but only use words 'if necessary' – with its implication that the verbal proclamation of faith is a secondary activity – has become an ecclesial cliché. But the practice of St Francis points in entirely the opposite direction. He and the friars were the centre of intentional church growth in the middle ages.

> In the thirteenth century as in the nineteenth, rapid urban expansion meant the disruption of historic parish connections and habits of churchgoing and domestic piety, and thus the need for evangelisation of a whole generation. It is well known that St Francis invented the concept of the Christmas crib: but it is less frequently appreciated that he did so precisely because there was a pressing need for new ways to teach the story of Jesus' nativity to an ill-educated population that knew nothing of the Christian story. The work of evangelism was foundational to the friars. Chapter 12 of St Francis' 1223 Rule was devoted to "regulating and promoting missionary activity", and for the rest of the medieval period and beyond friars were to be found preaching not only across Europe but also at the furthest reaches of the known world, in eastern Europe, India, China, Africa and the newly discovered Americas, often well in advance of official envoys or trade delegations.[56]

Realising that the middle ages were not a 'golden age' of churchgoing, that mediaeval congregations and Christians also struggled with indifference and struggled to grow churches, can be heartening in the late modern west, where it is tempting to assume that growing churches in the past was much 'easier' than now.

Where the friars did differ from much in the modern epoch was in their concern to convert people to a life of penance. Growth in the middle ages included a deep awareness of the 'weeds' that could accompany growth and had to be rooted out. This is an important lesson for the present, a reminder for contemporary congregations and ministers that numerical church growth needs to be accompanied by growing holiness, that the 'garden' of numerical church growth needs to be tended carefully if it is to bear good fruit. Threlfall-Holmes concludes that 'intentionality is key' – churches

[56] Ibid: 188–9.

grow numerically and qualitatively when people focus on this task – and cease to do so when that focus is lost.[57]

It could be argued that Reformation figures had no conception of 'church growth', in the sense that everyone was assumed to be a Christian. The debates of the Reformation were, mostly, about what kind of Christian one was supposed to be, *that* one should be a Christian was a given. Ashley Null, in Chapter 11, examines a central figure of the English Reformation, Thomas Cranmer. Null shows how strong the theme of personal conversion of life was for this key figure in the foundation of the Church of England.

Cranmer saw right desire as being as important as right doctrine. Saving truth would not of itself move sinful humanity. So the church's job is to proclaim right doctrine in such a way that its hearers are moved to accept it. Fascinatingly, Null shows how Cranmer's stress on 'feeling faith' was rooted in late mediaeval mysticism. But Cranmer recast it, based on the ideas of the reformers – stressing scripture as having a converting power. Thus, the way in which Cranmer stitched scriptural texts together to create liturgy was not only an illustration of the Reformation principle of '*sola scriptura*', it was an attempt to grow the church. Cranmer's homilies were 'affective evangelism'.[58] The 'comfortable words', comforting scripture quotations at the heart of Cranmer's eucharistic liturgy, are an example of Cranmer using scripture to address the pastoral needs of his generation, stressing God as merciful, in contrast to late mediaeval church wall paintings which stressed doom-filled judgement. For Cranmer 'the inherent drawing power of divine free forgiveness' was central to who God is and what the church is – and in turn acts as a deep force for growing the church, so that more and more people may know this forgiveness for themselves.[59]

In addition, unlike his fellow reformer John Knox, who outlawed anything not in the Bible, Cranmer allowed for context and tradition – a principle which supports the legitimacy of different expressions of church for different contexts and for diversity between denominations. This was illustrated most graphically in his determination to translate worship into the tongue of the common people and his stress, through the articles of religion, that variation between churches of different nationalities was legitimate. This created a distinctive theology which can underpin numerical church growth – a deep attentiveness to scripture and a concern to translate faith into the culture in which churches are to be grown. Null sees this as a model with wider applicability.

---

[57] Ibid: 195.

[58] A. Null, 'Thomas Cranmer and a Theology of Church Growth', in Goodhew (ed.), *Towards a Theology*: 207.

[59] Ibid: 215.

> Cranmer put his twin means of transforming human affections – scriptural rumination and cultural contextualisation – at the very heart of Tudor worship. The mission, vitality and expansion of the church today would be well served by doing likewise in our time.[60]

In Chapter 12, Dominic Erdozain extends the survey of the history of church into the modern period. This iconoclastic chapter subverts the assumptions of Christians and non-Christians alike: 'The past was not as uniformly Christian as social memory would suggest, and the modern period has been anything but secular.'[61] Most crucially, Erdozain shows how the myth of a past where 'everyone went to church' and the parallel myth of a present in which 'everyone' is secular has had a grip on the minds of many theologians.

> In the 1960s, a bold, integrated theory of secularisation emerged, combining theoretical and empirical analysis to assert that religion was finally dying. The end was nigh. Even though the "secularisation thesis" was an enormous piece of guesswork, resting on the weak assumption that the world follows where Europe leads, it became a kind of orthodoxy for social theorists and acquired the status of a social fact for a number of theologians.[62]

Erdozain argues that we can demythologise the secular eschatology that assumes that the world will inevitably become more secular:

> Secularisation functions as a theology of doom. People believe it. The goading analysis of "death" and "endgame" enters the Christian psyche. Experts with often-limited feel for the religious cultures they study are somehow allowed to set the agenda, the problem going beyond the numbing tyranny of statistics to an insidious language of disintegration and decay ... As David Martin, one of the leading exponents of secularisation theory, later reflected: "when we said the church was in trouble, we didn't expect the churches to believe us". Martin had not "anticipated how enthusiastically the churches would collude in their own demise" – rolling over to appease the new secular culture. This was not a scientific process unfolding. It was a self-fulfilling prophecy: a narrative of doom becoming a theology of panic.[63]

---

60 Ibid: 215.
61 Erdozain, 'New Affections': 232.
62 Ibid: 217.
63 Ibid: 219.

Erdozain argues that modernity has been more Christian that it is given credit for and that where it has declined, this has been sometimes positive – in that some of 'Christendom' was far from Christian. The eighteenth century contained much religious torpor and the mid-nineteenth century religious boom was less typical than is often assumed. Leaving aside the dramatically different trajectory of the church outside the west (and Davie's comment that it may yet be Europe that proves to be the exception rather than the norm deserves to be kept in mind[64]), different parts of the west have fared very differently in terms of church decline and growth. Contemporary signs of Christian vitality in the west should not be dismissed as exceptions that prove the secular rule. Conversely Erdozain critiques the assumption that high church attendance is, always, an inherent good – pointing out how the high levels of observance in Victorian Christianity were coupled with a culture that could, at times, be anything but Christian. Equally, just as 'Christian' covers a wide range, so does 'modernity'. There is substantial evidence that contemporary modernity is no more inevitably 'secular' than the Christendom of mediaeval western Europe was inevitably 'Christian'.[65]

Questioning Church Growth in the Context of Late Modernity

The notion of 'contextual theology' is fruitful and problematic. No one floats above their context and all theologies need to be seen through the lens their context provides. But no one has a single, simple context; contexts are multifaceted and interlock in complex ways. Moreover, insofar as Christianity sees itself as an eschatological faith, it will look beyond the horizon of the immediate context and the horizon of human history towards the horizon which the God of Jesus reveals. Theology seeks to operate between the two horizons of the context of the writer (and his or her readers) and the divine horizon from which we shall see things as they truly are. Eschatology may point beyond context, but everyone formulating theology speaks within a context that needs consideration if such theology is to be evaluated rightly.

---

[64] G. Davie, *Europe: The Exceptional Case: Parameters of Faith in the Modern World* (London: Darton, Longman and Todd, 2002).

[65] See, for example, T. Carnes and A. Karpathakis, *New York Glory: Religions in the City* (New York: New York University Press, 2001); G. Evans and K. Northmore-Ball, 'The Limits of Secularization? The Resurgence of Orthodoxy in Post-Soviet Russia', vol. 51/4, 2012, *Journal of the Scientific Study of Religion*; Brierley, *Capital Growth*.

Context is a word much used in modern theology. What is intriguing is the way the context of late modern theologians is rarely examined. Late modern western theology has been generated, for the most part, within academia and within a media-saturated world. Academic theologians work within institutions that, whilst they retain elements of past ecclesiastical prominence, have seen such prominence decline dramatically over the past two centuries. In the past hundred years departments of theology have tended to shrink, close, merge with other departments and/or be made more marginal to the academy in other ways. Academic theologians have worked within an academic environment in which the secularisation of society has been widely regarded as a given.[66] Core figures across a range of disciplines – such as Marx, Weber and Durkheim – regarded the decline of churches as inevitable and, for the most part, desirable. A vocal section of the scientific community has voiced the same opinion and, whilst such voices represent fewer of the scientific world than might be imagined, they have become increasingly influential.[67]

Modern theology has therefore had to operate within a context increasingly dominated by the assumption that the idea of God has no future, a kind of secular eschatology. The point here is not whether this secular eschatology is true (although there are many reasons to question its truthfulness).[68] Rather, what is significant is the fact that the context of a secularising modern academia and media has been the primary context within which western theology has been written. It would be remarkable if theologians were unaffected by such a context and did not, to some degree, internalise this secular eschatology, an eschatology which assumes that churches can only get smaller.

---

[66] D. Bebbington, 'The Secularisation of British Universities since the Mid Nineteenth Century', in G. Marsden and B. Lonfield, *The Secularisation of the Academy* (Oxford: OUP, 1992); G.M. Marsden, *The Soul of the American University: From Protestant Establishment to Established Unbelief* (New York: OUP, 1994).

[67] The Oxford academic, Professor Richard Dawkins is the best known example, but represents a larger phenomenon. Academics are one of the most prominent categories amongst the 'distinguished supporters' listed by the British Humanist Society. See: http://humanism.org.uk/about/our-people/distinguished-supporters/ accessed 4 June 2014.

[68] High profile dialogues between Archbishop Rowan Willams or Pope Francis and well known atheists do not suggest a convincing 'victory' for either party. See, for example: http://www.theguardian.com/science/2012/feb/23/richard-dawkins-rowan-williams-bout accessed 15 July 2014. The assumption that modern society is 'inevitably' getting more secular is based on questionable observations. Some parts of some western societies are getting more secular – but some are not. Most non-western societies are far from secular – and the assumption that they will secularise 'eventually' is both unproveable and has more than a whiff of colonialism about it.

The following examination of key modern theological and ecclesiological texts gives an indication of the extent to which numerical church growth is a subject for theological reflection – and the nature of that discussion. Jurgen Moltmann is one of the most influential protestant theologians of the twentieth century. Moltmann put great stress on ecclesiology but it is important to note how church growth does and does not feature within it. Church and kingdom are connected, but kingdom is by far the dominant factor, with the spread of the local church a much more minor theme: 'The real point is not to spread the church but to spread the kingdom.' Moltmann strongly emphasised qualitative discipleship and the calling of the church to work for socio-economic change. He saw numerical growth of churches as also legitimate, but this was a lesser theme of his ecclesiology. Moltmann stressed the need for churches to be counter-cultural, but saw this primarily in terms of resistance to human evil and avoidance of becoming a merely 'pastoral' church which never critiques its surrounding society, and not in terms of encouraging the proliferation of communities of faith. Apostolicity was defined primarily in terms of suffering, rather than as the foundation and nurture of new communities of faith. The necessity for churches to seek to grow and the possibility that they can grow has, therefore, a limited place within Moltmann's theology.[69] Moltmann wrote in the shadow of the Third Reich, which illustrated how large numbers of people could easily espouse hugely dubious beliefs and this understandably colours his thought. Equally, his thought is often applied to contexts very different from the Third Reich. There is much in Moltmann's theology with which to agree. The issue is not that the above emphases are wrong, but it is fair to ask whether the smallness of the space that Moltmann allows for concern for numerical church growth is theologically justified in the context of late modernity.[70]

A very different, but equally important, twentieth century theologian is the Roman Catholic, Karl Rahner. Rahner was acutely conscious of the context in which he wrote; the changing position of the church in the modern world 'dominated' Rahner's ecclesiology.[71] Rahner understood the church in the modern world in terms of the potency of secularity and the dramatic diminution of the influence of the church. For Rahner, the church was increasingly a little flock, a diaspora scattered across a world dominated by secular pluralism. He

[69] R. Bauckham, *The Theology of Moltmann* (Edinburgh: T & T Clark, 1995): 13–14, 119–150; J. Moltmann, *The Church in the Power of the Spirit: A Contribution to Messianic Ecclesiology* (London, SCM Press, 1977): 10–11, 84, 152–3 (and, more generally, 133–89), 357.

[70] Hence: Bauckham, *Theology of Moltmann*: 149–50.

[71] R. Lennon, *The Ecclesiology of Karl Rahner* (Oxford: OUP 1997): 213.

was pessimistic about the prospects for the church, continually stressing its sinfulness and assuming it would remain small. He took it as a given that Roman Catholics were or would soon be a minority in a world which did not share their views.[72] Rahner is best known for his notion of the 'anonymous Christian', but it should be noted that this notion is linked to his assumption that secularity was strong and Christianity weak.

> Rahner accepted that it [secularisation] probably meant that the Christian message would remain ineffective for the majority of people in any future world. Consequently it was not an articulated theism, but an "anonymous" response to God's offer of salvation which was likely to become the norm.[73]

Such pessimism had some basis in fact. Twentieth century church life in Germany and Austria, which formed Rahner's primary context, saw much secularisation and congregational life often operating at a low ebb.[74] But such pessimism was, and is, not the whole truth. Rather, Rahner had, to some degree, internalised the particular context in which he worked and the secular eschatology that dominated modern western thinking – and based his pessimistic assumptions regarding church growth upon that eschatology.

A different example is the leading American theologian, George Lindbeck. Lindbeck was deeply influenced by German theology. Consequently, systematics steeped in a culture of church decline could have a serious impact on areas (such as the United States) in which congregational decline has been less marked than in western Europe. An example of this process comes at the end of Lindbeck's key work, *The Nature of Doctrine*. Lindbeck sees the present age as one of 'progressive dechristianisation' and speaks of 'when or if dechristianization reduces Christians to a small minority' and of 'the by no means illegitimate desire of the churches to maintain membership'. Note that the best Lindbeck can hope for is to 'maintain' membership. Such phrases presuppose congregational decline without hope of growth. Lindbeck, as a seminal figure in post-liberal thinking, thereby injects decline theology into post-liberal DNA, which has

---

[72] Ibid: 178, 181, 183, 174–8, 254.

[73] Ibid: 178.

[74] In the context of a secularising Western Europe, Germany secularised first and furthest. See, for example: H. McLeod, *Secularisation in Western Europe, 1848–1914* (Basingstoke: Macmillan, 2000): 174–5; H. McLeod, *Piety and Poverty: Working Class Religion in Berlin, London and New York, 1870–1914* (Holmes and Meier: New York, 1996). Austria stood on the edge of the 'Iron Curtain', beyond which dramatic secularisation appeared to be happening after 1945, the period in which Rahner was most active as a writer.

tended to concentrate on 'strengthening' the faithful few, without conceiving of the possibility of growth. It is legitimate to ask whether such an *a priori* ruling out of the possibility of congregational growth must to be so.[75]

It is striking, also, to note the way in which Bonhoeffer's 'religionless Christianity' has been appropriated by later writers. 'Religionless Christianity' has been understood, principally via J.A.T. Robinson's work, as meaning that the secularisation and congregational decline of parts of the west in the 1960s is normative. Future churches will be small and marginal and this must be accepted as inevitable. There is considerable evidence to suggest that what Robinson took Bonhoeffer to mean was not at all what Bonhoeffer actually meant. By 'religionless Christianity', Bonhoeffer was using religion in Barth's parlance as a human way of trying to reach God. Using Bonhoeffer's phrase to refer to 1960s secularisation is, arguably, an anachronism.[76] Instead, the context of Robinson's own thinking deserves attention. Robinson was deeply formed by his particular experience of secularisation within Cambridge and London in the 1960s. Robinson's *Honest to God* could be seen as a universalising of such experiences, on the assumption that they embodied global trends.[77]

It is difficult to find major twentieth century theologians who strongly value the numerical growth of local congregations. From Barth to de Lubac, from Von Balthasar to Pannenberg, numerical church growth is not seen as a major part of church life. When such growth is mentioned, it is a minor theme compared to more dominant concerns – such as the growth in holiness of the believer, ecumenism, the church as constituted by the eucharist or the Christian community's engagement with wider society. Such concerns are entirely right in themselves. But the combination of such concerns with little, or no, stress on church growth raises questions. Originating in a secularising west, concentrated mainly in Germany, one of the most secularised parts of the west, it is fair to ask

---

[75] G. Lindbeck, *The Nature of Doctrine: Religion and Theology in a Postliberal Age* (London: SPCK, 1984): 133–4. I am grateful to Josh Penduck, curate of St Chad's, Lichfield and formerly an ordinand at Cranmer Hall, Durham for this insight into Lindbeck's thought.

[76] I am grateful to my colleagues Medi Ann Volpe and Jennifer Moberly for their insights on this point. For further elucidation, see their chapter, entitled, '"Let your light so shine": Rowan Williams and Dietrich Bonhoeffer', in *Engaging Bonhoeffer: The Influence and Impact of Bonhoeffer's Life and Thought*, edited by Matthew Kirkpatrick (Minneapolis: Fortress Press, 2014).

[77] E. James, *A Life of Bishop John A.T. Robinson: Scholar, Pastor, Prophet* (London: Collins, 1987): 161–2.

whether such theologies have been more shaped by their secularising context than they realise and more than they need to have been.[78]

Such writers are not saying that they do not wish the church to grow, but they are saying (explicitly or implicitly) that they see its numerical growth as of limited or even peripheral importance. By contrast, other aspects of church life are seen as 'kingdom' projects and accorded much greater prominence. Here are the ingredients for a 'theology of decline', in which congregational growth is assumed to be either impossible or irrelevant, or both.

Theology and church life interpenetrate. The visible channels of such influence can be seen in official church reports, which are frequently written by academic theologians or draw upon wider academic debates. It is therefore instructive to see what assumptions about the possibility or impossibility of numerical church growth are made in a sample selection of reports from the Church of England. Seminal reports – such as the *Tiller Report, Faith in the City* and *Faithful Cities* have internalised the secularisation thesis. Whilst valuable in many respects, such reports over-emphasise secularisation. They show little or no interest in the need or possibility of numerical church growth, often assuming a much more pessimistic scenario for church growth than has subsequently been shown to be the case. Growth tends to be seen as so unlikely as not to be worth worrying about, or as much less important than other, higher 'kingdom' matters. Future numerical church decline is often taken as a given. Such reports thereby promulgate a theology of decline to the wider church.[79]

---

[78] See, for example: K. Bender, *Karl Barth's Christological Ecclesiology* (Aldershot: Ashgate, 2005): 181; F. Kerr, *Twentieth-Century Catholic Theologians* (Oxford: Blackwell, 2007): 83–5; N. Healy and D.L. Schindler, 'For the Life of the World: Hans Urs von Baltasar on the Church as Eucharist', in E. Oakes S.J. and D. Moss (eds), *The Cambridge Companion to the Theology of Hans Urs von Baltasar* (Cambridge: CUP, 2004); S. Grenz, *Reason for Hope: the Systematic Theology of Wolfhart Pannenberg* (Second Edition, Grand Rapids: Eerdemans, 2005): 201–56. In making these points, I am grateful to Josh Penduck, curate of St Chad's, Lichfield and formerly an ordinand at Cranmer Hall, Durham for his insights, which have informed this paragraph.

[79] The Tiller Report assumes a static UK population, the continuing decline of the church in London, blanket secularisation across Britain and no significant migration to the UK. These assertions are all incorrect. See: J. Tiller *A Strategy for the Church's Ministry* (CIO Publishing, 1983): 11–17, 164. *Faith in the City* and *Faithful Cities* discuss urban ministry with almost no reference to numerical church growth – yet many inner city areas of Britain have seen marked church growth in subsequent decades, mostly outside the historic denominations – see: Archbishop of Canterbury's Commission on Urban Priority Areas, *Faith in the City* (Church House Publishing, 1985): 359–67; The Commission on Urban Life and Faith, *Faithful Cities: A Call for Celebration, Vision and Justice* (London: Methodist Publishing House and Church House Publishing, 2006): 89–91. It is striking that even the

Conclusion: Our Theology of Decline Must Go

> In his autobiography, *Steps along Hope Street*, David Sheppard recalled the advice that he received from his predecessor as he took over as Bishop of Woolwich in 1969: "Bishop John Robinson said he did not think there would be any visible church in the inner-city in ten years' time!"[80]

London has changed dramatically since the 1960s, when Robinson made this prediction. A recent detailed survey in the section of inner-city London where Bishop Robinson worked has shown that 240 new black majority churches had been founded there in recent years. And this survey does not include the many other new churches emerging in this part of inner-city London. Contrary to Robinson's view that there would be no visible church in the inner city a decade after his departure, London, especially inner city London, has seen marked numerical church growth in recent decades.[81] If 'church' is defined primarily as local communities of Christians (the primary definition used in this volume), then gloomy predictions regarding the future of 'the church' are not always correct.

In much of elite culture in western society it is a truth almost universally acknowledged that the church in the western world is in decline. Dominic Erdozain shows how often theologians and church leaders have internalised that 'truth'. Few stopped to ask whether the pessimistic eschatology of the Bishop of Woolwich was primarily the result of empirical observation – or the result of absorption of the surrounding culture.

Trying to grow the church numerically is often regarded as something that is just 'not done' in reputable theological circles – or is a concern adopted as a reluctant pragmatism made necessary by fear of ecclesial extinction. That such wariness of numerical church growth happened at the time when academia and media came to be markedly secularised is more than a coincidence. Theologians and church leaders have often internalised the horizon that their context set before them. The result has been 'a theology of decline' in which 'kingdom' often trumped (rather than included) the local church, in which church growth was

---

widely influential report *Mission-Shaped Church*, whilst much more explicit in its support of numerical church growth than the above reports, bases its analysis on academic research which strongly endorses the secularisation thesis and does not utilise analysis that questions the secularisation thesis – see: The Archbishops' Council, *Mission-Shaped Church*: 11.

[80] D. Erdozain, 'New Affections': 217.

[81] Rogers, *Being Built Together*; see also: Brierley, *Capital Growth*.

seen as impossible or even dubious and in which church decline was assumed to be the inevitable consequence of all-conquering secularity.

Christian theology should listen hard to context, especially the context of the culture in which it is written. But it does not need to be determined by that culture. It is called, in part, to be counter-cultural – by which is meant not the denial of culture, but a readiness to be creatively subversive. Much theology is fearful lest Christianity appear 'arrogant'. When Christendom was a meaningful reality, that was a legitimate concern. In the late modern west, when Christianity is far from a dominant entity, there is the opposite danger of assuming that Christianity has no capacity for agency. This is not humility. It is a form of ecclesial low self-esteem. It is part of the argument of this book that this theology of decline should go. It fits neither a nuanced epistemology, nor the narratives of the New Testament, nor core Christian doctrines, nor the experience of Christians across the centuries.

When we examine the New Testament, the core doctrines of the Christian faith and the history of churches down the ages, what is striking is how *positive* a view they have of local communities of Christians – churches. These central sources of theological insight give many examples of the frailties and fallibilities of such local churches, yet the overwhelming picture they present is of local churches as a good thing, deeply desired by God. It is a corollary that the numerical growth of congregations is a good thing, deeply desired by God. All local congregations are messy churches, in which the good seed of the kingdom springs up alongside quarrels, indifference, wrongdoing and foolishness. But the valuation of scripture, doctrine and history are unequivocal. These key sources for theology see congregations as at the heart of living out the Christian life and, as such, they see the numerical growth of congregations as heartily to be desired. Local churches are therefore never to be dismissed as 'merely' an agent of the kingdom.[82] Local congregations are never 'merely' anything. They are beloved by God. Who are we to devalue that which God values so highly? Since congregations are so highly valued by God, their growth and proliferation is at the heart of the kingdom and at the heart of the Christian mission.

Decline theology needs to go because it is intellectually problematic, but it also needs to go because it has deleterious consequences. The theology of decline has a dubious convenience. With such a theology in place, congregational decline can be explained away as the product of supposedly 'inevitable' social processes, with no hard questions asked as to whether alternative strategies and

---

[82] J. Hull, *Mission-Shaped Church: A Theological Response* (London: SCM Press, 2006): 2. 'The flowering of mission is the Kingdom; church is merely an agent.'

theologies could make a difference. Ironically, given the way decline theology often claims a 'high' view of 'kingdom', the numerical decline of congregations has a harmful (often terminal) impact on kingdom activities such as the alleviation of poverty and the wider leavening of civil society by Christ-like love. Dwindling congregations and empty churches are of limited use for furthering kingdom realities.

Conversely, a theology of church growth will contribute to numerical church growth. *Of course*, growth in the Christian life includes things other than numerical church growth. But since numerical growth has been so often sidelined, it is no bad thing to emphasise how important it is, within a wider definition of growth in the Christian life. Developing a nuanced theology of church growth will contribute to the numerical growth of the church and to the wider building of God's kingdom in changed lives and changed societies. Understanding how scripture, doctrine and history speak of numerical church growth will assist churches in growing numerically in the present and doing so in a healthy way. It gives a clear rationale for why numerically growing local churches is a good and godly thing and, via the experiences relayed in scripture and across history, a mine of examples of how to grow healthy congregations. Such growth, if it is of value, is always primarily the work of God, but it is a work in which Christians are called to share. That sharing in the work of God includes the discipleship of the mind which we call theology. And by working towards a theology of church growth, theologians and church leaders creatively subvert the secular elite culture of the late modern west.

Chapter 2

Dialogue, Proclamation and the Growth of the Church in Religiously Diverse Societies

David Marshall with William Glass

Defining a Problem: Religious Confidence in the Universe of Faiths

In the context of the increasing religious diversity of many western societies, the idea that Christians should proclaim the Gospel confidently to all people, and that they should hope and pray for the growth of the Church by the incorporation of new disciples from people of every background, including every religion, strikes many – including many Christians – as old-fashioned, arrogant and divisive. This essay addresses the tensions that exist among Christians over this issue. I shall argue that Christian engagement with religiously diverse societies should be marked both by the humility associated with dialogue and practical co-operation with all people, and also by the confidence associated with proclamation and the making of new Christian disciples.

First, however, a look at examples of how Muslims speak about the growth of the Muslim community in western societies helps to put current discussion of Christian thought and practice into a wider perspective. In May 2012 Abdal Hakim Murad (also known as Tim Winter), a lecturer in Islamic Studies at Cambridge University and one of Britain's best known Muslim scholars and leaders, published an article in *The Times* entitled 'Why the British are flocking to Islam's call'. Drawing on a report produced at Swansea University, Murad writes: 'There have been, it seems, a hundred thousand British conversions to Islam in the past decade, compared with sixty thousand in the 1990s. Despite the shock and horror of the 9/11 atrocities, Islam is thriving.'[1] This in fact appears to misrepresent the Swansea report, which does point to significant

[1] Available at http://www.thetimes.co.uk/tto/opinion/columnists/article3401700.ece accessed 18 December 2014.

growth, but on nothing like the scale Murad suggests.[2] For present purposes, however, it is not the accuracy or otherwise of Murad's account that matters. What is of interest is the fact that one of Britain's most respected Muslim leaders, writing in a national newspaper, displays no embarrassment or hesitancy at all in speaking of the conversion to Islam of large numbers of British citizens, most of whom one can assume were of at least nominally Christian background. The idea that there is any need to defend the growth of the Muslim community in a religiously diverse society seems not even to have occurred to Murad. And it should be stressed that he is not an untypical extremist on the margins of his community; on the contrary, he has regularly been involved in dialogues convened by the Archbishop of Canterbury; he addressed the Pope on behalf of Muslims involved in dialogue with the Vatican; he speaks regularly on BBC Radio's *Thought for the Day*.

Many other examples of the ease with which Muslims in the West speak of the growth of their community through conversion could be given. Two brief illustrations will suffice. At an interfaith panel discussion on the topic 'What do our scriptures say about "the other"?', held in February 2013 at Duke University Divinity School in the USA, Imam Abdullah Antepli, Muslim chaplain to the University, mentioned how Duke students regularly visit him to discuss their interest in converting to Islam. Imam Antepli, it should be stressed, is highly popular with his Christian colleagues and is noted for his commitment to dialogue with Christians and other non-Muslims. In a second example, on 14 May 2013 an email invitation from the Centre for Islamic Studies at the School of Oriental and African Studies, London University, advertised the launch of a report, co-sponsored by Cambridge University Press and the New Muslims Project at the Markfield Institute, entitled *Narratives of Conversions to Islam in Britain, Female Perspectives*. The launch was to be chaired by Kristiane Backer, a high-profile convert to Islam, and one of the speakers was to be Muhammad Abdel Haleem, a leading Muslim scholar and another regular contributor to Christian-Muslim dialogues.

The purpose in citing these examples is not to raise concerns or warn about conversion to Islam, but rather to show that, in the west, Muslims appear to be much more at ease than Christians in talking openly about the growth of

---

[2] The report states that there may be as many as 100,000 British converts to Islam in total, but it fixes the number of converts within the last decade at 40,000 *at most* ('there may have been between 30,000 and 40,000 conversions in total since 2001'). See M. Brice, *A Minority Within a Minority: A Report on Converts to Islam in the United Kingdom*, available at http://faith-matters.org/images/stories/fm-reports/a-minority-within-a-minority-a-report-on-converts-to-islam-in-the-uk.pdf accessed 18 December 2014.

their community, and do not appear to expect opposition or criticism for doing so. It is hard to imagine a Muslim publication on the growth of the Muslim community including a piece parallel to this essay, because there is no noticeable debate among Muslims about the desirability of non-Muslims embracing Islam. It should also be stressed that although we have dwelt at some length on conversion to Islam, the same essential point could be made with respect to very different worldviews. The robust proclamation of atheism by public figures such as Richard Dawkins indicates that confident, 'conversionist' proclamation of competing worldviews is a widespread, proper, and generally accepted feature of our culture. What is all the more striking, in light of such unabashed confidence among Muslims, atheists, and others is the contrasting reserve, anxiety, and sometimes polarised debate among Christians about the proclamation of their faith among non-Christians. We turn now to consider some reasons for this situation.

The Modern Turn Away from Proclamation

Major shifts in Christian thinking about mission in relation to adherents to other religions have taken place in the last few decades. John Hick was one of the most influential Christian theologians calling for a transition, which he compared to the Copernican revolution, from the view of Christianity as the one absolute truth and unique way of salvation, to which all people should be converted, to a view of Christianity as one among many equally valid and efficacious paths to God. Although Hick's vision for the reconstruction of Christian theology has probably been embraced in full by only a small minority of leading Christian theologians today, it is worth rehearsing his arguments because, even among those who have not accepted his radical approach in its totality, the questions he raised have had a pervasive influence.

In his essay 'The Non-Absoluteness of Christianity', Hick explains why many Christians, like himself, feel the need to move away from traditional Christian thinking and embrace the revolution for which he argues. Firstly, Christians have gained greater and more accurate knowledge about other faiths and, often, with that knowledge has come greater respect. 'The immense spiritual riches of Judaism and Islam, of Hinduism, Buddhism and Sikhism, of Confucianism and Taoism and African primal religion, have become better known in the West and have tended to erode the plausibility of the old Christian exclusivism.'[3] Secondly, as Christians come to know other faiths better they also become more aware of the quality of life of the adherents of other faiths. As they do so, fair-minded Christians tend to acknowledge the 'observable facts' that the fruits of individual and social transformation are just as apparent in other faith communities as among Christians. Thus, for Hick, there are 'no good grounds for maintaining that Christianity has produced or is producing more saints'[4] and, on a wider canvass, 'it seems impossible to make the global judgment that any one religious tradition has contributed more good or less evil, or a more favorable balance of good over evil, than the others ... as vast complex totalities, the world traditions seem to be more or less on a par with each other'.[5] A third point concerns the relationship between Christianity and colonialism in recent history. Awareness of this connection has led many Christians to feel that the claim that Christianity is uniquely true is inevitably bound up with an attitude that seeks to dominate and exploit the world politically, economically and culturally.[6] Finally, a particular example of how the sense of Christian superiority can lead to literally murderous results lies in a supersessionist Christian view of Judaism. For Hick, along with many other Christians, this view inevitably led to an attitude of contempt towards Jews which at the very least eased the way towards anti-Semitism, persecution and ultimately the Holocaust.[7]

Hick's arguments reflect ideas that are widespread in western culture and have deeply influenced Christian discourse and practice. One of the main practical outcomes of the influence of such thinking has been a radical decline in the sense that it is important or even appropriate for Christians to proclaim their faith to members of other religions and desire their conversion; dialogue and co-operation are instead emphasised as the most suitable approaches. This outlook is expressed by Stanley Samartha, an Indian theologian who became the first Director of the World Council of Churches' sub-unit on Dialogue with People of Living Faiths and Ideologies:

> ... when alternative ways of salvation have provided meaning and purpose for millions of persons in other cultures for more than two or three thousand years, to claim that the Judaeo-Christian-Western tradition has the only answer to all

---

[3] J. Hick, 'The Non-Absoluteness of Christianity', in J. Hick and P. Knitter (eds), *The Myth of Christian Uniqueness* (London: SCM, 1987): 17.

[4] Ibid: 23.

[5] Ibid: 30.

[6] Ibid: 18–20.

[7] Ibid: 18, referring to the essay by Ruether in the same volume.

> problems in all places and for all persons in the world is presumptuous, if not incredible. This is not to deny the validity of the Christian experience of salvation in Jesus Christ, but it is to deny the exclusive claims made for it by Christians.[8]

Before coming to the main proposal of this essay, in support of a Christian position that can be described as both/and in relation to dialogue and proclamation, we shall first consider a few points in critique of Hick's position. In an essay of this length, it is not possible to engage all of Hick's arguments noted above. In particular, it will not be possible to discuss his third and fourth points mentioned earlier, concerning colonialism and Christian views of Judaism, though both (and especially the latter) would need serious attention in a more extended essay.[9] The critique offered here, which will focus on those parts of his argument most directly related to the relationship of dialogue to proclamation, can be summed up in Gavin D'Costa's observation of a principal theological problem inherent in Hick's pluralism. Hick stresses 'the axiom of the universal and salvific will of God'.[10] Additionally, although Hick argues that both theistic and non-theistic religions are equally salvific in value, 'he holds that our final (and therefore presumably true) relation to the "Real" is one of eternal loving communion with a personalist, all-loving God'.[11] That is, although Hick

---

[8] S. Samartha, quoted in *The Mystery of Salvation: The Story of God's Gift: A Report by the Doctrine Commission of the General Synod of the Church of England* (London: Church House Publishing, 1995): 155–6.

[9] For a different approach to Hick's on colonialism and Christianity, see B. Stanley, *The Bible and the Flag: Protestant Missions and British Imperialism in the Nineteenth and Twentieth Centuries* (Leicester: Apollos, 1990). On Christian approaches to Judaism within the Church of England, a helpful brief overview is offered in *Sharing One Hope? The Church of England and Christian-Jewish Relations: A Contribution to a Continuing Debate* (London: Church House Publishing, 2001). Of particular relevance to the concerns of this essay are the discussion of different views on Christian mission and Jewish people (25–7). For a recent discussion of Anglican approaches, see M. Ipgrave, 'Remembering the Covenant: Judaism in an Anglican Theology of Interfaith Relations', *Anglican Theological Review*, 96.1 (2014): 39–56. See also P. Morrow, 'Christian Mission and Jewish Christian Particularities', in *Jews and Christians: Perspectives on Mission*: 23–45, available at http://www.woolf.cam.ac.uk/uploads/Woolf%20Mission%202011%20print%20version.pdf accessed 18 December 2014. For two contrasting Roman Catholic views on the question of Christian mission and Judaism, see the essays by G. D'Costa and J. Pawlikowski in the September 2012 edition of *Theological Studies* (*Theological Studies*, 73 no 3 S 2012: 590–613; 629–40).

[10] G. D'Costa, *Theology and Religious Pluralism*: *The Challenge of Other Religions*, Signposts in Theology Series (Oxford: Blackwell Publishing, 1986): 45.

[11] Ibid: 44. He quotes J. Hick's own admission that his post-Copernican conception of God at the end of the universe of faiths 'requires a "conception of God as personal Lord,

intends to relativise traditional Christian claims about Jesus as the determinative revelation of God, he at the same time implicitly maintains a picture of God that is essentially as revealed in Jesus. Yet it is not at all clear why this should be so. The religions of the world, taken on their own terms, do not all believe in a personalist God who seeks loving communion with all human beings. The Christian understanding of God looks rather unlike what some religious traditions speak of when they use the word 'God'. Hick at one moment tells us that we can't claim that Christianity gives us a uniquely true account of God and at the same time proposes a basically Christian understanding of God, placing that God as the divinity secretly at the heart of the world's religious traditions.

A related point concerns Hick's insistence that, despite the theological differences between the world's religions, there is at the ethical level a convergence and essential parity between them. A significant challenge to this view is found in the work of Charles Taylor, who disputes the idea that radically different claims about the nature of the world can produce basically similar ethical traditions. The tie between those claims and the ethics they inspire is much tighter; thus, religious beliefs should be understood as 'lived conditions, not just theories or sets of beliefs subscribed to'.[12] As Taylor observes, 'a moral order is more than just a set of norms; ... it also contains what we might call an "ontic" component, identifying features of the world which make the norms realizable'.[13] Accounts of the virtues depend on what a people holds to be most true about the world in which that people lives. By 'lived conditions', Taylor refers to a complex co-inherence of the way a culture lives, what it thinks it knows about the world, and how it thinks it can know. There simply is no way to explain the ethical traditions of Muslims, Christians, or anyone else without reference to the particularities of what they believe to be true about the world. Any attempt to do so requires an externally imposed vision of virtue that papers over particularities in community practices, and reflects its own bias as to which behaviours 'count' as individual and social transformation.

Hick's approach in fact presupposes the long history of Christian engagement with the world, and that history leaves its unmistakeable mark on his ethics. When he equates Christian *agape* with the negation of 'the present false ego' of Hinduism or the 'egoless openness'[14] of Buddhism and assumes the equality

---

distinct from his creation"', for only so can that God at the end of the universe be 'in loving communion with all humankind'.

[12] C. Taylor, *A Secular Age* (Cambridge: Harvard University Press, 2007): 8.

[13] C. Taylor, 'On Social Imaginary', available at http://blog.lib.umn.edu/swiss/archive/Taylor.pdf accessed 18 December 2014.

[14] J. Hick, *Problems of Religious Pluralism* (London: Macmillan, 1985): 70.

of these Hindu and Buddhist virtues with a commitment to liberating 'social structures', it appears that they are being uprooted from their own specific contexts and Christianised by Hick's assumption that they naturally lead to the political action commended by Christian liberation theology.[15] Nor is this surprising, because Hick is heir to a culture that values people who simply were not valued before Christianity emerged in the ancient world.[16] Christians, as David Bentley Hart argues, scandalised Greco-Roman sensibilities precisely because they 'were willing to grant full humanity to persons of every class and condition, of either sex'.[17] This willingness arose from the conviction that, in Christ, God had redeemed and dignified all human beings.

Thus, Hick's argument that there is no real difference between the distinct contributions made by the world's different religions to the ethics of its peoples suffers from the same internal contradictions as his theology. If Taylor is right, there is no way to understand the virtues of any given faith tradition except by the adoption of that tradition's dogmas – which is to say, their own way of seeing and being in the world. Likewise, to engage a religious tradition wisely requires attention to its own particulars: its own answers to its own questions, within its own universe of meaning. Questions of likeness and difference must not be assumed on the basis of some metaphysical *a priori*. It might be thought that Hick's pluralist theology offers the best possible basis for inter-religious dialogue, but in fact his prior convictions about what religions *are* and what they are *for*, seriously weaken the possibility of respectful and attentive engagement with another religious tradition in all its difference from one's own.

---

[15] Ibid: 79.

[16] This is what D.B. Hart means by calling western culture a 'culture that, in a sense, sprang from Peter's tears'. Hart argues that Christianity is largely responsible for creating a culture in which the tears of Peter, a peasant who denies his Master and regrets it afterwards, have any real sense of *pathos*. D.B. Hart, *Atheist Delusions: The Christian Revolution and its Fashionable Enemies* (New Haven: Yale University Press, 2009): 167.

[17] Ibid: 169. Further in this vein, Hart writes: 'It would not even be implausible to argue that our very ability to speak of "persons" as we do is a consequence of the revolution in moral sensibility that Christianity brought about. We, after all, employ this word with a splendidly indiscriminate generosity, applying it without hesitation to everyone, regardless of social station, race, or sex; but originally, at least in some of the most crucial contexts, it had a much more limited application. Specifically, in Roman legal usage, one's person was one's status before the law, which was certainly not something invariable from one individual to the next.' Hart, *Atheist Delusions*: 183.

Humility and Confidence in Interfaith Engagement

In contrast to Hick's kind of approach, I propose that dialogue and proclamation are equally necessary and inter-penetrating practices of a Christian engagement with other religious communities, reflecting the humility and the confidence that are both fundamental features of authentic Christianity. This approach recognises that there are salutary challenges in some of Hick's points, especially where he identifies tendencies to Christian triumphalism and an inability to recognise God's presence and activity beyond the Church; but it resists his conclusion that in order to meet those challenges Christians must radically revise and relativise their understanding of the heart of their faith, the uniqueness and universal relevance of the revelation and the redemption given by God in Jesus Christ.

I also suggest that the approach proposed here agrees with a broad Christian consensus. It is especially noteworthy that two recent official church reports, both published in 2010, support my argument about the need for both dialogue and proclamation – *Sharing the Gospel of Salvation*, from the Church of England, and *Meeting God in Friend and Stranger*, from the Catholic Bishops' Conference of England and Wales.[18] The emphasis in the two documents is somewhat different. *Sharing the Gospel of Salvation* was prompted by discussion in the Church of England's General Synod of the question of evangelism among people of other faiths, so naturally focuses on that theme, while also giving an account of the wider range of ways in which the Church should (and does) engage with other faith communities.[19] The primary concern of *Meeting God in Friend and Stranger* is to introduce the concept of dialogue to Catholics to whom the idea is unfamiliar and puzzling: 'Dialogue with believers of other religions is a new concept for many Catholics, and they may well feel that it is

---

[18] *Sharing the Gospel of Salvation*, available at http://www.churchofengland.org/media/39745/gsmisc956.pdf accessed 18 December 2014; *Meeting God in Friend and Stranger: Fostering Respect and Mutual Understanding between the Religions* (Catholic Truth Society: London, 2010). See also *Christian Witness in a Multi-Religious World: Recommendations for Conduct*, a brief 2011 document emerging from discussions between representatives of the World Council of Churches, the Pontifical Council for Interreligious Dialogue and the World Evangelical Alliance available at http://www.oikoumene.org/en/resources/documents/wcc-programmes/interreligious-dialogue-and-cooperation/christian-identity-in-pluralistic-societies/christian-witness-in-a-multi-religious-world accessed 18 December 2014.

[19] References to evangelism, proclamation, the making of disciples and such themes are frequent in *Sharing the Gospel of Salvation*. For example, see paragraphs 87 and 94 (the latter quoting R. Williams).

"one challenge too far".[20] But while its primary focus is on dialogue it repeatedly emphasises that the promotion of dialogue must not be understood to mean that the Church should no longer proclaim Christ to all people and desire their conversion.[21] In what follows I shall draw on both these official church documents, as well as making extensive reference to the highly relevant 1991 Vatican document *Dialogue and Proclamation*.[22]

Proper Humility and the Call to Dialogue

The days are gone, or very nearly so, when the churches could address western societies from a place of presumed authority and influence. In the wake of massive shifts in the religious demographic of western culture, Christianity finds itself not only part of the religious marketplace but also often the 'less interesting' part as new and intriguing voices appear. The Church cannot ignore those voices, nor simply dismiss the influence they are having in the culture. Although Murad exaggerates the number of Muslim converts in the United Kingdom, it is true, even so, that Muslim converts constitute a significant portion of a significant religious minority. Christian engagement with this phenomenon must consist, at least in part, of a willingness to hear the testimonies of those who have converted, thereby at least implicitly stating the failure of Christianity to provide what they were looking for. There is a proper humility for the Church in its approach to a religiously diverse culture: humility in relation to those outside the Christian fold, yes, but humility primarily before God, acknowledging our frailty before the truth, and attentive to what God might have to teach us through the other.

Christian humility, then, will motivate an openness to dialogue. Those who commit themselves to dialogue will soon learn that it is not possible for Christians to ignore the weight of history as it bears upon present inter-religious relationships. So openness to dialogue will compel a willingness to be challenged concerning the failure of the Church, past and present, to live up to its own explicit ideals.[23] It will also lead to a readiness to see God's work in people of other

---

[20] *Meeting God in Friend and Stranger*, Preface: 9.

[21] Ibid: paragraphs 51, 74, 87, and 89.

[22] Available online through the Vatican website, http://www.vatican.va accessed 18 December 2014. See M. Fitzgerald, '"Dialogue and Proclamation": A Reading in the Perspective of Christian-Muslim Relations', in D. Kendall and G. O'Collins (eds), *In Many and Diverse Ways: Essays in Honor of Jacques Dupuis* (Maryknoll: Orbis, 2003): 181–93.

[23] *Dialogue and Proclamation* refers to 'socio-political factors' and 'burdens of the past' as obstacles to dialogue (1.5.52, see also 2.7.74). *Sharing the Gospel of Salvation* refers to the 'dark side' of the history of mission in the Church of England, while adding that 'this is not a reason ... to give up on mission' (5, paragraph 32).

faiths and to learn from them. Thus the Catholic Bishops of England and Wales encourage us to expect that, through inter-faith encounter, 'God may sometimes lead us into further truth about himself, because God's mystery can never be fully within our grasp, and the journey into it is endless.'[24] Further, engagement in dialogue should give rise to a deep concern for universal religious freedom, fundamentally out of respect for the God whose working among human beings demands that they be able to respond without compulsion.[25] The dialogical process will also reveal areas of common concern between Christians and others. Christian humility before God and neighbour will thus motivate cooperative action for the common good, together with a concern that real goods in the earthly city be made available to all its citizens.[26]

Although there is a continuing need for the churches to work on this agenda for dialogue and the related attitudes and practices just described, there is no shortage of evidence of the commitment over recent decades of the historic Christian churches to inter-religious dialogue. Thus it was in the midst of the Second Vatican Council that the Secretariat for Non-Christians was created in 1964. Renamed the Pontifical Council for Interreligious Dialogue in 1988, it has initiated and taken part in numerous examples of dialogue in the following decades.[27] Three examples of the work of the Church of England and the Anglican Communion in the last decade, specifically in Christian-Muslim relations, are the creation of the Christian-Muslim Forum, the launching of an annual dialogue meeting with al-Azhar al-Sharif in Cairo, and Building Bridges, an annual seminar for theological dialogue, chaired by Rowan Williams throughout the decade in which he served as Archbishop of Canterbury.[28]

---

[24] *Meeting God in Friend and Stranger*: 14. This passage, significantly, goes on to say that at other times interfaith encounter will require Christians to confess, courteously, 'that what we are meeting is simply false, and not a glimpse of God's truth or holiness'. See also D. Marshall, *Learning from How Muslims See Christianity* (Grove Books: Cambridge, 2006).

[25] See the Vatican II declaration on religious freedom, *Dignitatis Humanae*, noting especially its grounding of this commitment in the revelation of God and God's ways (section 11). See also D. Marshall, 'Christians, Muslims and Religious Freedom', in S. Goodwin (ed.), *World Christianity in Muslim Encounter* (Continuum: London, 2009): 115–27.

[26] See L. Bretherton, *Hospitality as Holiness: Christian Witness amid Moral Diversity* (Ashgate: Farnham, 2006), chapters 4 and 5.

[27] See its bulletin *Pro Dialogo* for documentation of its work in this field.

[28] On the Christian-Muslim Forum, see: http://www.christianmuslimforum.org/ accessed 18 December 2014; on the dialogue process with al-Azhar, see: http://nifcon.anglicancommunion.org/work/declarations/al-azhar.cfm accessed 18 December 2014; on Building Bridges, see: http://berkleycenter.georgetown.edu/projects/the-building-bridges-seminar accessed 18 December 2014.

There is also increasing evidence that this emphasis in the senior councils of the churches on the need for a dialogical and co-operative approach to other faiths is also reflected in practical ways in many local churches.[29]

Proper Confidence and the Call to Proclaim the Gospel of Jesus Christ

Pre-supposing this commitment to dialogue as a fundamental and continuing characteristic of the Church – rather than a merely pragmatic necessity – we turn now to explore the Church's concurrent call to proclaim the Gospel of Jesus Christ. As we do so it is important to reiterate that although dialogue and proclamation are distinguishable, they are also inter-penetrating practices of the Church. As we will discuss further below, there can be practical difficulties in negotiating the relationship between them but it is nevertheless crucial for Christians involved in inter-faith relations to recognise the mutual indispensability of dialogue and proclamation. Thus, for those who emphasise dialogue, it is important to recognise that fruitful negotiation of the boundary between self and other in inter-faith engagement depends upon the proper confidence that motivates and accompanies proclamation. For Christians to attempt to occupy a space void of proclamation is to collapse the boundary between self and other in ways that make meaningful dialogue ultimately impossible. One cannot speak from nowhere. So proper humility depends for its authenticity on a simultaneous confidence in the place from which one speaks to others, even as one also hopes to meet God in them and to learn from them.

Dialogue and Proclamation argues that all Christians are 'called to be personally involved in these two ways of carrying out the one mission of the Church', but goes on to stress that they 'must always bear in mind that dialogue ... does not constitute the whole mission of the Church, that it cannot simply replace proclamation, but remains oriented towards proclamation ....'[30]

---

[29] The Church of England report *Sharing the Gospel of Salvation* gives numerous examples of how parish churches have sought to build bridges of dialogue and co-operation with other religious communities, while also witnessing to the Christian faith. One example is the Springfield Project in Birmingham (*Sharing the Gospel of Salvation*: 27–8, paragraphs 147–54), which is described in greater detail in '"Strangers and Neighbours": The Springfield Project and Barelwi Mosque Next Door – Edmund Newey in Conversation with Richard Sudworth', in F. Ward and S. Coakley (eds), *Fear and Friendship: Anglicans Engaging with Islam* (Continuum: London, 2012): 17–38.

[30] *Dialogue and Proclamation*: 4.3.82.

To be able to join with confidence in the Church's proclamation of the Gospel, Christians need strong foundations in the story that they are called to announce. As *Sharing the Gospel of Salvation* puts it,

> ... a rootedness in scripture and in an understanding of its originating contexts, provides a foundation for good practice in sharing the gospel. A Church which has generally been unused to reading and studying the Bible with its multi religious context in mind will find much to wrestle with and to be encouraged by.[31]

The Acts of the Apostles, for example, narrates the encounter of the Gospel with the religious and intellectual cultures of the Gentiles, giving much insight into the early apostolic proclamation, motivated by the utter singularity of God's saving action in Christ (4:12), but also indicating responsiveness to the particularities of different religious and cultural contexts (14:8–20; 17:16–34). The sending out of the disciples to proclaim Christ is indeed a pervasive theme throughout the New Testament, for example in the concluding sections of each of the four gospels. In the longer ending of Mark, the disciples are sent to 'preach the Gospel to the whole creation' (16:15). Matthew and Luke conclude with extended reports of appearances of the risen Jesus, in which he sends the disciples into all the world to make disciples (Matthew 28:19) and to preach forgiveness in his name (Luke 24:47). As John narrates it, one of Jesus' last prayers on earth is that God protect his disciples, whom Jesus sends into the world just as God has sent him (17:18), in order that the world should 'believe in [Jesus] through their message' (17:20). Also relevant here is Paul's narration of the events by which God has saved the world, and the proclamation to which this gives rise. Thus Paul moves in Romans from his account of the significance of the death of Jesus, as at 3:21–6 and 5:6, 8 ('While we were still powerless, Christ died for us ... God demonstrates his own love for us in this: while we were still sinners, Christ died for us') to his resurrection and the coming of the Spirit (8:11–16) and the future hope to which all this gives rise (8:18–25). And it is this story of what God has done in Christ that motivates Paul to proclaim the Gospel in order to bring about the obedience of faith among all the Gentiles (1:5; cf. 10:14; 15:18–20).

In line with this pervasive testimony of the New Testament to God's redemptive work in Christ and the proclamation to which it naturally gives

---

[31] *Sharing the Gospel of Salvation*: 15 (paragraph 90). *Dialogue and Proclamation* expounds the Church's call to proclaim Christ with extensive citation of scripture, for example at 2.1.55.

rise, the Roman Catholic Church is likewise at pains to stress the necessity of proclamation. While the Second Vatican Council is understandably and properly associated especially with the new emphasis on dialogue with the wider world, including people of other religions, it is also clear that the Council repeatedly reaffirmed the Church's task of proclamation to all people, notably in *Ad Gentes*, the Decree on the Mission Activity of the Church. It was also during the Council that Pope Paul VI insisted, in *Evangelii Nuntiandi* (5) that 'the presentation of the Gospel message is not optional for the Church. It is her duty, by command of the Lord Jesus, so that men may believe and be saved'. This complementarity of the calls to dialogue and proclamation continues to be affirmed, above all in *Dialogue and Proclamation* which, as we have seen, both affirms the importance of dialogue and also teaches that 'the Church's mission is to proclaim the Kingdom of God established on earth in Jesus Christ, through his life, death and resurrection, as God's decisive and universal offer of salvation to the world'.[32] Thus, 'there is no true evangelization if the name, the teaching, the life, the promises, the Kingdom and the mystery of Jesus of Nazareth, the Son of God, are not proclaimed'.[33]As we have seen, this dual emphasis is echoed more recently (2010) by both the Catholic Bishops of England and Wales in *Meeting God in Friend and Stranger* and by the Church of England in *Sharing the Gospel of Salvation*.

Holding Dialogue and Proclamation Together

This chapter has argued that Christian approaches to other faiths should be characterised, on the one hand, by the humility that is expressed in dialogue and, on the other, by the confidence that issues in proclamation of the Gospel of Jesus Christ. In practice, however, relating these two elements has proved difficult.[34] The very existence of the 1991 Vatican document *Dialogue and Proclamation*, cited frequently in this essay, is itself a pointer to this difficulty.

[32] *Dialogue and Proclamation*: 2.2.58.

[33] Ibid: quoting *Evangelii Nuntiandi*: 22.

[34] This might prompt the response that it is in the west that Christians find it difficult to hold dialogue and proclamation together, while this is not so to anything like the same degree elsewhere in the worldwide Church. There may be some truth in this, though the earlier quotation from S. Samartha shows that it is not just western Christians who oppose proclamation to non-Christians. Anyway, to the extent that it is true that western Christians find it especially difficult to hold dialogue and proclamation together, part of their task is to learn from the experience of Christians elsewhere in the world.

Its composition and publication jointly by both the Pontifical Council for Interreligious Dialogue and the Congregation for the Evangelization of Peoples arose from an awareness of how difficult some Christians found it to relate dialogue to proclamation. As the document puts it:

> The practice of dialogue raises problems in the minds of many. There are those who seem to think, erroneously, that in the Church's mission today dialogue should simply replace proclamation. At the other extreme, some fail to see the value of interreligious dialogue. Yet others are perplexed and ask: if interreligious dialogue has become so important, has the proclamation of the Gospel lost its urgency?[35]

The document thus seeks to draw into greater theological and practical harmony two areas of the Church's activity which all too easily drift apart or indeed exist in a state of some tension. Much the same can be said of other church documents in this area, such as the Church of England's *Sharing the Gospel of Salvation*. As one of the contributions to this report puts it: 'It has been said that most churches either obey the great commandment to love our neighbour, or the great commission to make disciples. They rarely manage to do both.'[36]

One reason for the apparent difficulty of holding dialogue and proclamation together is that proclamation, especially if accompanied by conversions or even a hint of the possibility of conversions, can appear to be the enemy of dialogue and inter-communal harmony. Even those who accept the principle of freedom of religion do not relish losing members of their community through conversion to another faith. For some religious communities this remains an extremely sensitive issue and any hint that Christians are seeking to convert their members can generate significant tensions. An example of this occurred in 1992 when it was reported that Michael Marshall, a Church of England bishop appointed to co-lead an initiative in evangelism, had written that 'the call to win Islam for Christ is on the agenda', leading to complaints from Muslim and Jewish organisations.[37] This issue recurs in various forms; for example, Hindu groups may make it a condition of dialogue that Christians should renounce any intention to convert Hindus.

---

[35] *Dialogue and Proclamation*, Introduction: 4 (c).

[36] *Sharing the Gospel of Salvation*: 35 (paragraph 186).

[37] *The Tablet*, 11 January 1992: 25–6, available at http://archive.thetablet.co.uk/article/11th-january-1992/25/decade-of-evangelism-offends-muslims-and-jews accessed 18 December 2014.

However, although it is therefore understandable that some Christians who feel called to promote dialogue see an emphasis by other Christians on proclamation as a threat to their work, the Church as a whole simply cannot remove proclamation and the possibility of conversion from its agenda. As Rowan Williams and John Sentamu put it, writing as the two Archbishops of the Church of England:

> ... conversion must never become a word of which Christians fight shy ... there should be nothing embarrassed or awkward about the Church's commitment to draw others to Christ. This we do, not in order to win favour for ourselves, nor to make others more like us, but simply because we want to share God's gifts as we have received them – freely and unearned.[38]

How Christians hold this commitment together with a commitment to seeking the common good and the harmony of society will often be taxing. There is no simple formula that can be offered here. While the Church should seek to be at peace with all people (Romans 12:18), it cannot be the Church of Jesus Christ and at the same time insist that its life in a religiously diverse society will be without tension and conflict. The Church cannot fulfil its commission from Christ to proclaim the Gospel and make disciples of all nations (Matthew 28:19) and expect never to encounter opposition. Nevertheless, as part of the commitment of the Church to intelligent dialogue with other communities about the common good, it should also seek peaceful ways in which all people can freely express their convictions. It is encouraging, therefore, that some progress has been made in frank inter-faith discussions about conversion. Notably, the Christian-Muslim Forum has produced a set of *'Ethical Guidelines for Christian and Muslim Witness in Britain'.*[39]

An authentic Christian motivation for desiring the conversion of all peoples to Christ is the conviction that the Church is only a pale reflection of what it is called to be, with an inevitably limited understanding of the full significance of Christ, until it is filled with people of every background, all bringing their distinctive contributions and insights to the diversity in unity that should characterise the life of the Body of Christ. *Sharing the Gospel of Salvation*, quoting the earlier Church of England report, *The Mystery of Salvation*, comments: 'It

[38] *Sharing the Gospel of Salvation*, Foreword. R. Williams also discusses the theme of conversion across religious traditions in his Afterword to *Fear and Friendship*.

[39] Available at http://www.christianmuslimforum.org/downloads/Ethical_Guidelines_for_Witness.pdf accessed 18 December 2014.

may be ... that our understanding of Christ will itself be enhanced when people of other faiths are gathered in'.[40] Kenneth Cragg elaborates on the same point:

> ... it takes a whole world to understand a whole Christ. Those who bring Christ are not vulgarly universalizing their own culture: they are conveying what, when apprehended, both they and their hearers learn ... . They who take Christ are in a state of perpetual discovery, and the discoveries they make are made through the discoveries they enable.[41]

In this same spirit that looks to how the Body of Christ will be enriched by the diverse peoples of the world, Christians may often contemplate aspects of the life of other faith communities with 'holy envy' and (to adapt the language of Hebrews 11:40) reflect that 'without them, we will not be made perfect'.

Christians who hold such a vision of the growth of the Church need also to be aware of the difficulties that may arise when people from other faith communities become Christians, and the consequent challenges for churches that wish to become welcoming communities to them. In particular, such converts may experience severe tensions with family and wider community, sometimes becoming alienated from them. The transition from being embedded within the close family and community life of a non-western culture to membership of a church community in the individualistic modern western world can be traumatic and experience of life in the Christian community can be disappointing. A British Christian from a Sikh background comments:

> ... those from other faiths often genuinely leave all behind them: families, friends and culture. What they often receive in return is a Sunday morning meeting! It's a poor trade-off because many of our other faith neighbours come from deeply interwoven and supporting communities. The hour or so we give to weekly worship and prayer, and the nodding, "Fine" to the cursory, "How are you?" over cheap coffee and rich tea biscuits can be an insulting parody of the kingdom community to which Christ calls us.[42]

Churches which desire to be faithful to the call to make disciples of all nations need to reflect on what it will mean for them to welcome, support, and truly integrate new Christians from other religious communities; they will also

---

[40] *Sharing the Gospel of Salvation*: 14 (paragraph 85).

[41] K. Cragg, *The Call of the Minaret*, third edition (Oxford: Oneworld, 2000): 168.

[42] Cited in R. Sudworth, *Distinctly Welcoming: Christian Presence in a Multifaith Society* (Bletchley: Scripture Union, 2007): 124.

need to reflect on the impact of such conversions on relations with other faith communities and the wider common good. While there may be no simple solution to the tensions that can arise, churches which are already at work on the dialogical agenda sketched out earlier, and have established good relations with other communities, can hope that their work of proclamation will be experienced not as an isolated and hostile activity, but as a part of the wider mission of the Church to love and serve all its neighbours.

Returning to the issue of differences in emphasis among Christians, in practice it tends to be the case that individual Christians and specific Christian organisations feel a call towards one activity or the other, dialogue or proclamation. It is true that this distinction can never be absolute, as dialogue always involves some communication of one's own faith and proclamation cannot really begin in the absence of any human dialogue. Nevertheless, a genuine distinction remains and there is an observable tendency for Christian groups to opt for one emphasis or the other. In general, the more established historic churches, partly because of their strong connections with civic institutions and their emphasis on responsibility for working for the common good, have tended to prioritise dialogue. We have seen that such churches will also often state (sometimes prompted by their more evangelistic members) that proclamation remains on their agenda; but in practice their official initiatives have tended to be in the field of dialogue.[43] In contrast, other Christian organisations, usually evangelical, will emphasise proclamation, or, if that word is not used, the sharing of the Christian faith in the hope that others will embrace it. Among such groups there is confidence that despite the difficulties involved, there has been a steady increase in the numbers of people coming to Christian faith from other religious backgrounds. For example, on the basis of his doctoral work at London University on the almost entirely unresearched question of the conversion of Muslims to Christianity in Britain, Tim Green writes: 'Today, in Britain and worldwide, more Muslims are turning to Christ than at any time in history.'[44] Of particular note are the numbers of Iranians converting to Christianity;

[43] In a conversation in 2005, a senior Roman Catholic expert in inter-religious relations, when asked about the commitment of the Roman Catholic Church to both dialogue and proclamation, as expressed in the document *Dialogue and Proclamation*, commented that while there were numerous examples of institutional commitment to dialogue, he could not name a single official church initiative promoting proclamation among non-Christians. That same broad trend is found in other historic Christian denominations.

[44] T. Green, 'Conversion from Islam to Christianity in Britain', in S. Bell and C. Chapman (eds), *Between Naivety and Hostility: Uncovering the Best Christian Responses to Islam in Britain* (Milton Keynes: Authentic Media, 2011): 101.

it has been calculated that there are probably two to three thousand of them in Britain.[45]

However, in recent years the dichotomy, in practice if not in theory, between dialogue and proclamation has perhaps become less stark. Church leaders, together with specialists and educators in the field of inter-religious relations, have begun to place more emphasis on the need for Christians to have greater confidence in articulating their own faith as well as on seeking a sympathetic understanding of their neighbour's faith and offering hospitality and support to communities which, in recent decades, were often new to Britain. Thus Archbishops Williams and Sentamu comment:

> The experience of parishes and people working in multifaith contexts is that, whilst stridency is counterproductive, failure to be open about our beliefs is equally unhelpful. Others want to know why we do things as well as seeing what we do. Because God loves all His people, encounters begin with respect for the other. If we are too cautious of sharing openly the foundations of our beliefs and the nature of our discipleship ... we put constraints on that respect and deny a little of God's nature.[46]

Of the many needs facing Christians as they address the opportunities and challenges of relations with other religious communities, I conclude by identifying two. Firstly, through experience of sustained personal encounter, study and prayerful reflection, Christian leaders need to develop a discerning intelligence as to what kinds of initiative in relation to other faith communities best express the mission of the Church at specific times and in specific contexts. As has been said before, there is no simple formula. Mistakes will be made; patience and perseverance will be needed.

Secondly, Christians need to be aware of the great range of ways in which the whole Body of Christ should express its multi-faceted mission towards all people. This awareness will enable them to recognise the partial and limited nature of any one initiative in this field and so exercise a charitable attitude towards fellow Christians whose emphases may be quite different. Those who are called towards an emphasis on dialogue may well feel nervous about the possible results of efforts towards evangelistic proclamation by other Christians, but need

---

[45] Ibid: 101, 105.

[46] *Sharing the Gospel of Salvation*, Foreword. For a similar emphasis from a senior Roman Catholic specialist in Christian-Muslim relations, see C. Troll, *Muslims Ask, Christians Answer* (Hyde Park, NY: New City Press, 2012); C. Troll, *Dialogue and Difference: Clarity in Christian-Muslim Relations* (Maryknoll, NY: Orbis, 2009).

to recognise that these too may be faithfully expressing part of the meaning of Christ for all people. Conversely, those with a zeal for proclamation need to see that it takes more than proclamation to witness fully to the 'grace and truth' that became incarnate in Jesus. No Christian individual or organisation will ever get the balance quite right, but all can pray that the whole Church, in its multiple activities, inspired by sometimes quite different theological convictions, may convey, however imperfectly, the full significance of Christ for the whole world.

The challenge outlined in this chapter might well suggest a daunting balancing act. It is as well to acknowledge that, in many ways, the encounter with religious diversity takes western Christians beyond their usual comfort zones and into places where they can be painfully aware of their lack of experience and their stark disagreements with each other. Viewed more positively, this is an opportunity for growth, growth in understanding of God-in-Christ and of God's ways in the world, but also growth of the Church in size and diversity as it learns to engage with all its neighbours with the humility and the confidence which have been our themes.

PART II:
Church Growth and the Bible

Chapter 3

The Kingdom of God and Church Growth in the New Testament

Mark Bonnington

Introduction

One of the most enigmatic verses of Acts comes in the second paragraph. The disciples ask the risen Lord Jesus the date of the restoration of the kingdom to Israel (Acts 1:6). Jesus gives an ambiguous response – and a series of still-not-quite-resolved theological hares are set running.

The disciples' question is an unsurprising one. Luke's Gospel, like the other Synoptics, has made Jesus' kingdom proclamation the central element of Jesus' mission and message (e.g., Luke 4:16–44), a centrality which is echoed in much contemporary missiology. The first paragraph of Acts continues the theme. The risen Jesus ... presented himself alive to them by many proofs, appearing to them during 40 days and speaking about the kingdom of God (1:3).

Asked whether he will now restore the kingdom to Israel, Jesus variously (depending on which commentator you follow): (a) denies an eschatological vision of the kingdom in favour of history – a history subsequently narrated in the rest of Acts; (b) denies a nationalist vision of the kingdom and signals a decisive turn to the gentile mission – foreshadowing one of the great themes of both the New Testament (NT) in general and of Acts in particular; (c) maintains a studious silence on the substance of kingdom eschatology and Israel's place within it and deflects attention from the time element – rebuking any unhelpful focus on eschatological timetabling operations; or (d) any two or three of the above.

To some degree we could take Acts' talk of the kingdom as characteristic of the NT more widely. First, in Acts, as in Paul's letters, talk of the kingdom is an intermittent but an assumed part of the theological furniture of the narrative of the apostolic mission. Secondly, kingdom language is not eliminated but has become defined by and subordinated to the great kerygmatic facts of Jesus' death and resurrection. Thirdly, where the content of the kingdom idea is clear it retains a distinctively eschatological shade of meaning.

So after Acts begins with the two kingdom references of the opening paragraphs, the phrase 'kingdom of God' appears four more times in summaries of missionary preaching (8:12; 14:22; 19:8; 20:25). Acts ends with Paul under house arrest in Rome: '... he lived there two whole years at his own expense, and welcomed all who came to him, proclaiming the kingdom of God and teaching about the Lord Jesus Christ with all boldness and without hindrance' (Acts 28:30–31). Luke neatly brackets his story of the spreading flame of the gospel and of the growing church with kingdom references. He sprinkles that narrative with kingdom language that assumes that the kingdom is essential to the gospel message, an insistence that persists pasts the NT and into the creeds.

To stick fairly strictly to the title of this chapter we will take our cue from Acts and take the same themes in two stages. The first is entitled: The (select) History of Interpretation of the Kingdom of God and what we could Learn from it. The second is similar: The Growth of the Earliest Christian Communities and what we can Learn from them. So this chapter contains a little bit of the history of interpretation, some reflections on early church life and some unsubtly laid trails to today's church for you to follow along the way.

The History of Interpretation of the Kingdom of God and What We could Learn from It

Weiss and Schweitzer

The modern era of discussion of what the NT in general, and Jesus in particular, meant by the kingdom of God began at the end of the nineteenth century when Johannes Weiss published his book *Jesus' Proclamation of the Kingdom of God* (1892). Weiss advanced a view which was later supported quite independently by Albert Schweitzer in his *The Mystery of the Kingdom of God* (1901) and *The Quest of the Historical Jesus* (1910).[1] Weiss and Schweitzer's explanation of the kingdom is usually called 'thoroughgoing' or 'consistent' eschatology and involved the idea that, for Jesus, the kingdom was essentially an imminent eschatological event – the sovereign divine in-breaking at the end of the world,

[1] A. Schweitzer, *The Mystery of the Kingdom of God: The Secret of Jesus' Messiahship and Passion* (ET: New York: Dodd Mead and Company 1914); A. Schweitzer, *The Quest of the Historical Jesus: A Critical Study of its Progress from Reimarus to Wrede* (London: A&C Black, 1910).

a view which they believed to have been taken over from Jewish apocalyptic thought. The fact that the kingdom was soon to appear led, as they saw it, to Jesus' emphasis on world-denying ethics for the interim between now and the End. Their emphases were different: Schweitzer wrote what is now a discredited outline of Jesus' life which finished with the desolate cry of a disillusioned man on the cross. Weiss concentrated more on Jesus' sayings. Weiss knew that there are passages in the Gospels which suggested that Jesus thought that the kingdom was present, but he explained them as a consequence of Jesus 'proleptic enthusiasm' in the light of the healing activity of his ministry. By this Weiss meant that Jesus thought that the kingdom was so close that it cast its shadow into the present age – moving Jesus occasionally to use present language of the future kingdom: '... the one great and foremost promise still remains to be fulfilled'.[2] The kingdom of God, in the form that Jesus expected it, is not yet established on earth.[3] Like the commuter on the railway platform who, on seeing the signal change and hearing the buzz of the rails, turns to his friend and says 'The train is here' when it isn't, Jesus occasionally spoke of the kingdom as present when it wasn't.

Weiss and Schweitzer represented a decisive turn against some previous trends in the kingdom interpretation. They set their face against pious renderings of the kingdom theme as being about the reign of God in the heart of the individual. They challenged domesticated and ecclesiocentric readings that too readily identified the kingdom with the church. And they firmly rejected liberal protestant optimism which interpreted the kingdom as largely about social progress – the gradual this-worldly development of an ethical regime of peace and justice, either in its colonialist or socialistic guises. This kind of interpretation – together with its more spiritual twin, optimistic revivalism, persists today. In his second book Schweitzer gave a dire warning: beware painting Jesus in your own image. It is all too easy to stand back and look at our portrait of Jesus and find that instead we are, in fact, looking at ourselves, or our cultures' religious and social preferences, preferences staring back in the mirror.

For Weiss and Schweitzer Jesus was a Jewish apocalyptic prophet expecting an imminent and divine in-breaking at the end of history. Whatever their mistakes here was a decisive turn. From two essential historical points made by Weiss and Schweitzer there has rarely been a hint of retreat – (i) Jesus makes most sense against his Jewish background and (ii) that background suggests that

---

[2] J. Weiss, *Jesus' Proclamation of the Kingdom of God* (Minneapolis: Augsburg Fortress, 1971): 74.

[3] Ibid: 79.

his message of the kingdom was the expectation of an eschatological regime of divine rule.

Many nineteenth century writers knew that Jesus talked about an eschatological kingdom but regarded it as a primitive and peripheral point, subordinated to the Pauline gospel of justification or secondary to his far more important ethical teaching. Weiss and Schweitzer drove a coach and horses through this analysis and established the centrality of the Jewish and eschatological emphasis of Jesus' kingdom message from which there has been no retreat.

From this flow four key challenges to our appropriations of NT kingdom language:

1. to recognise the centrality of the kingdom message to the mission and message of Jesus – a message which is embraced and not marginalised by the rest of the NT;
2. to acknowledge the kingdom as an eschatological reality for which disciples and believers are to long and pray;
3. to acknowledge the kingdom as God's work, not the culmination of human efforts or human progress which are therefore all cast as preparatory to the final victory of God in human history; and thus
4. not to conflate or identify the kingdom too easily with human and this-worldly experience, achievements or success.

C. Harold Dodd

If Weiss and Schweitzer thought that the kingdom was essentially a future eschatological act of God, C.H. Dodd thought of it as essentially present. Dodd is arguably the most influential British NT Scholar of the twentieth century. He expounded his notion of 'realised eschatology' in his famous book *The Parables of the Kingdom.*[4] Dodd argued that Jesus had taken up the Jewish language of the kingdom as the future eschatological act of God and transformed it into a reference to the present – reinterpreting it as a reference to the divine activity manifested in Jesus' own presence and ministry. Dodd focused particularly on those sayings of Jesus that suggested that the kingdom was a present reality, interpreted many of the parables in this direction and assigned Gospel references to the future kingdom to the editorial activity of the Evangelists. Dodd took the references to the kingdom being 'at hand' as references to the present

[4] C.H. Dodd, *The Parables of the Kingdom* (London: Nisbet, 1935).

(Mk 1:14f etc.), and he retranslated Mk 9:1 to read: '... there are some standing here who will not taste death before they see that the KG has *already* come with power'. Now only the perceiving of the kingdom was future – the kingdom itself is in the present.

Dodd's view has been subjected to a number of damning criticisms of which I mention two. First his use of the texts was often forced and arbitrary: he ignored some texts, retranslated others and assigned others to the early Church for no good reason.[5] Secondly Dodd concentrated on what he regarded as distinctive about Jesus, not characteristic. This was a method which implausibly rendered Jesus' meaning different to the future kingdom ideas of both earlier Judaism and later Church.

It was part of Dodd's agenda to present a Jesus who is relevant and accessible to modern man. Dodd's view of the kingdom as present overcame the problem of eschatology and, with it, Weiss and Schweitzer's problem that Jesus might have been wrong. By arguing that in his ministry Jesus was the embodiment of the kingdom Dodd could bridge the gap between the kingdom-centred message of Jesus and the Christ-centred message of the Church. These were both essentially about Jesus' uniqueness in different words, a claim to uniqueness during Jesus life without recourse to abstract theological speculation about his ontological relationship with God, unique not as Word incarnate but as kingdom embodied.[6] Dodd's reading closed the gap between Jesus and the church, but its underlying appeal to accessibility came at the cost of scepticism towards the Jewish roots of Christianity and of eschatology.

The Kingdom in Modern Discussion

Despite all this E.P. Sanders comments on Dodd that: '... readers of Dodd nearly universally agreed he had a point, but he overplayed it'.[7] The history of subsequent scholarly discussion of the kingdom can be seen as an attempt to come to terms with the different insights of Weiss and Schweitzer on the one hand and Dodd on the other.

---

[5] What Weiss took to be central Dodd simply ignored. One searches the Scripture index of Dodd's book in vain for any reference to Matthew 6.10: the prayer 'your kingdom come ...' – it is simply omitted without discussion. Faced with a number of authentic sayings with clear future references he suggested that they referred to the transcendent order beyond space and time where there is no before and after.

[6] The faint whiff of unitarianism hangs heavily over some of Dodd's writing.

[7] E.P. Sanders, *Jesus and Judaism* (London: SCM Press, 1985): 131.

The third phase of discussion about the kingdom of God is what we might call the post-war consensus: that Jesus thought that the kingdom was both present and future – that Jesus himself used the idea substantively in both ways. The list of those influenced by this kind of reading is almost endless but one influential advocate is G.E. Ladd:

> The kingdom of God is the redemptive act of God dynamically active to establish his rule among men, and ... this kingdom, which will appear as an apocalyptic act at the end of the age, has already come into human history in the person and mission of Jesus ... the kingdom of God involves two great moments: fulfilment within history, and consummation at the end of history.[8]

This is the both/and solution to reconciling present and future uses of kingdom language and is nicely, if rather philosophically, summed up in Ladd's own book title *The Presence of the Future*. Ladd exerted direct influence on the Vineyard movement, which more or less began with an explicit acknowledgment of John Wimber's debt to Ladd because of their contact at Fuller Theological Seminary.

Others concur but with different language and emphasis. Swiss theologian Oscar Cullmann, in his book *Christ and Time*,[9] argued, against Dodd's use of the Platonising notion of a timeless eternity, that the NT concept of time was essentially linear. In Judaism the decisive mid-point of history still lay in the future at the end of the age whereas, for Christians, it lies in the past – Christ himself is the midpoint of history. So believers live in the great run-in to the end of the world, between D-day and V-day, in the tension between the 'already' and the 'not yet'. For Cullmann the crucial battle is over, the 'already' is decisive and outweighs the 'not yet'.

This 'already' and 'not yet' view has key strengths inherent within it. It provides an exegetical synthesis of future and present sayings in the Gospels, fits well with the kingdom language of the rest of the NT and shows us a Jesus who adds a creative Messianic twist to Jewish eschatology. Most importantly for our purposes, the great practical consequence for theological praxis is the *ethical balance of its implications.*

By retaining future eschatology the possibilities for human progress in this world, whether social, political or spiritual are relativised. We are reminded by the 'not yet' that the results of all human effort and activity are necessarily

[8] G.E. Ladd, *The Presence of the Future: The Eschatology of Biblical Realism* (Cambridge: Eerdmans, 1974): 218.

[9] O. Cullmann *Christ and Time* (London: SCM, 1955).

provisional. We are robbed of the illusion of the possibility of ultimate solutions in this world and all our efforts are contextualised by the dramatic scope of the God's ultimate kingdom purpose. On the other hand the 'already' serves as a basis for hope, a reminder of the potential of divine work and power in everyday life and a call for reliance on God. It provides a starting point for constructive engagement in purposeful activity and guards against any other-worldly escapism which sees this-worldly activity as a pointless gesture.

Subsequent discussion of Jesus' kingdom language has mainly been a subset of the so-called 'Third Quest of the Historical Jesus' since about 1990. Serious rapprochement with Jewish studies and a more complex and subtle understanding of first century Judaism have led to a much less monolithic view of eschatology. This has been allied to a shift towards more synthesising interpretations of the mission and teaching of Jesus which embrace his actions as well as his words. The hailing of Jesus in kingly messianic terms at his baptism[10] or Jesus' act of riding into Jerusalem on an ass to fulfil the prophecy of Zechariah 9:9 are actions relevant for understanding Jesus' mission on his own terms. Constructive renderings, like N.T. Wright's,[11] have recognised clearly the need to show how Jesus' embracing of the cross as his Messianic vocation fits with his kingdom message and within his overarching mission. Without a good answer to the question: *What has the cross to do with the kingdom?*, there can be no convincing rendering of Jesus' ministry and mission. Without a good answer to this question there can be no authentic kingdom theology.

Loisy's famous saying that 'Jesus announced the kingdom, but it was the church that came'[12] is a sharp observation but it can now be seen to exaggerate the tension between Jesus and the Church and the kingdom and the cross. Eschatology need be neither so naively imminentist nor so other-worldly that it fails to resist escapism that leaves no room for the kind of constructive engagement in mission and service that is so clearly evident in the NT.

In short, recent developments in the discussion of the mission of Jesus and the meaning of the kingdom of God are challenging us to integrate our understanding of the message of Jesus with the preaching of the Church and theologies of the cross with theologies of the kingdom. Those who read the gospels and see the cross need to show how this is anticipated by the message of the kingdom and those who read the gospels and hear the message of the kingdom need to show how the cross continues and complements Jesus'

10 Mark 1:11/Matt 3:17/Luke 3:22 or similar, cf. Psalm 2 and Isaiah 42:1.

11 Mainly N.T. Wright, *Jesus and the Victory of God* (London: SPCK, 1996).

12 A. Loisy, *The Gospel and the Church* (Philadelphia: Fortress, 1976): 166.

kingdom message. We are challenged to see the relationship between kingdom and church as complementary.

The Kingdom and Church Growth

What might we conclude about kingdom theology and the growth of the church today? As we have gone along I have tried to draw out the key implications of the century old conversation in scholarship over the kingdom. Despite its limitations, each constructive reading is worthy of attention, in both the strengths and weaknesses of each one, as we hone our own sense of how the kingdom message contributes to the mission of today's church. For example, in some popular circles today there is an understandable reaction against too ecclesio-centric a vision of the kingdom, too close an identification of kingdom with church, and with it often comes resistance to ecclesiastical control. The alternative is often a use of kingdom language to claim Gospel authorisation for a broader, supposedly less self-interested, 'progressive' movement, free of ecclesiastical control and authority, perhaps fed by disillusionment with the church or just with 'church' (which is perhaps seen as stale rather than fresh).

It seems rather obvious from what we have seen about the kingdom that, whilst there are important insights here, this is not how the NT works the kingdom message of Jesus into its theology. Kingdom and church are not the same thing in the NT but they are complementary and coordinated realities. It seems obvious that the language of the kingdom stands in constructive tension with the message of Easter. For the post-Easter proclamation of the death and resurrection of Jesus, the kingdom consciousness of the church provides an eschatological and teleological orientation to Christian living, mission and suffering.

With this kingdom backdrop the vision of early Christianity could never narrow to a this-worldly movement, even a successful and growing one. The discovery of a purposeful and forward thinking church – a teleological church if you like – can never merely have survival/mission/growth* (*delete as appropriate) in its sights as its final goal. To do so is to reduce teleology to missiology rather than eschatology. We may be looking up at the sky at last but we must not mistake the edge of our bunker for the horizon. To do so is to fail to do justice to the Bible's vision of the goal of both humanity and the cosmos which worship anticipates and towards which it points.

In early Christianity the sights are always higher and the canvas broader – Christian community has more even than a global scope and a missionary goal. It has a cosmological context for both of these. The Easter message in the context of the kingdom locates believers within the purpose of God in all human history. This makes the victory of the cross and resurrection a foretaste of a fuller and deeper triumph being worked out in the lives of the growing movement as it looks for its final, God-given and complete vindication under the Lordship of Christ.

The Growth of the Earliest Christian Communities and What We can Learn from Them

We now turn from more theological matters to a very practical set of questions about the NT church. How did it grow?

Geographical Spread[13]

The most obvious way in which the early church grew is given clear prominence by Acts. Jesus commissions his disciples to be witnesses in Judea, Samaria and the ends of the earth – it is surely right to take Acts 1:8 as a key programmatic statement for the whole book. The early church cannot be accused of lacking in geographical ambition. It is evident, for example, in Paul's own determination, expressed in Romans 15, to keep moving on to virgin mission territory (in fact Spain), in James commending Jewish Christian wisdom to the 12 tribes of the Dispersion or the Apocalypse's vision of the people of God made up of every nation, tongue, tribe and people. The spreading flame of the Gospel envisages, in embryo at least, the church as a global phenomenon. It is a simple observation that the earliest churches grew because they spread to unevangelised areas and unreached peoples and when the gospel came it came with all the advantages and disadvantages of a novel faith. There is still some of this to do – take your twenty-first century computer in your hand, go to a well-known search engine and look with a 'heaven's eye' view at where some of these places remain. In general today it is the places where the church is geographically closer and the distance is social or cultural or linguistic where you will find the places unreached by the gospel of Christ.

Acts is also interested in the numerical growth of the church and notes it when success is out of the ordinary, even within its own remarkable narrative:

---

[13] E. Schnabel, *Early Christian Mission* (Downers Grover: InterVarsity Press, 2004); E. Adams, *The Earliest Christian Meeting Places: Almost Exclusively Houses?* (London: T & T Clark, 2013); W. Meeks, *The First Urban Christians* (New Haven: Yale University Press, 2003); D. Horrell, *After the First Urban Christians* (London: T & T Clark, 2009).

3,000 converted on the day of Pentecost (2:41); despite opposition to Peter and John many of those who heard the word believed and the number of men converted reached 5,000 (4:4); many priests in Jerusalem became obedient to the faith (6:7) indeed James later points out that thousands in Jerusalem believe in Jesus but remain faithful to the Law (21:20); many in Joppa believed in the Lord (9:42); a great crowd was converted in Antioch (11:24); Paul and Barnabas made many disciples in Derbe (14:21); many of the devout Greeks and not a few leading women converted in Thessalonica (17:4); many of those hearing Paul believed and were baptised in Corinth (18:8).

Many is not a number and the only place where we hear of thousands of converts is Jerusalem (2:41) where it is clear that the boundaries between the church and practising Judaism were understandably, and perhaps rightly, vague. Since thousands are mentioned we are perhaps right to read into the meaning of 'many' something like: 'more than was usual but not more than a few hundred'. Enough to cause a stir if they started to refuse to follow the pagan practices of festivals, guilds, processions and sacrifice and to look more like Jews in their religious practice without actually converting to Judaism. Not least, all these passages leave us with a sense that the early Jesus followers felt themselves to be part of a burgeoning movement – a movement facing opposition but also enjoying extraordinary divine favour.

Key to this geographical and numerical growth were two closely related mechanisms: (i) the deliberate choice of some to act almost exclusively as itinerant evangelists and church planters; and (ii) the less deliberate work of others travelling the seas and roads of the empire to join with others in passing on the faith as they travelled and settled and moved on again, Priscilla and Aquila seem good examples of this latter phenomenon – they turn up in at least three places (Ephesus, Corinth and Rome) that Paul also visits.

The impression given by the Bible maps of Paul's missionary journeys starting out from and returning to the mother church of Antioch lacks the calendar that we need to see what is really going on. Paul spent a year in Philippi in 48–9 AD; 18 months in Corinth in 50–51 AD (and another two or three months there in the winter 56–7 AD), over two and a half years in Ephesus in 52–5 AD, two years imprisoned in Caesarea in 57–9 AD and at least two years imprisoned in Rome in 60–62 AD. Paul hunkers down for the winters but good weather most of the year, relatively speedy travel by sea and road between the main centres, a *lingua franca* and his artisan's trade that could support his ministry virtually anywhere all contributed to a mobile ministry.

Travelling leaders like Paul and his associates stayed long enough to build relationships, establish their authority, shape the life of an emerging community and find others to whom he could pass on the leadership of the churches. Though he liked to be, Paul was not first in all the places he visited. He was not always free and not everything went well in a place like Corinth. But it is precisely the fact that he made the most of difficult circumstances, was horrified and proactive when it went wrong and in periodic pastoral contact with his churches by message, letter and personal envoy that offers ample testimony to his efforts to build a network of sustainable and self-resourcing churches. Paul works hard, lives sacrificially, and appears to follow the instruction of Jesus to travel in a pair (for he often writes in a pair). He claims an extrinsic authority that appeals both to the commission of the risen Christ and the intrinsic authority of his own behaviour, speech and lifestyle. This itinerancy (formal and informal) was designed to leave behind not merely converted individuals but established communities with a distinct and clear new identity.

Travelling then, as now, effectively meant much social contact with passing acquaintances. Everyday living was much closer than virtually anywhere today. The population densities in ancient cities were as high as anywhere in the modern world and might have been twice that of modern Manhattan or Calcutta. Rubbing shoulders with people was part of the way of life of the *polis* that is simply foreign to the modern west with the isolating effect of more sanitary living conditions and modern motor transport. Close living, close working and even closer travelling made for a plethora of social contacts in the course of which the gospel was preached or gossiped in occasional, regular, deliberate or incidental contacts alike.

The Gospel and Conversion

It seems almost too obvious to say but the gospel itself and its impact in the transformation of lives of both individuals and households is the key element in its own spread and the growth of the church. The early church was a message-led not an organisational, or even community focussed, movement. Discussion of social history or missionary strategy cannot dislodge one relatively obvious but simple fact: hearing the gospel and responding to it was a life-transforming experience for many Jews and gentiles alike in the Greco-Roman world. The freshness and novelty of this change of heart and life worried and attracted others by turns.

Many of course did not respond. The numbers of those who converted or actively opposed Christian preaching must presumably have been many fewer than those who just shrugged and walked away. In Acts there always seems to be a rather general crowd who can be stirred up by activists on either side to sympathise or oppose the faith depending on the mood.[14] This is the stuff of both the narratives and the theology of the early churches. Acts may record the remarkable and the noteworthy but it pays ample testimony both to the struggles and triumphs of a movement confident in the God-given commission to preach and to the life-transforming effect of the gospel. Paul's theological answer to why this happens is powerful and resonant: the gospel is the power of God for salvation (1 Cor. 1:18–25). In it the Spirit of God is at work to change lives, invert values and create communities of people called together under the Lordship of Jesus Christ (1 Cor. 2:6–13; 4:9–11).

As we have seen, behind the centrality of the proclamation of the cross and resurrection was the bold canvas of God's work in all of human history. At least part of the genius of the gospel message was its combination of the simplicity with which its basic thrust could be apprehended (even when this was in a series of unfamiliar and rather Jewish concepts for many Greeks). This was combined with the theological and spiritual depth and power to generate novel, convincing and life-transforming models for human self-understanding and personal re-orientation. The early church did not look quite like old Judaism, except perhaps superficially, but it drew on the story of the Jewish Scriptures, whilst recounting and living out a couple of novel supplementary episodes of its own.

The message of the gospel is deeply rooted in the past, particularly in the Jewish Scriptures, but perhaps even more dramatically contextualised in a teleological and eschatological orientation to God's ultimate purpose in Christ. Despite the claims of some that Acts is an apologia for a delayed parousia, the sense of an ending dots the preaching of the book and motivates its call to repentance as it does the passages of the epistles (and the Apocalypse).

The first churches grew because the gospel was foundational to their life and through it the life transforming power of God created its own dynamics of conversion and community. Perhaps this is also the genius of many contemporary forms of church, especially in their more evangelical and Pentecostal varieties, which generate communities where the power of word and Spirit are vital forces in their common life.

Especially for gentiles, Christian conversion was a high commitment activity. We must allow for some blurring of the sharp lines of being in or out on

[14] Acts 17 is a microcosm of variable responses.

occasion, especially for Jews.[15] In general, conversion meant quite radical social and religious change. It meant giving up many practices and withdrawing from social activities with religious overtones. There was no such thing as a secular mindset in the ancient world. Everyone had some religion and early Christianity made exclusive claims that had radical, social and relational consequences.

The big claims of the gospel at a theological level were matched in practice by changes of patterns of life and behaviour. A slave converted and wanted to go out early or late to meet other believers. He made up for it by working harder. A household converted and the household gods disappeared from the corner of the room. The master avoided the temples of the gods but instead invited people to dine with him at his own house. When he did so he omitted the traditional libation to his guild's divinity and instead thanked the God of heaven for the meal. Insider and outsider alike knew something had changed and the reasons why were freely on offer. When this was questioned or opposed, and believers still persisted, the new faith was taken more seriously and the reputation of the church grew. Coming up against the authorities, the believers made the case for their faith respectfully, accepted protection gladly and carefully kept their theological distance from Roman divinities and power. Perhaps Jews had to change less or less obviously than pagans. The fact that everyone had given up something from their past for the sake of Christ surely created communities where the sense of joint ownership of the new was universal and challenged people to change. The gospel and conversions were themselves key elements in the growth of the earliest churches.

Leadership

It is worth noting at this point that the earliest churches had established leadership from the beginning. Yes, it is true that Paul's claim to apostleship bridged an uneasy divide between his claimed independence, stemming from his commission by the risen Christ, and recognition of him by the Judean apostles. The early church had leadership from the beginning that came directly from the ministry and resurrection of Jesus and it was clear from whom authorisation of the next generation was to flow. Some are impressed by how rarely leadership is appealed to, others by how often or how quickly it emerged. It is certainly modified by a clear sense of the giftedness of many in the body of the local church. Within at least Paul's vision of the church was the idea of diverse ministries and

[15] Hebrews and James are perhaps two NT books which, in different ways, testify most clearly to this phenomenon.

at least some of these are orientated towards outsiders. But authority is never ceded completely by the apostles.[16]

Where personal knowledge of leaders was indirect or fading in the memory, material like the Pastoral Letters sets out criteria for leadership and looks for local appointment, but the basic central principle remained the same – the apostles were the key authority. They held authority that was backed up in most cases by their evident preparedness to suffer. Apostolic leadership existed from the beginning. It gave the churches basic cohesion. There were tensions between leaders, but foreign to the NT is the kind of model advocated in some circles – summed up by Von Campenhausen's famous nineteenth century book title *Ecclesiastical Authority and Spiritual Power*.[17] This sees an inverse relationship between ecclesiastical authority and spiritual power and advocates a return to primitive egalitarianism in the Spirit as the key to the renewal of the church. The testimony of the NT is different: it grows with recognised leadership from the beginning, but that leadership is not unfamiliar with the life and power of the Spirit. The question is not whether to have leadership but what kind of leadership to have for the growth of the church.

Local Congregations: How Did the Churches the Apostles Left Behind Grow?

The basic thrust of the apostolic mission seems to be to the strategic centres. Called by the man of Macedonia from Asia Minor to new mission work in Europe for the first time, Paul goes straight past the port of Neapolis and heads inland to the great city of Philippi.[18]

Perhaps a growing *local* church did as they did in Corinth. Phoebe's status as a deacon of the church at Cenchreae[19] (9 km away from Corinth on the eastern Saronic Gulf) gives us a clue: they planted a daughter a few miles away which had a separate identity and leadership but which still saw itself as within the Pauline sphere. We know Paul passed through there and the church could have originated from his first mission but it is just as likely that it began under

[16] Paul's limitation of ambition to ministry within the Corinth church to prophets is subtle but noteworthy (1 Cor. 14:1; cf. 12.28).

[17] H. von Campenhausen, *Ecclesiastical Authority and Spiritual Power in the Church of the First Three Centuries* (trans. J.A. Baker (Stanford: Stanford University Press, 1969). Available at http://books.google.co.uk/books?id=ZYmaAAAAIAAJ&printsec=frontcover&source=gbs_ge_summary_r&cad=0#v=onepage&q&f=false accessed 7 January 2015. For a helpful summary of this trajectory see R. Campbell, *The Elders: Seniority Within Earliest Christianity* (Edinburgh: T & T Clark, 1994): chapter 1.

[18] Acts 16:11ff.

[19] Romans 16:1.

Phoebe's patronage after he left. In other places, where Paul himself did not specifically stay or evangelise, an associate like Epaphras in Colossae would do the work on behalf of Paul, and the church would fall indirectly but clearly under Paul's apostolic care. Epaphras was a local, and the most likely scenario is that, having been converted somewhere else and spent time working with the apostle, he headed home and planted a new church in Colossae.

We don't know the precise sizes of early Christian congregations. Eutychus fell from the fourth floor window in one of the Roman blocks of 'flats' or *insulae*[20] – encouraged no doubt by the late hour and a warm room full of olive oil smoke. Given the room sizes in the *insulae*, or in the villas of a city like Corinth, even with the understanding that people lacked modern western perceptions of necessary personal space, churches of no more than 150 were possible in villas and perhaps, typically, a few dozens at most in an *insula*.

Diversity within a congregation of this size is socially powerful – large enough for nearly everyone to find someone like them, small enough for people to know each other's lives and engage in regular inter-personal contact. We don't know exactly what churches did if they grew but church plants, more meetings and more meeting places seem to be likely and obvious solutions, with all the attendant dangers for internal cohesion that come with this strategy.

From what we can glean it also looks as if churches maintained a dual strategy of going out to reach people and drawing people into their gatherings. Acts bears ample testimony to preaching in streets and market places, synagogues and public spaces. Going to these strategic places of public interaction with a fresh and challenging message stirred interest and opposition and the occasional cheeky strategic move may have been very effective – like departing the synagogue and then holding meetings in the house of Titius Justus next door (Acts 18:7). It looks here very much as if not one but two leaders of the synagogue were converted in turn – Crispus and Sosthenes. Clearly early churches knew a good thing when they saw one. Alongside this we should place many, many more informal contacts. Paul met Prisca and Aquilla as refugees from Rome in his workplace. We also know that they met in homes for worship and that Paul could have a reasonable expectation in Corinth that an outsider might come in and find the worship both strange and arresting by turns (1 Cor. 14:23–5).

The internal makeup of the churches that were established looks as if they were as socially and economically mixed as their host cities, a diversity mitigated and challenged by common allegiance to Jesus and the new movement emerging in his name. Arguments have long raged over the social status composition of the

---

[20] Acts 20:7–12.

earliest churches. Views have swung from one extreme – the notion that they were successful because they appealed to an educated elite – while, on the other, there is the persistent suggestion that early churches consisted particularly of the poor. This is an issue made more complex by arguments about the social condition of the populace in general.[21] The gleanings of Paul's letters and Acts narratives seem to point to an unsurprising conclusion for a movement proclaiming a universal gospel: people of all backgrounds were attracted to Christ and the churches, like society as a whole, contained a few educated, rich, influential and high born members but most were ordinary poor people, artisans, wage labourers, clients of the great houses, the free, the freed and slaves of both sexes and all ages. In other words, when we take into account the dominance of the poorer groups in Greco-Roman society as a whole, it looks as if the churches were rather typical of their host society as Paul says in 1 Cor. 1:14: 'For consider your calling, brothers and sisters: not many of you were wise by worldly standards, not many were powerful, not many were of noble birth ...' (cf. 1 Cor. 1:26). That each stratum of society could find in the church some of its own can only have been a help in spreading the gospel: 'We have someone here like you' remains a powerful tool for drawing the enquirer into church.

It cannot be stressed enough that the early Jesus movement did not just make converts, it created communities too. The focal strength of commitment to Christ and the boundary marking effect of the moral and ethical transformation expected of converts made for inclusive but transformative communities of grace:

> Do you not know that the unrighteous will not inherit the kingdom of God? Do not be deceived; neither the immoral, nor idolaters, nor adulterers, nor sexual perverts, nor thieves, nor the greedy, nor drunkards, nor revilers, nor robbers will inherit the kingdom of God. And such were some of you. But you were washed, you were sanctified, you were justified in the name of the Lord Jesus Christ and in the Spirit of our God. (1 Cor. 6:9–11)

Churches like this, churches of inclusion and transformation, grew.

---

[21] So J. Meggit, *Paul, Poverty and Survival* (Edinburgh: T & T Clark, 1998).

Conclusions

Two thousand years of Christian history and a presumed familiarity with the Christian church, its faith and the gospel that drives them are brute facts of our national religious (or irreligious) landscape.

Nonetheless we are left wondering whether some key contributions to church growth in earliest Christianity are not basically the same now as then: a gospel and movement rooted in the ministry and message of Jesus; a combination of fixity and itinerancy in ministry; sacrificial missional leadership; a combination of deliberate and incidental evangelism; convincing living to back the claim of a life-changing message; human-sized communities where relationships are real and discipleship serious; sacrificial life-styles that reflect the seriousness with which the message is taken; a focus on the communal context of discipleship as communities of resistance in a dominant culture; a degree of daily social openness and vulnerability that offers bridges for the good news; evidence of changed lives as a spur to sustained discipleship and further mission; a serious balance between inclusion and transformation where everyone experiences the cost of change; diversity in the local church which highlights common life in Christ. And a sense of a momentum – that by the wind of the Spirit, ultimately, they are running with the tide of history. Which we are.

Chapter 4

The Ecclesiology of Acts[1]

C. Kavin Rowe

Introduction

In a certain sense, dealing with the ecclesiology of Acts ought to be as easy as any topic in New Testament theology. The entire book of Acts, after all, is most fundamentally a story about the church. It seems we should be able to read Acts carefully and discern its teaching about the church. But, of course, this is not so easy.

There are several reasons why it is difficult to speak well about the ecclesiology of Acts. For one thing, Acts presents multiple Christian communities throughout its narrative, and it hardly takes much thought to see that in important ways the church in Corinth, for example, differs from that in Ephesus, which in turn differs from that in Lystra and Antioch and Jerusalem, and so on. For another, studying Luke's 22 uses of the word *ekklesia* in Acts sheds surprisingly little interpretive light on the dynamic theological moves of the narrative as a whole. As NT scholars have often observed, it is difficult – perhaps frustratingly so – to find a particular pattern of usage. But absent such a pattern, our study of the word produces little more in the way of results than restatements of the context in which the word receives its meaning. Still more difficult is the fact that, almost reflexively, we tend to think of ecclesiology in relation to particular structures of various Christian denominations. Does the Acts of the Apostles lead to or support the Lutherans? the Presbyterians? the Methodists? the Baptists? the Pope? Or none of the above? Such a focus does not necessarily produce the wrong questions – we should ask Scripture questions about church governance – but neither does it get to the heart of Acts' vision. The simple reason is that ecclesiology in Acts is less about the particulars of church order

---

[1] An earlier version of this essay was given as the 2011 Harrison Lecture at Mount Olive College and published as an article in *Interpretation*, vol. 66/3, 2012. The editor and publishers are extremely grateful to the editors of *Interpretation* and to Professor Rowe for their allowing this article to be reprinted here.

(though there is some of that) than it is about how to be Christian in a world that did not know what being Christian was. That is the ecclesiology of Acts: a way of reasoning and habit of being that makes Christianity a visible human witness to the Lord Jesus Christ in a world that did not know him.

Precisely because of this lack of knowledge, the best way to see the ecclesiology of Acts is to situate its political vision within the wider Roman world. This allows us to see clearly the particular tension that constituted the heart of Christianity's public witness and made it such a potent force. I will proceed in three steps. First, I will discuss one of the most memorable scenes from the second half of the book, the riot in Ephesus (Acts 19). Second, I will examine the series of scenes from Acts 25–6 that depict the trial of the apostle Paul. Third, by looking closely at a short scene in Thessalonica (Acts 17), I will explore the picture that emerges when the scene in Ephesus is held together with Paul's trial. The scene in Thessalonica provides the interpretive lens through which to look at the ecclesiology of Acts as a whole – because it captures in abbreviated form the animating theological moves that fund the Acts narrative.[2]

Christianity and the Destabilisation of Greco-Roman Culture (Ephesus: Acts 19)

The first scene to consider is a riot in Ephesus, one of the most important cities in the ancient Mediterranean world. The story occurs in Acts 19:1–41. The central narrative line of this lengthy passage is as follows: the Christians arrive with their typical missionary programme, and many people convert. Because conversion to the Christian movement involved the simultaneous rejection of the practices of magic, soothsaying, and the like, the new converts hold a public book burning in which they destroy their magic books. Shortly thereafter, an Ephesian silversmith named Demetrius accuses Paul and the other Christians of destroying his business in Ephesus and threatening the city's major temple. (This temple was the temple of Artemis, and Demetrius; his co-workers made shrines of the goddess and sold them in conjunction with the temple. Their business was directly dependent upon the flourishing of the temple.) Demetrius' accusation is not a formal legal one – a particular kind of crime such as treason or improper use of magic – but is rather more of an attempt to incite a crowd against the

[2] What follows is an abbreviation of the argument I made in C. Rowe, *World Upside Down: Reading Acts in the Graeco-Roman Age* (New York: OUP, 2009). For a discussion of the proposals of that book, along with my response, see the March issue of *Journal for the Study of the New Testament* (2011): 317–46.

Christian missionaries. It works: the people cry out, 'Great is Artemis of the Ephesians' and drag some of Paul's companions into the city theatre, and there they riot. This riot lasts for some time before the chief official of Ephesus arrives and quiets the crowd by reminding them that, because of their disorderly tumult, they are all in danger of being charged by the Romans with riotous sedition. The Christians then slip away more or less unharmed.

Out of all the interesting details in this story, I focus on only three. First is the importance of the Ephesian silversmith's charge. To his colleagues in business, Demetrius says:

> Men, you know that from this business we have our wealth. And you know that this Paul has persuaded and turned away a considerable crowd of people by saying that "gods made with hands are not gods". And you [therefore] know that there is danger not only that our business may come into disrepute but also that the temple of the great Artemis may count for nothing, and that she may even be deposed from her magnificence, she whom all Asia and the world worship. (19:25–7)[3]

Two millennia later, Demetrius' charge may appear somewhat overdone. But as abundant evidence demonstrates, it would be difficult to overestimate the importance of Artemis to Ephesian life. As a first century inscription put it, the temple of Artemis was known as 'the jewel of the whole province [of Asia] on account of the grandeur of the edifice, the age of its veneration of the goddess, and the abundance of its revenue'.[4] It functioned not only as a 'house of worship' but also as the arbiter for regional disputes, a bank, a holding facility for important civic archives, and an asylum for debtors, runaway slaves, and other persons in dire trouble. The temple sent its own representatives to the Olympic Games, was the beneficiary of private estates, had abundant sacred herds, owned considerable real estate from which it drew its famous revenue, and so on. In short, as one scholar wrote, Artemis of the Ephesians was 'an indispensable pillar in the cultural structures and life of Asia, and was therefore a crucial factor in the lives of all ... whom Christianity hoped to convert'.[5]

Taking seriously the cultural role of the Ephesian Artemis cult prevents the possibility of reading Demetrius' charge simplistically, as if Luke were simply exhibiting the cunning with which the silversmith enlisted others to rescue his business. On the contrary, the words of Demetrius articulate a more radical

[3] All translations are my own unless otherwise noted.

[4] See Rowe, *World Upside Down*: 45 (cf: 204, n. 209).

[5] R. Oster, 'The Ephesian Artemis as an Opponent of Early Christianity', *JAC*, 19 (1976): 24–44 (esp. 34).

possibility: the potential for cultural collapse. As readers of Acts would know from earlier portions of the narrative (especially chapters 7, 14, 16 and 17), theological criticism of the kind Paul advocates does in fact depose Artemis and, hence, would dismantle this 'indispensable pillar in the cultural structures and life of Asia'. Through the mouth of Demetrius, Acts thus juxtaposes starkly the competing perspectives that form the clash of the gods: to understand the Christian mission is to perceive the theological danger posed to Artemis of the Ephesians. Consequently, it is to witness, says Demetrius, to the prospective disintegration of religiously dependent economics.[6]

It is no wonder, therefore, that after the compatriots of Demetrius hear his argument, they become 'full of rage and cry out, "Great is Artemis of the Ephesians!"' (19:28). Acts continues, 'The city was filled with confusion and they rushed into the theatre, dragging ... Paul's travel companions' (19:29). That those whose livelihood depends upon the Ephesian goddess should vigorously defend her greatness is only natural. Demetrius speaks of a Christian politics that collides with fundamental features of Greco-Roman life on the basis of competing theologies.

For my limited purpose, the second important feature of this scene is the chief official's persuasion of the crowd. His basic point, with which many an ancient civic official could sympathise, is that rioting will not bring the desired outcome, but might well instead lead to profoundly undesirable consequences for them all. In order to get the crowd to agree with him – and therefore quit the theatre and go home – the Ephesian official makes essentially two interconnected arguments. First, he skilfully negates Demetrius' charge against the Christian missionaries by drawing attention to the fact that the central cultic object of the Ephesian Artemis, a sacred stone, was not, strictly speaking, 'made by hands'. The sacred stone, so says the official, had been given by heaven/Zeus, i.e., it had fallen from the sky.[7] For the ancient Ephesians, this meteorite was a religiously charged cultic image. The official's point is thus clear: Paul's central criticism – 'gods made by hands are not gods' – does not apply to Artemis, because, in actuality, the cultic object was *not* made by hands. Moreover, the official points to the fact that business is booming as usual. 'Is there anyone', he says, 'who does not know that the city of the Ephesians is the temple warden of Artemis?' In short, the

[6] That this problem would come to be associated with the Christians very soon after the composition of Acts can be seen in Pliny the Younger's famous correspondence with the Emperor Trajan about the Christians (ca. 110/112 AD).

[7] Meteorites were not infrequently the objects of cultic veneration in the ancient world.

official argues that the missionaries are neither blasphemers nor temple robbers; there is no reason to worry about economic disaster on their account.

The chief official's second argument against the tumult is quite simple, and it makes an immediate impact. After reminding Demetrius and his group that there are legal means by which to deal with any official accusations (the Roman governor and the open courts), the Ephesian official informs the people that they are in danger of being accused of *stasis*. In this context, *stasis* means 'riot-interpreted-by-the-Romans-as-sedition'; i.e., a breach of the civic order required to sustain the *pax Romana*. That Rome was particularly nervous about crowd violence – and therefore particularly heavy-handed in their discipline thereof – is well known. One could think, for example, of Gaius' merciless slaughter of rowdy tax-protesters in the circus, or of the decade-long revocation of Pompeii's ability to hold gladiatorial games, or Claudius' reduction of the revolting Lycians to slaves.[8] Whatever the specifics of the imagined response, the official's threat is clear enough to achieve its aim: he dismisses the people from the theatre, and they go away. The Ephesian official's argument works: 'the Christians are no worry to us'; therefore, the people should 'go on home before we get into real trouble'.

The third crucial feature of this scene is that focusing on the charge of Demetrius and its counter-argument by the Ephesian official brings us to an interpretive choice *vis-à-vis* Christian politics according to Acts: should we follow Demetrius (the Christians are culturally destabilising and are therefore politically problematic), or the Ephesian official (the Christians are no worry to us)? To which voice in the narrative should we listen? With few exceptions, modern scholars have sided with the Ephesian official: the Christians do not fundamentally threaten larger cultural patterns and can even make rather good citizens. Indeed, to many readers of Acts, the Ephesian official's argument seems to cohere with Luke's overall vision of early ecclesial politics: because the Christians regularly appear before Roman officials (or those who represent their overall political interests) and because these officials speak of the innocuousness of the missionaries' efforts, Christianity according to Acts – so this reading goes – is compatible, perhaps even cosy, with the wider political nexus named the Roman Empire.[9]

The problem with this reading is that Demetrius is actually right. Yes, the city official's words are clever and slick, but they also miss the point: as readers

---

[8] See Rowe, *World Upside Down*: 48.

[9] Acts would thus on this reading be the first great piece of Constantinian Christian literature. Indeed, it has often been read that way (e.g., Haenchen, Conzelmann et al.).

of Acts and any other early Christians would know, Jesus and Artemis are not compatible. If there are numerous conversions to the Christian movement, Demetrius will likely go out of business. The Christians are thus fundamentally disruptive to the practices necessary to sustain the worship of Artemis. That such disruption unfolds economically and politically is the necessary consequence of the inseparability of ancient religion from the rest of life.

If we take this kind of politics seriously, we could infer that the political shape of early Christianity is worrisome to the Roman world precisely because its theology strikes at the religio-economic heart of Roman order. The Christians are rebellious in a very basic sense and therefore, in the view of the Romans, need to be punished. Before concluding that the Christians are politically problematic for Roman order, however, we must consider carefully another scene where the issue of the Christian mission and its potential to engender *stasis* is on prominent display.

Christianity is Not *Stasis* (Paul on Trial: Acts 25–6)

In contrast to Acts 19 where there is no formal trial, Acts 24:1–26:32 narrates Paul's actual trial for the crime of *stasis* (i.e., 'sedition', again in the sense of riot-causing revolt). This is the last of several times in Acts in which the early Christians have been brought before Roman officials and yet one more in a series of confrontations where the accusation of disruption has been raised in relation to Christian life. In this particular case, Paul's judge is first Felix and then Festus, the successive Roman governors of Judaea. The main narrative line of this complex scene is as follows: because of Paul's apparent role in causing a riot in Jerusalem, a military tribune named Claudius Lysias apprehends him. When Lysias learns, however, that Paul is a Roman citizen, he sends him on from Jerusalem to the Roman governor Felix in the seaside city of Caesarea (the location of the governor's residence for the majority of his tenure). After hearing the case against Paul – wherein Paul is charged formally with inciting a seditious riot – Felix decides to put Paul in custody rather than to release him or have him executed (in Roman law, sedition was a capital crime). Two years pass with Paul in custody, and Felix is replaced by Festus, who also hears Paul's case. To make sure he understands the particularities of the Jewish argument, Festus invites the Jewish King Agrippa II along with some other important political officials to hear Paul's defence. Paul then makes his case, which he does by telling the story of his awakening to belief in Jesus of Nazareth's resurrection from the dead. Festus cannot make any sense of Paul's account as a legal defence speech (an *apologia*) and so turns to Agrippa for help. Agrippa then offers his judgement, which confirms Festus' rather vague intuition: Paul has committed no political crime worthy of death. The charge of leading a revolt (*stasis*) cannot be sustained.

I am again limited to only three central observations. First, quite in the face of the accusations brought against him, Paul resolutely maintains his innocence: 'I have done nothing against the law of the Jews, against the Temple, or against Caesar', he says to Festus and the rest (25:8). By this point in the narrative, readers of Acts know of course that Paul speaks as a reliable character in that story – after all, next to Jesus, Paul is Luke's hero – and we are therefore to read his declaration as the political truth (indeed, he has already made this declaration earlier in the story). As Paul represents it, the early Christian movement is not a direct attack on the Roman political system, a kind of religiously-based bid for insurrection or imperial power. As far as Acts is concerned, Paul's declaration speaks rightly of the political shape of the Christian mission. The Christians are not out to stage a coup.

Second, it becomes all the more puzzling to take note of Festus' statement to King Agrippa about Paul. Because he cannot understand Paul's talk about the resurrection of Jesus, Festus does not know what to write to the emperor in his letter of transfer that would accompany Paul on his way to appeal his case in Rome. Festus thus says to Agrippa, 'I have nothing to write to my Lord about [Paul]' (Acts 25:26). This is the only time in the NT that the Roman emperor is actually called 'Lord' (*kyrios*). It was the correct thing for the emperor's officials to call him, as numerous texts, papyri, and inscriptions show. In fact, the emperor was not only styled as 'Lord' *simpliciter* but, more comprehensively, as 'Lord of all the world', as an inscription from Greece has it, or as we can read in Lucan, Martial, or Epictetus, for example.[10]

In Acts, however, the emperor is not called 'Lord of all'; among human beings, that title is reserved for Jesus alone. Indeed, in Acts 10, the apostle Peter tells a centurion named Cornelius that Jesus is the one who is 'the Lord of all':

> You know the word which he sent to the people of Israel preaching peace through Jesus Christ: this one is Lord of all. You know what has happened throughout the whole of Judaea, beginning in Galilee after the baptism which John preached, as God anointed in the Holy Spirit and power Jesus of Nazareth, who went about benefacting and healing all who were oppressed by the devil, for God was with him. (Acts 10: 36–7)

[10] See Rowe, *World Upside Down*: 106.

When readers of Acts later encounter the statement of Festus, we are thus required to think through a startling juxtaposition. In Acts, both Jesus and the Roman Caesar are called *kyrios*; yet it is Jesus Christ – not the Roman emperor – who is the Lord of all. The obvious implication is that, according to Acts, the Christians' most basic and final allegiance is not to the Roman emperor but to the Lord of all, Jesus of Nazareth.

Third, the reason that Jesus is Lord of all – in the view of Acts – has to do with his resurrection from the dead. And that is Paul's point in his speech before Festus. Jesus, says Paul, must suffer, rise from the dead and proclaim light both to the people [Israel] and to the nations [Gentiles] (cf. 26:23). That is, in maintaining his innocence of sedition, Paul does not articulate a normative general political scheme – monarchy, democracy, communitarianism, and so forth – but instead says that he is innocent of leading a revolt because Jesus has been raised from the dead: a confirmation of his life of peace and the beginning of the formation of peaceful communities of Jew and Gentile throughout the Mediterranean world. In effect, Paul says, 'I'm not leading a revolt because obedience to the resurrected Jesus commits us to peace of just the kind he himself exemplified in his willingness to go innocently to his death and be raised by God.'

On the face of it, to say the least, this is a rather odd defence in a Roman court setting. It is therefore unsurprising that a Roman official such as Festus – who has no Jewish theological sensibilities about resurrection from the dead and knows virtually nothing of Jesus of Nazareth – is genuinely perplexed. Indeed, Festus interrupts Paul and cries out, 'Paul, you're crazy!' (Acts 26:24). Festus literally cannot understand Paul's defence as a proper legal defence. He thus turns to consult the Jewish King Agrippa, who has actually heard of the Christians. After discussion with Agrippa, Festus and his council decide that Paul is innocent. Quite crazy he may be, but he is not the ringleader of a politically seditious faction.

What is critical is the interpretive conundrum that arises when this passage is read together with the scene in Ephesus. In that scene, as we saw, Acts portrays the Christians as fundamentally disruptive to the patterns that sustain a culture – and therefore as threatening in a decisive sense to the wider world in which the rule of Rome is unfolding. But in the trial before Festus, Paul is flatly declared 'unworthy of death', that is, innocent of the capital crime of treasonous sedition. On the one hand, Luke narrates the movement of the Christian mission into the Gentile world as a collision with culture-constructing aspects of that world. From the perspective created by this angle of vision, the Christian mission and basic features of Greco-Roman culture are competing realities. On the other hand, Luke narrates the threat of the Christian mission in such a way as to deny that it is in direct competition with the Roman government. Of treason and sedition, says Luke, Christianity is innocent. The Christians are a basic threat, but they are not out to establish Christendom, as it were. New, threatening way of life? Yes. Coup? No. The question thus becomes: How do we account for this tension?

The history of NT scholarship – as well as Christian politics – demonstrates that it is all too easy to neglect one side of the tension and focus entirely on the other. The culturally destabilising reality of the Christian mission is overlooked, and Christianity becomes a politically innocuous or even irrelevant 'spiritual' movement; or the declaration of innocence of sedition is overlooked and Christianity is read as a liberating, overt frontal challenge to the Roman Empire. But, in fact, we should not be forced to choose one side or the other. Indeed, precisely because they are both parts of the same narrative, we should read them together. The task is to inhabit the narrative's tension and refuse to dissolve it. To that end, we turn to our final scene in the Acts of the Apostles.

Jesus the King: The Tension of Christian Politics (Thessalonica: Acts 17)

The scene in Acts 17:1–9 takes place in the city of Thessalonica. The central relevant matter is rather clear. As a consequence of their missionising and the conversions that take place therewith, the Christians are hauled before the local authorities and accused in this way: 'These people who have turned the world upside down have come here also, and Jason has received them; and they are all acting against the decrees of Caesar, saying that there is another king – Jesus' (17:7).

Much scholarly ink has been spilled in the effort to determine the precise nature of the imperial 'decrees' against which the Christians are acting. But for the most part, such labour has been unnecessary for the simple reason that the text says directly what the accusation is: the Christians are accused of saying that there is 'another king'. The word 'another' makes clear that the question is one of rivalry: 'another', as in 'not the one you now have'. If we ask who the king is that Thessalonica now has, the answer is not hard to find. Indeed, the only historically plausible answer to this question in the mid to late first century is the Roman emperor. In Thessalonica the Christians are thus accused of challenging the throne of Caesar. It is precisely in setting Jesus up as king that the Christians run afoul of the 'decrees of Caesar'.

It is with good reason that many interpreters of the NT have thought that these charges were false. As we have seen with Paul's trial before Festus, Acts does speak of the Christians' innocence of sedition. Moreover, at the end of the scene here in Thessalonica, the Christians are forced to give collateral for their good behaviour but are then set free, thus once again illustrating narratively their innocence of treasonous sedition.

But in exegesis, as in life, things are seldom as easy as they appear. In point of fact, it was no secret that the early Christians acclaimed Jesus as king. No reader of early Christian literature could think otherwise. The Gospel of Luke and the Acts of the Apostles are no exception. Throughout Luke's Gospel, Jesus is cast in a royal role. Indeed, he both enters Jerusalem and is crucified there explicitly as king. And in Acts, the missionaries repeatedly preach about the reality brought by Jesus' advent and resurrection as 'the kingdom of God'. The final sentence of Acts has Paul preaching in Rome itself about 'the kingdom of God and the Lord (of all) Jesus Christ' (28:31). In short, the accusers in Thessalonica actually have a rather good case. Jesus is king. The interpretive question is thus what we should make of the fact that Jesus is actually another king – that in some way, his kingship is juxtaposed to that of the Roman emperor – and that, at least as Acts tells it, such a kingship does not lead to a seditious revolt.

It has long been tempting for Christians to resolve this tension by insisting on a dualistic nature of the two kings or kingdoms. God's kingdom – in which Jesus is king – does not overlap in any kind of earthly or strictly political way with Caesar's (or, later, the rule of the state). It is possible to have both kings, because their sovereignty can be referred to different spheres (heaven and earth), modes of communal life (church and state), and so forth. In this reading, it would be true that Jesus is 'another king' as the accusers in Thessalonica say, but inasmuch as his kingship is politically innocuous it is compatible with Caesar's. 'Another' here would thus mean in its positive Christian construal a second, non-rival, different-kind-of-king.

But we have already seen that Acts would teach us to think with more nuance about this tension. In Acts, the kingdom is obviously not a 'human kingdom' in the straightforward simplistic sense – and in this way, the Christian mission does not threaten Rome as did, for example, the Parthian kingdom on the eastern frontier. Yet, against all Gnostic or pietistic tendencies, the vision in Acts is of a kingdom that is every bit as much a human presence as it is a divine work. The kingdom of which Jesus is king is not simply spiritual, but also material and social, which is to say that its takes up space in public. It competes with Artemis in Ephesus, for example. And because public space is not neutral but contested space – the arena in which various readings of the world make their bid for adoption – the Christian mission's challenge to basic aspects and patterns of Greco-Roman culture is simultaneously a challenge to the order of Caesar, and thus in a crucial or fundamental sense to his claim to be the lord of all.[11]

To think with Acts, we must thus say both 'yes' and 'no'. Yes, the resurrection of Jesus threatens the stability of Roman life; no, the Christians are not guilty of *stasis*; yes, the Christians are bad for religiously based economics; no, they are not trying to take over the public market; yes, Artemis will be deposed; no, the Christians will not tear down the temple; yes, Jesus and not Caesar is Lord of all; but, no, the Christians are not violent revolutionaries. And so on.

If we take both the yes and the no seriously – if we take the tension described earlier and refuse to dissolve it – then it becomes apparent that the charges in Thessalonica are at once both true and false. They are false in that they attempt to place Jesus in an outright competitive relation to the Roman emperor. Such a positioning can lead only to a politics of revolt. But in Acts, the Christians have no dreams to expel the Romans from Jerusalem or rise up and march on Rome, or take over the empire. Jesus is not, strictly speaking, that kind of a rival to Caesar, as if they were in the same contest competing for the same prize.[12]

And yet, the charges are true in that Caesar is not the highest political authority (he is demoted, to say the least). The Christians owe their allegiance to the true Lord of all, and the politics of the Christian mission entail a call to a way of being that threatens to undo basic habits and practices of Greco-Roman life. As we saw in Ephesus, and as could be seen in many other places in the Acts narrative, the Christian missionaries really do, in the words of their accusers in Thessalonica, turn the world upside down.[13]

Focusing on the scene in Thessalonica highlights the irreducible conflict over the interpretation of the Christians – what their public space is about, as it were – precisely because we can answer both yes and no to the question

---

[11] Thinking analogically about Caesar's claim to be Lord of all, for Christians to kill other Christians because they are separated by different citizenships is to say in a very painful and practical way that Christian identity is subordinate to national identity – which in turn, is to say that Caesar trumps Jesus, or, as my colleague Paul Griffiths puts it, 'citizenship trumps baptism' (see his 'Allah is my Lord and Yours', *Christian Century*, October (2006): 8–9). Caesar, that is, is the one who can command final, ultimate allegiance to the point of death.

[12] Acts presupposes no deeper ontological basis upon which Jesus and Caesar play out their respective roles as claimants for the title Lord of all. In Acts, Jesus simply is the Lord of all as the self-revelation of the God of Israel; and that is, as it were, the cosmic ontology – the arena in which everything else takes place.

[13] See Chapter 2 of Rowe, *World Upside Down*.

of whether they turn the world upside down by proclaiming another king (or Lord). With respect to the examples above, when we focus upon the conflict with Artemis of the Ephesians, we must answer 'yes'. But when we focus upon Paul's trial before the Roman governor Festus, we must answer 'no'. The narrative programme in Acts – of which these scenes are, to repeat, paradigmatic instances – thus resists interpretive reduction and requires for its interpretation complexity and constant movement in our political thought.

The programme as a whole can be summarised in this way: Jesus is Lord of all, the king of the way of life called the kingdom of God. The early Christian mission is a new, worldwide, and publicly identifiable instantiation of this reality and, as such, calls into question religious/economic/ political norms that both help to produce and sustain Greco-Roman culture. In this sense, the Christians are profoundly destabilising and will continue to be so insofar as the wider Roman world remains unmoved by their call to a new pattern of life. Yet, the political objectives of such destabilisation are not in any way directly revolutionary (particularly not in the sense of an attempt to depose Caesar and place a new, Christian emperor on the throne). 'Sedition' and 'treason', therefore, are not the right vocabulary to describe the shape of Christian politics. In the Acts of the Apostles, the stark either/or of Roman politics is refused (either for Rome or against her, either innocent or guilty, either Caesar is Lord of all or there is revolt). In its place, Acts proclaims the possibility of another way of life. The lordship of Jesus in Acts leads neither to an *apologia* to/for Rome nor to an anti-Rome polemic. It is simply, but really, a new and different way. In short, theology here is politics.

Conclusion

Inasmuch as the deeper currents of Western (or North Atlantic) culture continue to flow against the normative commitments of Christian life,[14] we may be entering a time of reading Scripture that both requires and enables a richer analogical relation to the ancient world than has been possible or necessary in a very long time. Our world will doubtless not forget what Christianity is any time soon. Many of the commitments needed to sustain care of the sick and dying, for example, depend upon a specifically Christian view of the human being. Yet, the fact is that it grows increasingly difficult to develop and maintain a Christian imagination that correlates with an all-encompassing pattern of life. Moreover, it

[14] See C. Taylor, *A Secular Age* (Cambridge: Harvard University Press, 2007).

is possible to imagine a future in which the Christian way of being is a minority whose life-pattern is at odds with much of what the wider Western world will consider normal.[15] We return to Acts, therefore, at a propitious time in the life of the church to learn or relearn things that will allow our children in the faith to continue the form of life in the world that earned the name 'Christian' – or to live out the life that proclaims Jesus is Lord of all in a world that will not recognise his lordship.

Of the things we should learn from Acts' ecclesiological vision, none is quite as important as the very basic sense that thinking theologically about the church requires us to discern the interconnections that make up a total way of life. That is, the church in Acts has really nothing to do with a discrete sphere of life or thought, as if ecclesiology could name a particular, limited set of ideas or practices in distinction from Christology, eschatology, anthropology, and so on. Rather, if we wish to talk about ecclesiology according to Acts, we must talk primarily about a theologically explicated habit of being that is noticeably different from the larger practices and assumptions that shape daily life in the Greco-Roman world. According to Acts, ecclesiology is simply the communal form of life that is living in obedience to the Lord of all; it is a form of life that is at once political and theological, or public and private, or, to say it only slightly differently, all-encompassing. This refusal to locate particular parts of the church in different spheres of life is the necessary presupposition to the existence of a people with the mode of being that is publicly identifiable in Acts' sense – the 'Christians'. If we, too, wish to live so that our children and grandchildren in the faith – and their children and grandchildren – can be known as 'Christians', then according to Acts, our ecclesiology will have to keep alive the distinction between church and world not merely on this or that contested point (e.g., euthanasia, abortion), but also in the concrete practice of a whole way of life that marks publicly its practitioners as those who live under the lordship of the Lord of all.

---

[15] See D. Hart, *Atheist Delusions: The Christian Revolution and Its Fashionable Enemies* (New Haven, CT: Yale University Press, 2009).

PART III:
Church Growth and Doctrine

Chapter 5

Theology, Eschatology and Church Growth

Alister McGrath

Commitment to mission is now seen as essential to the future of the church – and rightly so. Most dioceses of the Church of England now expect their bishops to show leadership in this field, and galvanise their clergy into growing their congregations. Admittedly, this notion of 'mission' is often framed in terms of increasing church attendance, in the anticipation that this will also increase parish contributions towards the cost of running diocesan administration. Yet there is a valid insight here: that we ought to expect churches to grow and to start asking awkward questions if they do not.

Many have urged the adoption – or at least the recognition of the importance – of managerial solutions to church growth, noting how good management is often able to turn a failing organisation around, thus enhancing corporate morale and increasing turnover and market share.[1] There is unquestionably something to be learned from this. Poorly organised churches rarely grow. Yet this pragmatic approach can only be part of a solution; indeed, when regarded as the defining solution in and of itself, it can easily lead to a potentially fatal redefinition of 'vision' in terms of what is to be achieved (growth) rather than what might enable that growth to be achieved in the first place (the gospel). Reaching the goal thus comes to take priority over preserving the resource which enables that goal to be reached.

Theology matters to church growth, precisely because it aims to sustain the luminous and captivating vision of God which lies at the heart of the Christian

---

[1] For example, see the issues debated in C. Watkins, 'Organizing the People of God: Social-science Theories of Organization in Ecclesiology', *Theological Studies*, 52.4 (1991): 689–71; N. Healy, *Church, World and the Christian Life: Practical-prophetic Ecclesiology* (Cambridge: CUP, 2000); R. Roberts, 'Personhood and Performance: Managerialism, Post-Democracy and the Ethics of "Enrichment"', *Studies in Christian Ethics*, 21.1 (2008): 61–82; M. Torry, *Managing God's Business: Religious and Faith-based Organizations and their Management* (Aldershot: Ashgate, 2005).

faith, defending it against well-meaning attempts to reduce it to something manageable and culturally accessible, which ultimately robs it of its depth and vitality.[2] Yet theology does not simply seek to defend; it also aims to encourage a defensible cultural translation of the realities of faith, ensuring that the proclamation of the church connects up with contemporary culture without reducing the gospel to cultural banalities and platitudes.[3] If the church is to grow, it needs to tend the vision of God which stands at its heart, and ultimately underlies worship, mission, and theology.

In this chapter, I propose to offer a general reflection on the importance of theology for church growth, before moving on to focus on the specific topic of eschatology.

Why Theology Matters

For some in the church growth movement, theology is an irrelevance, perhaps even a hindrance. While this concern is not ungrounded, it needs to be treated with a certain degree of caution. Systematic theology aims to provide the church with a toolkit. Each of the tools has been tested and calibrated. Yes, these tools are meant to be used. Yet the discipline of systematic theology is not primarily about using these tools; it is more concerned with ensuring that they work and their proper function is understood. It is up to others – including those concerned with church growth – to work out how best to use them and how they bear upon the issues that specifically focus on their concerns.

More importantly, one of the fundamental tasks of theology is to provide us with a 'big picture' of the Christian faith.[4] The first task of Christian theology is to appreciate this 'big picture' in all its fullness. We need to be captivated by its comprehensiveness, by its richness, by its capacity to make sense of things and offer hope and transformation.[5] It discloses a glorious, loving and righteous God, who creates a world that goes wrong, and then acts graciously and wondrously

2 A point emphasised by A. Louth, *Discerning the Mystery: An Essay on the Nature of Theology* (Oxford: Clarendon Press, 1983).

3 Examples of this might include the culturally adapted 'moralistic therapeutic theism' which some discern within contemporary American approaches to faith: see C. Smith and M. Denton, *Soul Searching: The Religious and Spiritual Lives of American Teenagers* (New York: OUP, 2005).

4 For a popular exploration of this point, see A. McGrath, *Faith and the Creeds* (London: SPCK, 2013): 26–39.

5 See further A. McGrath, *Surprised by Meaning: Science, Faith, and How We Make Sense of Things* (Louisville, KY: Westminster John Knox Press, 2011).

in order to renew and redirect it, before finally bringing it to its fulfilment. And we ourselves are an integral part of this story, which discloses our true purpose, meaning and value – who we really are, what is really wrong, what God proposes to do about this and what we must do in response.[6]

Theology thus aims to provide a panorama – the big picture that makes sense of the snapshots, the grand narrative that weaves together and interprets lesser stories, including the stories of individuals and communities. It gives us a lens that helps us bring things into focus, allowing us to see things more clearly than might otherwise be the case. Yet most importantly of all, it reassures us that there is a big picture – that what we observe and experience can be fitted in to a grander pattern, like individual threads woven together in a tapestry, disclosing a rich pattern. Shadowlands remain – yet even here, we see them more clearly than otherwise. As C.S. Lewis once put it, 'I believe in Christianity as I believe that the Sun has risen, not only because I see it, but because by it, I see everything else.'[7]

The ability of the Christian faith to make sense of things, connecting up with both our desire for understanding and our quest for meaning, is one of its most appealing aspects. If the church is to grow, it needs to ensure that the gospel is understood and appreciated in all its fullness. When I have taught university classes in theology, I have sometimes been aware of having created the impression that Christian doctrines are like watertight compartments, each of which can be studied in isolation from others. We begin with the doctrine of creation and end up with eschatology.

It is a neat idea and may be helpful pedagogically in managing the complex business of instructing people in the basics of faith. But it is misleading. Christian beliefs are not a set of individual, unrelated ideas. They are interconnected, like a web, held together by the compelling and persuasive vision of reality made possible by the gospel. We see a breathtaking landscape and marvel at its beauty; then we move on to take in its details. To understand the beliefs, we must first catch the vision. To make sense of the snapshots, we need to take in the panorama.

Now there is nothing wrong with snapshots, which often provide welcome detail of complex landscapes. Yet there is, I think, a danger that certain approaches to theology offer us nothing more than those snapshots and fail to show us the panorama. It is one thing to say – as I would say – that we have to

---

[6] For an influential exploration of this theme, see N.T. Wright, 'How Can The Bible Be Authoritative?', *Vox Evangelica*, 21 (1991): 7–32.

[7] C.S. Lewis, 'Is Theology Poetry?', in *Essay Collection and Other Short Pieces* (London: HarperCollins, 2000): 21. For detailed comment on Lewis's remark, see A. McGrath, 'The Privileging of Vision: Lewis's Metaphors of Light, Sun, and Sight', in *The Intellectual World of C.S. Lewis* (Oxford: Wiley-Blackwell, 2013).

find some way of teaching the Christian faith in an educationally realistic way. It is quite another to suggest that Christianity consists of a series of individual disconnected theological boxes, each of whose contents may be inspected at any time without needing to see what is contained in the others or considering the relationship between them.

In this chapter, I will be considering the importance of eschatology for church growth. Yet I must concede immediately that it is impossible to detach eschatology from other doctrines – such as the doctrine of creation and the doctrine of salvation. All of these have eschatological perspectives. Or, to put this more helpfully, all interconnect with eschatological issues. An obvious example, of no small importance in reflecting on church growth, is the eschatological dimensions of the church. John Calvin was one of many theologians to argue that a distinction was to be made between the present empirical reality of the church (the 'visible church') and the eschatologically perfected church (the 'invisible church').[8]

Yet many would argue that it is only in recent years that the full impact of eschatology for church growth has been debated fully. This has been catalysed – and to some extent influenced by – the growing interest in eschatology in popular American evangelicalism, perhaps seen in the *Left Behind* series of novels.[9] Those who adopt such an eschatology favour an approach to church growth which disengages with the world and sees its tribulations as a sign of hope, in that they are harbingers of the return of Christ. In reaction against this, many within the 'Emergent Church' movement insist on the need for engagement with the world. Brian McLaren, for example, dismisses what he terms a 'skyhook Second Coming', which speaks of God 'wrapping up the whole of creation like an empty candy wrapper and throwing it in the cosmic dumpster so God can finally bring our souls to heaven, beyond time'.[10]

In this chapter, I shall not have space to engage with these more recent debates, which are often framed within a dispensationalist theological paradigm. Rather, I shall focus on more classic eschatological themes, as we find these reflected

---

[8] For differing interpretations of the implications of this distinction, see the classic studies of P. Barth, 'Calvins Verständnis der Kirche', *Zwischen den Zeiten*, 8 (1930): 216–33; O. Weber, 'Calvins Lehre von der Kirche', in *Die Treue Gottes in der Geschichte der Kirche* (Neukirchen-Vluyn: Neukirchener Verlag, 1968): 19–104.

[9] C. Gribben, *Writing the Rapture: Prophecy Fiction in Evangelical America* (New York: OUP, 2009), pp. 129–44. More generally, see A. Frykholm, *Rapture Culture: Left Behind in Evangelical America* (New York: OUP, 2004).

[10] B. McLaren, *A Generous Orthodoxy* (Grand Rapids, MI: Zondervan, 2006): 237.

in the writings of Augustine of Hippo and others.[11] Nevertheless, we cannot disregard some themes in more recent discussions of this doctrine, particularly the notion of 'participatory eschatology', which – when rightly stated – offers a helpful perspective to practitioners of church growth.

So where shall we start? Perhaps the most fundamental theme that needs to be enunciated in any theology of church growth is that the seed of the gospel is good. In what follows, we shall consider this in more detail.

The Seed is Good: but what about the Soil?

Perhaps we know the parables too well to appreciate to the full their vivid depiction of the spread of the kingdom of God.[12] The characteristic images of the kingdom – yeast spreading in dough, seeds growing in the ground – indicate that some kind of growth is integral to the New Testament vision of the gospel. While it remains to be clarified how 'kingdom of God', 'gospel', and 'church' relate to one another, it might reasonably be suggested that an innate capacity to grow is built into the genetic profile of the Christian faith.[13] Consider the Parable of the Sower:

> Listen! A sower went out to sow. And as he sowed, some seed fell on the path, and the birds came and ate it up. Other seed fell on rocky ground, where it did not have much soil, and it sprang up quickly, since it had no depth of soil. And when the sun rose, it was scorched; and since it had no root, it withered away. Other seed fell among thorns, and the thorns grew up and choked it, and it yielded no grain. Other seed fell into good soil and brought forth grain, growing up and increasing and yielding thirty and sixty and a hundredfold. (Mark 4:3–8)

The parable – and others dealing with biological growth – emphasises both the fundamental goodness of the seed on the one hand, and the importance of

---

[11] See J. Oort, *Jerusalem and Babylon: A Study into Augustine's City of God and the Sources of His Doctrine of the Two Cities* (Leiden: Brill, 1991).

[12] R. Longenecker (ed.), *The Challenge of Jesus' Parables* (Grand Rapids, MI: Eerdmans, 2000); M. Getty-Sullivan, *Parables of the Kingdom: Jesus and the Use of Parables in the Synoptic Tradition* (Collegeville, MN: Liturgical Press, 2007): 1–15. Note also 1 Corinthians 3:6; see R. Collins, *The Power of Images in Paul* (Collegeville, MN: Liturgical Press, 2008).

[13] B. Witherington, *The Gospel of Mark: A Socio-Rhetorical Commentary* (Grand Rapids, MI: Eerdmans, 2001): 160–68; Getty-Sullivan, *Parables of the Kingdom*: 57–8.

'preparing the ground' on the other. Seed will not grow unless it falls in 'good soil'. A vineyard will not bear fruit unless it is tended properly (Isaiah 5).

There are two points that need to be made here; first, that the gospel seed *is* good. It does not need to be *made* good, as liberal writers of an earlier generation assumed, by reformulating or reconstituting its identity in terms of contemporary cultural resonances. As history makes clear, this inevitably led to the gospel being reduced to such resonances, in effect adding a religious or spiritual veneer to essentially cultural imperatives. The churches' task is fundamentally to exhibit and communicate the goodness of the seed, not to alter it in the light of transient cultural trends.

Secondly, the reaffirmation of the goodness of the seed does not obviate the need for serious reflection on the nature of the soil into which it necessarily falls. The church's evangelistic tasks extend beyond the mere 'sowing of the seed'. What can be done to break up the ground and make it receptive to the seed taking root? How can weeds be removed, to give the growing seed more space and light? What can be done in the face of external threats?

The parable's striking emphasis upon the importance of establishing roots cannot be overlooked and must be incorporated into our reflections on church growth. It is evident, for example, in Andrew Walker's notion of 'Deep Church', which is intended to convey the 'championing of a common tradition' and a 'commitment to a "thick" or "maximalist" form of Christianity', set within a context of an 'hospitable, orthodox approach to the Christian faith' that is more concerned with thinking about 'the nature of faithful and enlivening witness in the contemporary context' than with policing denominational boundaries.[14]

For Walker, the key to the growth and resilience of faith envisaged in the Parable of the Sower lay in the selective retrieval of the believing past. This was a move that resonated with many in the 1990s and beyond, especially within evangelicalism. Some were anxious that the movement appeared rootless, ungrounded in a deeper tradition of biblical engagement and interpretation. Older evangelical writers – such as James Orr and J.I. Packer – saw themselves as exponents of such a 'Great Tradition'. Yet evangelicalism's historical origins in the eighteenth century led to it being shaped by at least some core assumptions of

[14] A. Walker, 'Recovering Deep Church: Theological and Spiritual Renewal', in A. Walker and L. Bretherton (eds), *Remembering our Future: Explorations in Deep Church* (Milton Keynes: Paternoster Press, 2007): 1–29. Similar ideas have also been expressed in a North American context by J. Belcher, *Deep Church: A Third Way Beyond Emerging and Traditional* (Downers Grove, IL: InterVarsity Press, 2009). Both Walker and Belcher borrow the phrase 'Deep Church' from C.S. Lewis: see his letter to the Church Times, 8 February 1952 in C.S. Lewis, *Collected Letters* (vol. 3; San Francisco: HarperOne, 2004–6): 164.

the Enlightenment – perhaps most notably, its tendency towards individualism and seeing the past as a burden to be discarded. Many evangelicals now consider that the rise of postmodernity posed a threat, not to evangelicalism itself, but to the modernism that the movement had absorbed through the circumstances of its historical origins. Was this an opportune moment to correct this imbalance through a recovery of the importance of tradition?[15]

Focussing on the soil, and not simply the seed, creates conceptual space for reflecting on the significance of the context in which the gospel is proclaimed and embedded. This observation serves to emphasise the importance of the empirical study of how congregations grow and respond to changes in their environment.[16] How does ecclesial growth depend on cultural context? A theological affirmation – the goodness of the seed or, to transpose this apologetically, the self-authenticating actuality of the gospel – does not excuse us from giving serious consideration to other factors implicated in the germination and flourishing of the seed. Theology is an excellent starting point for reflections on church growth. But they cannot stop there. Other issues come into the frame.

One such issue is the cultural translation of the gospel into terms that connect up with our culture. Perhaps there is something to be learned from C.S. Lewis here. During the early 1940s, Lewis found himself facing the question of theological translation.[17] How could he express academic theological notions in plain language? How could he use ordinary English as a medium for often quite complex theological ideas, such as the rationality of the incarnation? Lewis gradually learned how to adapt his style and vocabulary to meet the needs and concerns of an audience he had never encountered before.

Lewis summarised some of the issues he was forced to confront in a post-war lecture of 1945 on 'Christian Apologetics'. The two points that Lewis emphasised were the empirical necessity of discovering how ordinary people speak *through observation and encounter*, followed by reflection on how religious ideas might best be translated into language that was within their experience and comfort zones. 'We must learn the language of our audience. And let me say at the outset that it is no use at all laying down *a priori* what the "plain man" does

[15] For useful pointers to these discussions, see J. Cutsinger, *Reclaiming the Great Tradition: Evangelicals, Catholics & Orthodox in Dialogue* (Downers Grove, IL: InterVarsity Press, 1997).

[16] See, for example, P. Ward (ed.), *Perspectives on Ecclesiology and Ethnography* (Grand Rapids, MI: Eerdmans, 2011).

[17] For Lewis's role as a wartime apologist, see A. McGrath, *C.S. Lewis – A Life. Eccentric Genius, Reluctant Prophet* (London: Hodder & Stoughton, 2013): 205–13.

or does not understand. You have to find out by experience ... You must translate every bit of your Theology into the vernacular."[18]

Lewis's notion of 'translation' is about more than the interaction of two languages – the academic or technical and the everyday or popular. Long before the more general realisation of this point in the 1980s,[19] Lewis appreciated that words are culturally embedded, having developed meanings which echo their cultural contexts. What is required is a 'cultural translation',[20] which attempts to express ideas from one language, embedded in its social context, to another language, embedded in a different social context. Translation is thus a cultural, not simply a linguistic, matter.

Yet Lewis's genius lay only partly in his acquired capacity to translate theological idioms into the cultural vernacular; it lay also in his intrinsic ability to transpose such idioms into other literary genres – above all, narratives. Where *Mere Christianity* is a rational exploration of the themes of the Christian faith, the *Chronicles of Narnia* are its imaginative counterpart.[21] The *Chronicles of Narnia* often provide a narrative framework within which to consider a doctrine that we had hitherto analysed conceptually – such as eschatology, so intriguingly re-presented in *The Last Battle*.[22] Austin Farrer perhaps captured Lewis's achievement best when he spoke of his 'imaginative realizations of doctrine'.[23]

But we must now turn to a specific consideration of eschatology in its own right. How does an eschatological perspective help us think about church growth?

Eschatology and Church Growth

The rediscovery of eschatology in the last century is linked with a new interest in the Christian hope, and the recognition of the need to distinguish this

---

[18] C.S. Lewis, 'Christian Apologetics', in *Essay Collection*: 153, 155.

[19] For the emergence of this awareness at that time, see S. Bassnett and A. Lefevere, *Translation, History, and Culture* (London: Pinter Publishers, 1990).

[20] T. Asad, 'The Concept of Cultural Translation in British Social Anthropology', in J. Clifford and G. Marcus (eds), *Writing Culture: The Poetics and Politics of Ethnography* (Berkeley, CA: University of California Press, 1986): 141–84.

[21] G. Meilander, 'Theology in Stories: C.S. Lewis and the Narrative Quality of Experience', *Word and World,* 1.3 (1981): 222–30; R. Wood, 'The Baptized Imagination: C.S. Lewis's Fictional Apologetics', *Christian Century*, 112.25 (1995): 812–15.

[22] S. Connolly, *Inklings of Heaven: C.S. Lewis and Eschatology* (Leominster: Gracewing, 2007): 87–91.

[23] A. Farrer, 'The Christian Apologist', in Jocelyn Gibb (ed.), *Light on C.S. Lewis* (London: Geoffrey Bles, 1965): 31.

from its secular alternatives and more generic optimistic outlooks on life.[24] Yet eschatology is about more than the affirmation of a hope for the future which impacts on the present. It is also about seeing the present in its proper perspective. An eschatological perspective challenges the privileging of the present, forcing us to realise the transiency of our culture. We have to take the long view – thinking in terms of centuries, not years. None of us sees the 'big picture', which allows us to grasp the significance of our present moment in the greater scheme of things.

This theme recurred in the prophetic literature of the Old Testament, as Israel tried to make sense of what was going on the in world around it and how it should respond to the rise and fall of great imperial nations, such as Egypt, Assyria and Babylon. An eschatological viewpoint allowed Israel to assert God's ultimate authority over history, without requiring that the future can be known or predicted.[25] Eschatology is about hope in the face of apparent chaos, meaninglessness and opposition, reflecting a trust in God's capacity to make all things new, rather than expressing a naively optimistic attitude.[26]

The Christian is a citizen not just of this world but of the kingdom of God and thus lives in accordance with a reality which is not yet fully present or seen but which we can nevertheless imagine.[27] The Christian hope is about longing for and hoping for this coming reality, which, in the meantime, we try to display and enact in our individual lives, in the church, and in the world. The church is called on to realise what might otherwise only be imagined – not something that is *imaginary*, a product of our hopeless longing, but something that is *imagined*, seen in the light of the gospel promises and the actions of a creating and recreating God.

Eschatology thus demands a proper perspective on our situation. We naturally see our own time as momentous, privileged and unique. We stand at

---

[24] R. Bauckham and T. Hart (eds), *Hope against Hope: Christian Eschatology at the Turn of the Millennium* (Grand Rapids, MI: Eerdmans, 1999).

[25] See, for example, P. Hanson, 'Second Isaiah's Eschatological Understanding of World Events', *Princeton Seminary Bulletin*, 3 (1994): 17–25. For a similar theme in the New Testament, see G.E. Ladd, *The Presence of the Future: The Eschatology of Biblical Realism* (Grand Rapids, MI: Eerdmans, 1974).

[26] For reflections on this principle in connection with the recent rise of the 'New Atheism', see A. McGrath, 'Empires of the Mind', in J. Hughes (ed.), *The Unknown God: Sermons Responding to the New Atheists* (London: SCM Press, 2013): 49–54.

[27] For an excellent study of this theme, see T. Hart, 'Imagination for the Kingdom of God? Hope, Promise, and the Transformative Power of an Imagined Future', in R. Bauckham (ed.), *God Will be All in All: The Eschatology of Jürgen Moltmann* (Edinburgh: T & T Clark, 1999): 49–76. For further reflections, see J. Alison, *Raising Abel: The Recovery of Eschatological Imagination*, second edition (London: SPCK, 2010): 159–77.

an unprecedented juncture between two worlds. To the church historian, this is a puzzling judgement. What about Augustine of Hippo, who tried to position Christianity as the settled certainties of the thousand-year Roman Empire collapsed around him? Or the massive outpouring of anxiety in the Christian west following the fall of Constantinople to Islamic invaders in 1452? Or the shifting of the cultural sands in nineteenth century Europe, so memorably captured by Matthew Arnold (1822–88) in his *Stanzas from the Grande Chartreuse*, written around 1850. Arnold framed his own personal journey in terms of

> Wandering between two worlds, one dead,
> The other powerless to be born,
> With nowhere yet to rest my head.[28]

We must avoid the presumption that we somehow occupy a privileged and unprecedented place in history. The prophets of Israel saw the great empires of the Ancient Near East rise and fall, confident in their belief that only the Word of God would remain forever (Isaiah 40:8). We cannot foresee; we have to trust. The real questions we must face are these: What wisdom and treasure can we salvage from the past? And what new opportunities and openings can we grasp in the future?

Yet adopting an eschatological perspective on church growth also alerts us to another issue, which is perhaps unsettling, but needs to be confronted. We don't see the distant horizon. Situations change – and we cannot predict the manner and nature of that change, even though we can make sense of them afterwards. We can retrodict, but not predict. Wolfhart Pannenberg made this point back in the 1960s.[29] To understand the full significance of anything – such as events in history, or our own ministry – we need to see things from the perspective of the end of history.

If we knew how things worked out in the long term, we could determine what needs to be done to expedite them – an idea famously explored in Karl Marx's now-discredited quasi-eschatological doctrine of the historical inevitability of socialism.[30] We can only make sense of things properly when we see their final

---

[28] M. Arnold, *The Poems of Matthew Arnold, 1849–67* (Oxford: OUP, 1906): 260. For the context, see R. Wolff, *Gains and Losses: Novels of Faith and Doubt in Victorian England* (London: John Murray, 1977).

[29] W. Pannenberg, 'Dogmatic Theses on the Doctrine of Revelation', in W. Pannenberg (ed.), *Revelation as History* (New York: Macmillan, 1968): 123–58.

[30] For its dismantling, see the classic critique of K. Popper, *The Poverty of Historicism* (London: Routledge & Kegan Paul, 1957).

outcome. And that perspective is denied to us. We don't know how things are going to work out. For example, is the present travail within Anglicanism the beginning of the end? Or the end of the beginning? Is it a barrier to church growth? Or does it remove barriers to church growth? We just don't know how the future will judge these questions.

Yet we still have to live and minister in this context, where we don't see the big picture, and have to make judgements about where we are and how best to act in that context. It's all about faith and discernment, not the cold and clinical judgements of a technocrat. I recall a conversation with a senior British army officer some years ago, as he tried to explain to me the idea of the 'fog of war'. His point was that tactical decisions have to be made in a theatre of conflict, without a full understanding of the situation. We can't do nothing!

Taking eschatology seriously has one very significant outcome: it causes us to be 'attentive' to the local and the present – or, to frame this in terms of the British context, the parish. The 'fog of eschatology' – if I might be allowed this phrase – calls into question how much we can know about both the wider context and the future, and leads us to focus on the local and the present. We cannot fully grasp the 'big picture'; we therefore focus down on the local and particular, trying to understand how to proclaim and embody the gospel in this specific place that has been entrusted to us. The growing interest in a 'theology of place' reflects this new interest in the particularity of local situations.[31]

So what insights does eschatology offer us concerning our own roles and responsibilities within this 'big picture'? How are we to understand our roles as agents within the growth of churches? In what way do our individual stories fit into this greater story, of which we realise that we are part? Faith, after all, is about embracing and inhabiting this greater story and recalibrating and redirecting our own stories in its light. We find proper meaning and value through being part of this grand narrative, which transcends our individual narratives yet gives them a new significance and signification.

One approach is to see the future as predetermined, so that our role is merely to catalyse the inevitable. To be faithful is thus to be predictable – to accept passively one's preordained role in the greater scheme of things. Thinkers within the 'Emergent Church' tradition have been highly critical of this way of thinking. Brian McLaren, for example, suggests that such approaches simply 'provide a detailed timeline for the end of the world', within which we are called upon to

---

[31] See E. Casey, *The Fate of Place: A Philosophical History* (Berkeley, CA: University of California Press, 1998): 285–330; J. Inge, *A Christian Theology of Place* (Aldershot: Ashgate, 2003): 59–122; M. Fulkerson, *Places of Redemption: Theology for a Worldly Church* (Oxford: OUP, 2007): 231–52.

find and accept our proper place.[32] This is, for McLaren, about the creation of destiny, not simply our passive acceptance of something that is predetermined. In McLaren's judgement, much of popular American dispensationalism is shaped by an 'eschatology of abandonment' – the inevitable outcome of a modernist Christianity that is preoccupied with the decline of the church and the threat of future global destruction.[33]

A similar concern is expressed by Doug Pagitt in his *Christianity Worth Believing*.[34] He protests against the pessimism of such eschatological outlooks, seeing such an emphasis on the rapture as rendering the salvation of the individual the primary concern of Christian ministry. As McLaren notes, this modernist preoccupation sidelines concerns about ecology and social reform, focussing instead on an individualist agenda.[35] This is hardly a credible interpretation of the New Testament's concerns or focus.

Yet this concern is not exclusive to the 'Emerging Church' movement. N.T. Wright argues that some forms of Christian theology misinterpret the idea of believers being 'citizens of heaven' (Philippians 3:20) in terms of heaven being a supraterrestial destination that offers us an escape from this world, instead of seeing it as a hidden realm of God's promises.[36] His notion of 'collaborative eschatology' is grounded in his understanding of the resurrection:

> Because the early Christians believed that resurrection had begun with Jesus and would be completed in the great final resurrection on the last day, they believed that God had called them to work with him, in the power of the Spirit, to implement the achievement of Jesus and thereby to anticipate the final resurrection, in personal and political life, in mission and holiness ... [T]hose who belonged to Jesus and followed him and were empowered by his Spirit were charged with transforming the present, as far as they were able, in the light of that future.[37]

---

32 B. McLaren, *Everything Must Change: Jesus, Global Crises, and a Revolution of Hope* (Nashville, TN: Thomas Nelson, 2008): 94.

33 McLaren, *A Generous Orthodoxy*: 237.

34 D. Pagitt, *Christianity Worth Believing: Hope-filled, Open-armed, Alive-and-well Faith for the Left Out, Left Behind, and Let Down in Us* (New York: John Wiley & Sons, 2008).

35 McLaren, *A Generous Orthodoxy*: 237.

36 N.T. Wright, *Surprised by Hope: Rethinking Heaven, the Resurrection, and the Mission of the Church* (London: SPCK, 2011): 26.

37 Ibid: *Surprised by Hope*: 27.

So how does this way of seeing things impact on the church growth agenda? This reworking of a classic theological theme encourages us to believers, not as divine pawns in a predetermined game of chess but as creative participants in the divine story. Wright's 'collaborative eschatology' and McLaren's 'participatory eschatology' both highlight human activity and responsibility within the grander scheme of things. While God dominates the storyline, our stories are part of that narrative. McLaren puts this nicely, using a homely analogy.

> God intended to create our universe the way a parent gives birth to a child; the child is given limits and guidance, but she also has freedom to live her own life. That means that the future of the universe is not determined as if it were a movie that's already been filmed and is just being shown to us. Nor is it completely left to chance like dice on a table. Rather, God's creation is maturing with both freedom and limits under the watchful eye of a caring parent.[38]

The same basic point is made by others within mainstream Christianity. Some of its threads may be found within the missional writings of Lesslie Newbigin, particularly his notion of the church as the pilgrim people journeying towards the grand climax of God's consummation. As Newbigin put it in one of the early works, 'the Church is not to be defined by what it is, but by that End to which it moves'.[39] The church is thus not to be understood as a fixed or predetermined entity; rather, its existence within the flux of history is a sign of its calling to inaugurate the realm of God.[40] The recognition that we are called to be active agents within history is a theological commonplace. The biblical commands to 'do' and 'go' can be framed in various ways; they cannot, however, be overlooked, or reformulated in essentially passive manners.

This mandate for activism does not entail the abrogation of divine sovereignty, but is rather to be seen as a recognition that God acts sovereignly to permit believers to advance and develop the storyline. It is not about the denial of grace or providence, but is rather an acknowledgement of God's delegation of certain

---

38 McLaren, *Everything must Change*: 173.

39 L. Newbigin, *The Household of God* (New York: Friendship Press, 1954): 19. Note that the American edition of the work incorporates some improvements made by Newbigin to the original British edition of 1952.

40 For the importance of eschatology for Newbigin's ecclesiology, see P. Weston, 'Ecclesiology in Eschatological Perspective: Newbigin's Understanding of the Missionary Church', in M. Laing and P. Weston (eds), *Theology in Missionary Perspective: Lesslie Newbigin's Legacy* (Eugene, OR: Pickwick Publications, 2012): 70–87.

responsibilities to individual believers and to the church. God makes space for us to act, *faithfully and creatively*, within history.

Such an approach thus gives us theological space to understand our roles in church growth. We are not to see ourselves as cogs in an impersonal machine, or as extras in a movie that has already been shot and whose outcome is predetermined. Rather, our stories are taken up within the overall story of God's purposes and intentions, so that they thus become part of this greater story without ceasing to be our own stories. We can make a difference, precisely by exercising those gifts and talents which have been bestowed upon us by a gracious God – gifts which are meant to be discerned and used.

Eschatology is not about the passive acceptance of the unknown, like some kind of theological *che sarà, sarà*; it is about actively working to transform this unknown future, trusting in the presence and power of the God who raised Christ from the dead and daring to imagine what this future might look like. The church is best seen, not as a fixed institution defined by a specific cultural context of the distant past, but as a living organism, capable of adapting to change in the present without losing its true identity. It is both a sign of God's presence in the future and a symbol of God's capacity to transform that future.

Conclusion

This chapter has offered some brief reflections on the importance of theology for church growth. I have sketched a rough theological framework for reflection and action, which I hope will be useful both in safeguarding the fundamental resource on which the church depends for its present existence and future growth and in providing a lens through which we can see our own situation and possibilities more clearly. A more specifically eschatological perspective enables the church to see the struggles and perplexities of the present age in a new way, enabling us to work for growth, not as an act of cultural defiance, but as an act of faithful obedience, grounded in the future hope inaugurated through the resurrection of Christ. Despite the platitudes of the pragmatists, we all need a theoretical framework to make sense of what we are doing – and enable us to do it better.

Chapter 6
Incarnation and Church Growth

Martin Warner

Introduction

The planning for this collection on Church growth sought a breadth of vision that includes the catholic tradition of the Church of England. I want to applaud that as good in itself and also as characteristic of the tradition of Durham's Cranmer Hall at its best. I am glad to contribute as a catholic Anglican whose formative undergraduate years at St Chad's College, also in Durham, nurtured a robust sense of rivalry with St John's College and Cranmer Hall, our evangelical neighbours.

Life beyond my student years has revealed a theological landscape more complex than the one I expected. Certainties about what is and is not catholic look far less reliable or important. Evangelicals have stolen some of the tools of catholic devotion and imagery (I blame Taizé for much of this!). Conversely, catholic Anglicans have gleefully used evangelical choruses for purposes far removed from the theological intentions of their composers (e.g., a service called Benediction, hitherto regarded by some as illegal).

So far, so ecumenical. But are there, really, any differences left, these days? The question is important, not in order to retain a definition of tribal boundaries, but so that we do not lose sight of what the gifts are that each of us can bring to the party. And the party reference is not a superficial one. I do seriously have in mind the context of Christian celebration.

The environment of worship is essential to us all as Christians. A catholic contribution to a theology of Church growth begins with an assertion that this environment is itself a gymnasium of imaginative exploring, encounter and transformation. That may or may not be a distinctive contribution, but it is very clear in its assertion that the liturgical environment of celebration is where human beings are invited into a matrix that plots the indices between time and eternity. That is why this contribution focuses on sacramentality as a medium of revelation and authority: it is an extended reflection on the implications of the incarnation as the archetype of Church growth in which the body of Christ, the Church, reaches its fullness in being coterminous with the human race.

However, we also need a reality check on this rhetoric. And the reality check is very simple: it clocks the numbers. In today's culture, driven by consumerism and the market economy, if you are not attracting the numbers, it's likely that you are not connecting with the market. Here is a serious challenge for all Christians. We are not being realistic, or faithful, if we simply seek to live in a bubble that is self-defined and deluded, talking to ourselves about our faith, and failing to connect with anyone else.

But the Christian tradition also warns us not to be conformed to this world. We are called to be transformed by the renewing of our minds.[1] The challenge for us lies in the engagement between the world we inhabit for the purposes of language and the processes of life, and the life indivisible from that of our spiritual selves, our life in Christ.

It is in that context that I wish to set out four convictions that are foundational to the substance of this chapter. On them we shall build an understanding of growth that follows from worship and apologetics as the means by which Christians take their part in the mission of God.

Foundational Convictions

First, it is always about Jesus. He is our constant point of reference. He is, uniquely, the way to the Father, the one to whom the Spirit leads, the revelation of our true identity. He is our life; our 'merciful redeemer, friend and brother', in the words of St Richard de Wych, of Chichester.

Second, I wish to assert that, for the Church today, numbers do matter. If we close our minds to the pressing issue of attracting new people into the company of believing Christians we have failed the Lord we serve. Jesus still invites us to 'make disciples of all nations'.[2]

This outline of worship and apologetics as vital contributions to an understanding of Church growth presupposes the use of that wide range of evangelistic strategies that are creatively employed in seeking expansion of the number of believing Christians. Messy Church, Godly Play, Alpha, Emmaus, Pilgrim!, Fresh Expressions, pioneer ministry and church planting are all

---

[1] Romans 12:2. All references to the Bible are from the New Revised Standard Version unless otherwise stated.

[2] Matthew 28:19.

examples of this, together with conferences and similar events that are sponsored by the networks of Christian association, such as Greenbelt, Spring Harvest, New Wine, etc.

Third, I want to be clear that concern about numbers must not be driven by a desire for power – 'success' in the terms of this world and its commercial criteria. Our concern about numbers must be driven by love in all its divine, eternal, triune fullness and beauty. That is the only motivation for the Mission of God. How often have you quoted the text, 'God so loved the world'?[3] Has it, on every occasion been a statement of worship, adoration and the mandate for Christian service? It must always be that, not a health warning to our detractors and those not yet in our pews. Our conviction is, in the words of the Book of Common Prayer, that God desires 'not the death of a sinner, but rather that he may turn from his wickedness and live'.

In this regard, it is important that we also take note of the ecumenical imperative that compels Christians to find their unity in Jesus. Increasingly we are aware of the need for us to be reconciled with each other as ecclesial groupings, in order to be a reconciling presence that serves the common good in the world at large. The growth of Christian commitment to food banks across England is one example of how service of those most in need becomes its own apologetic for Christian faith. It offers demonstrable expression of what we say we believe.

Fourth, I believe that Christianity is the best outworking there is of human life and love within creation. This point leads to the substance of the rest of this chapter, so I would like to explain it in greater detail.

The Introduction of Anthropology

In a recent interview with the Italian atheist Eugenio Scalfari, Pope Francis spoke of the vision of his predecessors Pope John XXIII and Pope Paul VI in the Second Vatican Council.[4] Here, in a Church still coming to terms with the social and technological impact of world war, the Roman Catholic Church sought to look afresh at the modern world and seek how to engage with it.

The documents of the Second Vatican Council were on our 'Church, ministry and sacraments' syllabus when I was a student in Durham. Words that open the

---

3 John 3:16.

4 E. Scalfari, 'The Court is the Leprosy of the Papacy', K. Wallace (trans.), *The Tablet*, 5 October 2013: 12–13.

1965 Pastoral Constitution of the Church in the Modern World (Gaudium et Spes) are etched on my heart and mind as a statement of contemporary Christian commitment to the common good: 'The joy and hope, the grief and anguish of the people of our time, especially of those who are poor or afflicted in any way, are the joy and hope, the grief and anguish of the followers of Christ as well.'[5]

In response to Pope Francis and his affirmation of this vision of the Council, Scalfari made a significant observation: 'Modern society throughout the world is going through a period of deep crisis, not only economic but also social and spiritual ... Even we non-believers feel this almost anthropological weight. That is why we want dialogue with believers and those who best represent them.'[6]

The reference by an atheist to a sense of 'anthropological weight' is an indication of why an approach from within the catholic tradition that takes anthropology seriously might have a distinctive and valuable contribution to make. The area of concern that I wish to tackle is really one of apologetics.

The atheist has thrown down the gauntlet to the Christian by asking how we account for the nature of being human in this era of turmoil that it is 'economic, social and spiritual'. It is incumbent on us to provide some kind of answer, but this is not in any way offered with the expectation that one can lead another person by philosophical argument into a living faith in Jesus Christ – though that possibility should not be discounted as a strategy inspired by the Holy Spirit.

The context in which we undertake this apologetics is complex, however. In both Yorkshire and Sussex my visits to parishes include an opportunity for conversation with clergy and laity about what helps and what inhibits them in sharing their faith. One thing that inhibits many people is fear of ridicule. This should not be disregarded lightly; it is a serious comment on the perception of contemporary systemic hostility to the enterprise of faith in God generally, and to institutional Christianity in particular.

What follows in this paper is an exploration of how we might tackle the perception of systemic hostility and proceed with greater confidence to enter into dialogue with those who experience the 'anthropological weight' of contemporary life and are looking for answers to their questions. A hostile response to them from the Church is sub-Christian and to be resisted. Even a patient account of why Christianity 'is right' seems unlikely to make much progress. We should by now have learned that effective communication is also

[5] A. Flannery O.P. (ed.), *Vatican II: The Conciliar and Post Conciliar Documents* (Dublin: Dominican Publications, 1975).

[6] Scalfari, 'The Court is the Leprosy': 13.

hugely complex and, in terms of apologetics, the message we intend to convey can escape our control. Let me give an example.

In the matter of same-sex marriage the debate in England has been generally robust and wide-ranging. Although it has made reference to religious traditions beyond those of Christianity, it was church leaders who were at the forefront of resistance, articulating shared views on marriage that were widely held. There was also, I believe, an equal conviction among them that homophobia is incompatible with Christian faith and practice.

Within the diocese of Chichester, the City of Brighton and Hove is home to the largest concentration of gay and lesbian people outside London. I have been very strongly challenged by the Christians that I serve to help them respond to the impact that the same-sex marriage debate has had on attitudes towards the Church. What they tell me is this: the case for sustaining a traditional Christian view of marriage was well made and with no concession to homophobia. What was heard by the community outside the Church in Brighton felt very different.

The people of Brighton, protective and supportive of their gay and lesbian community, heard us say, 'God does not love you very much', even though we said no such thing. It will not help matters, if now we embark on a campaign to tell them that they have got us wrong. That only amounts to more negative output from us.

So communication that speaks into our turmoil of 'anthropological weight' and uncertainty can also carry a sub-text at least as loud as the words we utter and possibly be more persuasive. It is for this reason that a Christian apologetic would do well to direct its attention to areas that suggest commonality of experience, interest and need, rather than areas of divergent opinion and conflict.

This is why the use of anthropology is potentially helpful. It refers us to the human condition in ways that are universal and therefore relate to us across the distinctions of gender, race, sexual orientation, social status, etc. In this regard an anthropological approach to apologetics neatly references Paul's understanding about the nature of salvation, namely that 'there is no longer Jew or Greek, there is no longer slave or free, there is no longer male or female; for you are all one in Christ Jesus'.[7]

Commonality as expressed by a Christian anthropology is where I want to begin this account of incarnation and Church growth, seeking to find positive narratives that respond to the challenge from the atheist's question posed above.

I wish then to look at an aspect of being human that makes a statement about our spirituality in an area of endeavour common to Christian and

---

[7] Galatians 6:28.

non-Christian alike. This gives us scope for a Christian apologetic that draws on a non-contentious issue, avoiding the damage of unintended sub-texts. Finally, I want to look at how an explicitly Christian environment of liturgical celebration gives a similarly positive narrative to areas of social and economic concern, also providing positive scope for apologetic communicated in verbal and non-verbal ways.

How Does this Relate to Growth?

The use of Christian anthropology as a basis for apologetics can facilitate growth in two ways, indirectly within the life of the Church and directly in our engagement with the world.

Indirectly, it is about strengthening the Christians who attend our churches to be more confident about resisting the fear of ridicule and knowing that they have something to offer from our household store (Matthew 13:52) that meets every human need and condition.

Directly, this is about the Church's contribution to the common good. Our strategy for growth, inspired by Jesus Christ, is based on love and our capacity to exemplify it. It is well expressed by Pope Paul VI in his 1957 call to love the modern world: 'Let us love and try to understand, esteem, appreciate, serve it and suffer for it. Let us love it with the heart of Christ.'[8]

So to sum up, there are four points on which a catholic contribution to Church growth might be made. It is always about Jesus; numbers matter; the Church is not in a power game about numerical strength; our conviction is that Christianity is the fullest expression of how to be human.

It is to an outline of Christian anthropology that I wish now to proceed, in order to identify the ground for an apologetic that has indirect and direct application to Church growth. We shall then go on to explore an area of common aspiration in the creativity of art, and conclude with some observations on how we celebrate the Christian commitment to the common good that can similarly provide us with grounds for apologetics and growth.

[8] Quoted in S. Platten (ed.), *Anglicanism and the Western Christian Tradition* (Norwich: Canterbury Press, 2003): 221.

A Christian Anthropology

Our starting point must be in the accounts of creation in Genesis. The key verses about the creation of the human person are in Genesis 1:26 'Let us make man in our image, after our likeness' (King James Version) and Genesis 2:7 'And the Lord God formed man of the dust of the ground, and breathed into his nostrils the breath of life; and man became a living soul' (KJV). In both cases a statement is made that early Christian theologians recognised as foundational to our anthropology.

At this point it is also worth noting that the creation of mortals is itself an expression of growth as part of God's plan. To man and woman God says, 'be fruitful and multiply, and fill the earth and subdue it' Genesis 1:29 (KJV). In this regard the human race is, from the outset, given a share in God's role of creativity. The growth, however, is not chaotic. The stewardship that God gives to the human race carries the responsibility for extending the order of creation as God has willed it. Mortals are given dominion over creation for this reason; it is the exercise of their dignity as made in the image of God.

So Gregory of Nazianzus (fourth century) writes in one of the Dogmatic Hymns: 'The soul is the breath of God ... He spoke, and taking some of the newly minted earth his immortal hands made an image into which he imparted some of his own life. He sent his spirit, a beam from the invisible divinity.'[9] The connection here between spirit and breath is a powerful one, but is about more than simply the function of living: there is in the breath the capacity for rationality as well. It is simply stated by seventh century John of Damascus that God, 'by his own inbreathing gave him a rational and understanding soul, which we say is the divine image'.[10]

Perhaps the foundations of a Christian anthropology has already been laid, however, by Irenaeus in the early third century, as he begins to set out a template for our understanding of the incarnation. He writes of creation as establishing a potential in mortals that was not revealed because 'the Word according to whose image man was made was still invisible. Therefore man easily lost the likeness. But when the Word of God was made flesh, he confirmed both image and likeness' (Against heresies 5.16.2).[11]

---

[9] Quoted in H. Bettenson (ed. and trans.), *The Early Christian Fathers* (Oxford: OUP, 1956).

[10] John of Damascus, *Orthodox Faith* 2.12.

[11] Irenaeus, *Against Heresies*, Book V. All following references to Irenaeus are from *Against Heresies*, Books IV and V.

For Irenaeus, it seems that creation prior to the fall contained within itself the need and expectation that the Word would become flesh in order that mortals might achieve the purposes God intended for them. The relationship between the Word and the mortal creature is intentional from the beginning.

In this respect, the Christian writing of Irenaeus echoes the eschatological and cultic mood of contemporary Jewish devotion. In the targum on Exodus 12:42 (… That was for the Lord a night of vigil to bring them out of the land of Egypt. That same night is a vigil to be kept for the Lord by all the Israelites throughout their generations …), the *Poem of the Four Nights* provides a list of revelatory moments through which God's intention and mission to bring creation to perfection is accomplished.[12] They are 'the First Night, when the Lord was revealed over the world to create it'; the Second Night, when the Lord was revealed to Abram, Sarai asks whether she will indeed bear a son, Isaac is offered on the altar, and 'the heavens were bowed and descended, and Isaac saw their perfections, and his eyes were dimmed because of their perfections'; the Third Night, 'when the Lord was revealed against Egypt in the midst of the night' and 'the Fourth Night, when the world will reach its end to be redeemed … this is the night of the Passover to the Name of the Lord'.

The significance of the night as a context for revelation will not be lost on the children of the new Israel, the Church. The night of the birth of Jesus is the point at which Wisdom sees the word leap down from heaven; the night is the context of betrayal in which Jesus, the new Isaac, is bound, a willing victim: the night is the context in which the tomb is broken open and the resurrection light of the eighth day, the day of perfection, begins to dawn in human history.

Anyone who has ever negotiated the way through the plainsong of the *exultet* and paschal *praeconium* at the Easter Vigil will know just how strong the emphasis is on the significance of the phrase, 'this is the night'. And it is in this very context that the works of God are done and, literally, brought to light.

The liturgical text of the *exultet* invites the congregation to use their sense of sight imaginatively. This is a visual parallel to what Ignatius of Antioch imagines when he invites his readers to think in terms of sound, not sight, suggesting in a very similar way that God works these deeds of creative salvation in silence. Imagine what is happening. That is a constant refrain in the catechetical narratives that we have from Cyril of Jerusalem on these rites.

The significance of Cyril's interest is that the candidates can imagine themselves into what is happening; that is no small part of the statement

---

[12] See R. Hayward, 'The Present State of Research into the Targumic Account of the Sacrifice of Isaac', *Journal of Jewish Studies*, 32 (1981): 127–50.

of dignity in those who are worthy of baptism. The imagination from which sacramental experience draws is described by Cyril as imitation. It is a human exercise through which God the Holy Spirit works in order to disclose reality to us. So Cyril instructs his newly initiated pupils in these terms: 'O strange and inconceivable thing! We did not really die, we were not really buried, we were not really crucified and raised again, but our imitation was but in figure, while our salvation is in reality.'[13]

Imagining redemption in all its phases of history is what the human person is capable of by God's intent. This anthropological statement about a capacity marks the human as different from the animal species; it is a statement about our spiritual capacity that also gives content to how we understand the image of God within us.

Imaginary vision is the medium of prophecy. Prophets are seers and as such they exemplify the capacity of the human person to intuit the vision of God. In book four of *Against the Heresies*, Irenaeus makes reference to prophecy as a foundational medium of revelation in a way that is similar to the tracking of salvation history in the *Poem of the Four Nights*. He also charts the stages of revelation through which we are brought to a point of realisation and identity that determines the outcome of all history. This point of realisation is what Irenaeus most often seems to mean in his use of the term 'recapitulation': Jesus came 'in fulfilment of God's comprehensive design and consummates all things [recapitulates all things] in himself'.

Jesus holds all history in his hands and invites us similarly to share in being its governors not its slaves. So Irenaeus writes:

> The Son makes known the Father from the beginning. For he has been with the Father from the beginning: and he has shown to mankind the visions of the prophets, the different kind of spiritual gifts, and his own ministry, and the glorification of the Father in due sequence and order.

Thus the Word 'became what we are that he might make us what he himself is'.

There is something very important here about likeness and attraction and it resides in the capacity to imagine and so to see. When the Word is still invisible, our self-understanding of the image of God within is so weakened that it is easily lost. This is a description of a people with a pitifully weakened and impoverished imagination. But of itself, the vision of the Word made flesh reconfigures our

---

[13] F. Cross (ed.), *St Cyril of Jerusalem Lectures on the Christian Sacraments* (London: SPCK, 1978): 61.

very minds and nature so as to re-establish our identity. So with lapidary force, Irenaeus is able to say that 'the glory of God is the living man; and the life of man is the Vision of God'. Here, indeed, is the contrast with the types and shadows of the older rite[14] to which the *Poem* points: for the outcome, as Isaac experiences it, is vision dimmed by the brightness of God's glory; for the child of the New Israel that vision is precisely the destiny to which we are called and can begin to practice even now.

The words of Irenaeus about the glory of God and the vision of man were chosen by Michael Ramsey in exactly the form quoted above for the memorial stone that would mark where his ashes were to be interred in the cloister of Canterbury cathedral. It would be a gigantic leap to claim that their use in such a context by a former archbishop of Canterbury is indicative of how Anglicans do their anthropology. The use of this quotation by Ramsey does remind us that there is a strand of theological reference within our Anglican tradition that builds on the wisdom of Irenaeus for its understanding of the scope of being human.

This is a strand that is expanded in the late eleventh century by Anselm in his account of faith seeking understanding and his perception that what we would refer to as the imagination is how the human person probes the very nature of God and discovers that it is always greater than the capacity of our minds.[15]

Richard Hooker makes a sixteenth century contribution, with reference to the scope of law, as does Joseph Butler two centuries later in his exploration of how analogy works. More recently the twentieth century moral theologian Kenneth Kirk explored this theme in a wide-ranging account of what we imagine a good life to be. The 1928 Bampton Lectures, entitled *The Vision of God*, draw explicitly on the work of Irenaeus and his description of vision as the medium of prayer and sanctification is an exercise of imagination in the informed Christian mind and life.

William Temple touches on the theme, a few years later, of our imaginative reading of creation in Nature, Man and God. He asserts that from nature we learn to read the mystery of redemption, seeing the rising of the sun in the sky as the fundamental metaphor of the resurrection and our salvation. It is the basis of Temple's application of the gospel to our social context.[16]

A similar application is undertaken by David Brown in the contemporary context. He relates imagination to tradition and discipleship and explores the withdrawal of Christian interest from a variety of human activities that we have

---

[14] A reference to the Office hymn for Corpus Christi by St Thomas Aquinas. See A. Caesar et al. (eds), *New English Hymnal* (Norwich: Canterbury Press, 1986), no. 268.

[15] See R. Southern, *St Anselm: A Portrait in a Landscape* (Cambridge: CUP, 1990).

[16] W. Temple, *Nature, Man and God* (London: Macmillan, 1935): 306.

previously engaged with spiritually. He points to art as an obvious arena for this engagement; gardening and sport are perhaps more surprising examples.[17]

The significance of these writers is that they depend on the use of the imagination for their theological methodology. As a statement of human capacity, the term imagination is probably better suited to our own era of self-awareness and psychological definition. But it is there in what the theologians from earlier generations, quoted above, have described as imitation, seeking, analogy, conscience and, most powerfully, as vision.

In Kirk, Temple and Brown there are interesting statements about what Christians believe being human is like. They draw from older wisdom and cover much of the terrain of economic, social and spiritual weight – the content – of the anthropology that was being surveyed by the atheist Eugenio Scalfari in his conversation with Pope Francis.

The human person that emerges from the outline of a Christian anthropology is one who is endowed with physical, intellectual and emotional powers, with rationality and a capacity for understanding the laws of God in ways that lead to a knowledge of God akin to that of the angels (that's an excellent Anglican contribution from Richard Hooker's first volume in his *Books of Ecclesiastical Polity*[18]).

What might this mean for Church growth in specific terms? To answer that, I wish to move to a consideration of the exercise of imagination as a narrative in art. This is a narrative that shapes our environment; art has the power to do that. It is one that conveys profound emotions and spiritual intuition and has been a powerful medium for evangelisation.

The Vision of God: Caught Internally, Sought Artistically

I hope that this might not be so arrogant an age that we fail to learn the evangelical lessons of the past. Bede records that when Augustine landed in Kent, nervous of a hostile reception, he and his mission team took to their meeting with King Ethelbert 'a silver cross as their standard and the likeness of our Lord and saviour painted on a board'.[19]

In no way does Bede claim supernatural properties for these items, but he is referencing a piece of wisdom known to the evangelists of those days and

---

[17] D. Brown, *God and Enchantment of Place* (Oxford: OUP, 2004).

[18] R. Hooker, *The Works*, 3 vols, J. Keble (ed.) (Oxford: OUP, 1845).

[19] Bede, *A History of the English Church and People*, L. Sherley-Price (trans.) (Harmondsworth: Penguin, 1968): 69.

worthy of consideration in our own time. Nor am I suggesting that England will experience a Christian revival if the Archbishop of Canterbury simply turns up at Buckingham Palace bearing a silver cross and an icon. The point being made by Augustine and recorded by Bede is valid today. They are noting that the response to evangelistic preaching occurs at a variety of levels within the human person. A visual presentation can prompt the imagination in ways that engage both mind and heart.

Augustine's action in taking with him a picture was in keeping with the edgy and controversial evangelistic method of his time. A little after Augustine arrived in Kent, Pope Gregory wrote to bishop Serenus of Marseilles to clarify what the danger and value of the use of images might be:

> It is one thing to adore a picture [the danger], another to learn what is to be adored through the history told by the picture. What Scripture presents to readers, a picture presents to the gaze of the unlearned. For in it ... the illiterate read.

Michelle Brown, Curator of Illuminated Manuscripts at the British Library, comments on this observation by Gregory. She notes that the convention of illustrating the text of scripture, in manuscripts like the Lindisfarne gospels for example, indicates an imaginative reading and cross-referencing of texts 'founded upon a wealth of scriptural and exegetical sources and multivalent levels of 'reading' from which our sophisticated electronic age might well learn'.[20]

The imagination is the engine of 'multivalent levels of reading'. It is not a process of thought that is foreign to us, or to the authors of scripture itself. For example, the evangelists Matthew and John engage markedly in this kind of reading when they speak of the actions and words of Jesus as fulfilling the words of the prophets. They are seeing an event, and imagining themselves into the vision of those who have seen something similar as a sign of God's self-revelation. So Matthew observes in Jesus as he heals the sick some words from Isaiah that exactly capture the scene: 'Here is my servant, whom I have chosen ... I will put my Spirit upon him.'[21] This is the raw material of the artist's imagination.

There is a good example of the explicit relating of one piece of scripture to another in the painting of Fra Angelico in the Dominican monastery of S Marco in Florence.[22] In each of the friars' cells Fra Angelico and his team have painted a meditation on some aspect of the life of Jesus. Their work is an artistic expression

---

[20] M. Brown, *The Lindisfarne Gospels* (London: The British Library, 2003): 77.

[21] Matthew 12:15–21; cf. Isaiah 42:1–4.

[22] P. Morachiello (ed.), *Fr. Angelico: The San Marco Frescoes* (London: Thames and Hudson, 1995).

of what might be meant by multivalent reading. The artists play with time and texts in order to invite the contemporary viewer to enter into the mystery of salvation that they have shown. So, for example, St Dominic is often depicted as present in one of the scenes of the birth or passion of Jesus. The elements of the scourging of Jesus are shown in one cell and St Dominic is tenderly portrayed as pondering on the scriptures to find the references, from Isaiah 53 perhaps, that give meaning to this moment in the work of our salvation.

In a picture, the illiterate read. This is a profoundly anthropological insight that does not simply relate to the ability to read words on a page. It is equally valid for the kind of reading that we describe as reading the signs of the times. This is intuitive reading; it is about the stuff that touches our soul. The reading of an image in this context is akin to the way in which we read the emotions on the face of another person, who might be a stranger or a person we know and love deeply. In both cases it could well be that no words are uttered, and yet the communication between us can be profound and unmistakable.

In terms of evangelism today, the recognition of a multivalent reading that engages the imagination should be a vital strand in our apologetics. The fact that it works at a universal, anthropological level makes it the more important. Recognition also that, as perhaps never before, we live in a data-rich, multi-media age, suggests that we should be more robust and articulate in our communication and visual intelligence than we seem to be.

A challenge has been offered to us by one of the greatest evangelists in this area, Neil MacGregor. He was the director of the National Gallery who celebrated the Millennium year with the exhibition entitled, 'Seeing Salvation'. Early in 2001 the BBC noted that this was the most visited exhibition of 2000. An arts editor observed that 'it is very interesting that such a Christian theme could be a crowd puller. It was a gamble but it paid off'.[23] Nor should we easily dismiss the blockbuster success of that exhibition as an aberration. The 'Sacred Made Real' exhibition at the National Gallery in 2009 was also a resounding success, followed by a more challenging contemporary sculpture collection by Michael Landy in the autumn of 2013, entitled 'Saints Alive'.

In terms of evangelism, these exhibitions are functioning at the level of direct apologetics. Funded by public money, in one of the great art galleries of Europe, they invite an audience to consider how and why the artistic imagination has been brought to bear on the narrative of Christian faith. The exercise is not simply the scholarly exploration of an episode in human history consigned to the

[23] Available at http://news.bbc.co.uk/1/hi/entertainment/1162175.stm accessed 16 January 2015.

past. It is not simply about nostalgia for a Christian past. It is also asking where this capacity and need has gone in today's irreligious and consumerist society.

We should be noting the interest in such a gamble and asking more about why it occurred and what place it has in our evangelistic thinking. We should be more creative and enterprising in using resources such as our art galleries as gymnasia for the exercise of enquiry about the Christian story.[24] I have sometimes listened in on teaching sessions for schools or adults in the Sainsbury Wing of the National Gallery, which houses the Gallery's collection of early renaissance paintings, the majority of which are Christian in content and purpose. The question and answer exchanges have been amazingly instructive exercises in Christian apologetic outside the Church. The questions are simple. They are about what you see. The answers demand an explanation of faith: you see what it is that Christians say they believe.

This is all very well, you might think, for those who live in London, but it has no relevance for the majority of the nation that cannot afford the luxury of dropping into the National Gallery. This might be so, except for the presence of a cathedral in every diocese that will have some resources to offer in the gymnasium of this apologetics by imagination. And if we were a little more attentive to our church surroundings, we might benefit from the inheritance we have within those buildings.

I have become increasingly fascinated by stained glass, most of which is nineteenth century, some of which is simply ghastly. However, sitting through Evensong in a Sussex church recently, I became absorbed in the window opposite me that showed St Matthew the evangelist with his emblem of the human face (referencing Ezekiel and Revelation)[25] and the prophet Isaiah holding a roundel of the lamb of God. It took me a bit of time to unravel the very subtle line of imaginative thinking that leads from one to the other.

The value of the window was not in primary evangelism; it was in the statement of imagination at the service of the narrative of faith in its artistic expression. This was an interesting experience, in a village church, of seeing salvation. I suspect that most members of the congregation there would have little awareness of the narrative in their stained glass, and yet an exploration of that image might evoke more from them than some sermons using just words.

---

[24] For further exploration of the point that art opens up vistas that nothing else can, the observation by Rowan Williams is worth pursuing: 'The non-secular character of art, in this context, is its affirmation of inaccessible perspectives. It would not be too glib to say that this somehow constituted art as a religious enterprise.' Rowan Williams, *Faith in the Public Square* (London: Bloomsbury, 2012): 14.

[25] Ezekiel 1:10; Revelation 4:7.

The point is not that a fresh interest in stained glass is going to renew the Church's engagement with the world. More pressing is a concern about the profound lack of curiosity that so many congregations seem to have about the content of their faith in relation to scripture, tradition, reason and how these relate to their experience in primary ways. This seems to be compounded by an inattention to the environment of sacred space as a primary resource for communicating imaginatively the content and immediacy of Christian faith. This inattention impairs our confidence in apologetics at a very basic level.

Let's return for a moment to my experience of listening in to teaching sessions in the National Gallery. It is in the environment of worship – what we see, say, sing and do, that we narrate what we believe. The primary apologetics that emerges from that is the capacity for simple description. What is characteristic of Christian faith is that we worship; how, why and what we worship is expressed in these imaginative processes that are evidenced by the environment of our sacred spaces. What is also obvious about gatherings of Christians that attract large numbers is that the quality of worship is one of the drivers in sustaining and expanding their number.

My reference here is deliberately to sacred spaces, avoiding the use of the term 'church'. A significant percentage of Christians in Britain today understand themselves to be the Church that meets in a building that is not 'a church'. Most of these Christian communities are rapidly growing in number. But they rarely function without recourse to the elements of the imagination that I have been exploring.

Stained glass by Kempe and Burne-Jones might not be part of the fabric of the building, but the use of modern technology supplies visual images in abundance. And often these images are drawn from creation, using a process of imagination that invites us to an emotional response to God as our creator. Look, for example, at the Hillsong website. The images are a profoundly anthropological meditation on the theological quality of communion, *koinonia*, in Greek. Imagery is used very provocatively as an apologetic for the self-understanding of this Church which is 'about God and people'.[26]

The need to recover a spiritual dimension in the relationships that we form (being a people, not simply a person) is profoundly expressed in a variety of contexts. It is here that Christian apologists might wish to engage with the apparently secular world of contemporary art.

Antony Gormley is one of the most thoughtful of contemporary artists in the sphere of social analysis. His 2007 exhibition at the Hayward Gallery,

---

[26] Available at www.hillsong.co.uk accessed 16 January 2015.

entitled Blind Light, explored the theme of environment, especially the built environment and the experience of seeking human identity and relationship within it.

In the preparation for two of the exhibits, Allotment and Space Station, Gormley researched the demographics of modern urban life. He noted 'the number of single bedroom apartments that are being built in Western cities. It does seem that people want to be very close but at the same time to have nothing to do with each other'.[27] As an artist Gormley touches on the same point that is being made by the Hillsong website: the contrast is between being people and being alone. The Church is always about being people and thereby enriching the experience of being a person. That is the hallmark of our relationship with Jesus Christ through baptism and thereby with the interrelated life of the divine Trinity. But the relationship is also made specific to us in terms of time and space. This is what constitutes the scandalous particularity of the sacraments; in each time and place they communicate what is true for every time and place.

In order to move this exploration towards some concluding remarks about how we function evangelistically within the imaginative environment, I wish to refer to the installation from which Antony Gormley's exhibition took its title, Blind Light. This was described by Gormley as 'something clean, square, well-designed, safe and dry that is completely inverted by being used to contain all those elemental things that Modernism was supposed to have protected us against ... [namely] from weather, from darkness, from uncertainty'. The content of the box was re-created cloud, lit so as to become blinding when you entered it.

The environment that Gormley describes fits with astonishing aptness the descriptions of the presence of God in the Old Testament and in the New. The story of the transfiguration in the gospels attests to this, as does the Exodus account of Moses on Mount Sinai. Perhaps the most explicit account of the cloud as the presence of God is in the Chronicler's description of the dedication of the temple built by Solomon: 'the house of the Lord was filled with a cloud, so that the priests could not stand to minister because of the cloud; for the glory of the Lord filled the house of God'.[28]

As a definition of worship at its best this seems to me to be very important. The work of worship is, ultimately, the work of God in which we are given the privilege of doing service. Our service is the offering of life in sacrifice, motivated by love of God. This is what St Paul urges upon us: 'I appeal to you therefore,

---

[27] A. Vidler et al. (eds), *Antony Gormley: Blind Light* (London: Hayward Publishing, 2007): 55–6.

[28] 2 Chronicles 5:13–14.

brothers and sisters, by the mercies of God, to present your bodies as a living sacrifice, holy and acceptable to God, which is your spiritual worship.'[29] This is the point at which we conform ourselves to the sacrifice of Jesus Christ in the great act of giving thanks, the Eucharist.

It is to the demonstration of that act of thanksgiving within the imaginative environment that we now turn by way of conclusion to this contribution.

Making a Eucharistic Community

The Eucharist is about the formation of the Church. In that context a different way of being human is enacted and we demonstrate what we mean when we speak about being a Christian.

Having argued the case (in dialogue with an atheist or any other critic) for faith in God by reference to the apologetics that come from a Christian anthropology, we are next required to show how this works. I stated at the outset that a catholic contribution to reflections on Church growth will focus on worship and sacramentality. This should not be confused with the detail of how the mechanics of worship function. Unhealthy fascination with the mechanics, to the detriment of the meaning, is however a real danger in this tradition. But in a more positive vein, I wish to point to the nature of the society that takes its shape from the Eucharist.

The Eucharist is the means by which incorporation (a body language word) into Jesus Christ is registered and lived out. It is about growth because that is intrinsic to the nature of food and drink. In terms of Christian life, this growth is focused on the particular relationship with Jesus as the one from which we derive nourishment, restoration and joy. These things are also practised in relationships with the others whom we meet through life in Christ, for they too are like him and bear his name.

It has been observed above that a church that is growing is dependent on the quality of its worship: it is at the same time dependent on the quality of its relationships if that numerical growth is to deepen through commitment and holiness. One of the good news stories in the Church of England is the growth of people from all age groups who attend worship in cathedrals. That is great as a statistic. However, cathedrals have quickly realised that the statistic means little if they are simply being used as a service provider (in every sense). They have

---

29 Romans 12:1.

rapidly developed patterns of pastoral care and nurture that enable attendance to deepen into conversion – of the mind, heart, family, wallet and diary.

The Eucharist is a forum in which time is put back together. We live in an age that is obsessed with itself and greedy for its future. The Eucharist requires us to remember the narrative that got us here. That is why the Eucharist begins with an extended study of the Bible. The Sunday pattern of readings from Old and New Testaments and from the gospel require us to reflect seriously on the story of salvation as scripture reveals it to us.

Sitting under the judgement of scripture is not necessarily comfortable but it is corrective. One of the most impressive evangelists I met in Middlesbrough was a man who had got into trouble in his teenage years and been brought to faith by a family friend who was a Christian. Ultimately he and his wife decided to set up a charity that would enable him to minister to youngsters on Teesside who were like him as a teenager. The passage of scripture that spoke to him was the phrase 'a father to the fatherless', from Psalm 68. This transition from scriptural reflection to ministry in daily life is what the final dismissal from the Eucharist is about: 'Go in peace to love and serve the Lord.'

The Eucharist is also the fulfilment of the worship of the temple. It is how the law achieves its purposes.[30] Within the dispensation of this fulfilment comes the attention to the covenant between God and creation, God and Abraham, God and Israel. In the temple worship the focus on the earth and the justice of human relationships is strongly present. Some may seek to diminish the importance of this as simply a manifestation of the concerns of an agrarian people with a nomadic past. However, in today's global society, the environmental issues that confront us raise again the questions of justice and the treatment of the earth. At the heart of the Eucharist is the great prayer which gives thanks for creation and redemption. Its vision is orientated towards the revelation of the new heaven and the new earth and the coming of the Lord in judgement and glory. Christian social teaching on how we live our lives finds its home in worship as these themes are rehearsed.

Today, there are many people of goodwill who look for voices in support of their concern for greater care of the earth, a more equitable use of its resources and a clearer sense of responsibility to future generations. The Eucharist, with its emphasis on creation as the sacramental material in which God conveys truth and self-giving, offers Christians a narrative with which to draw such people into our communion.

---

[30] Jesus says, in the Sermon on the Mount, 'not one letter, not one stroke of a letter, will pass from the law until all is accomplished' (Matt 5:18).

Finally, the Eucharist is the educational environment in which we are schooled in what morality looks like. At the altar all are equal before God. This emphatically includes the ordained minister who leads the celebration and approaches with everyone else by saying, 'Lord, I am not worthy to receive you'.

Morality is not about keeping rules: it is about the worship of God that makes us into people who have a distinctive character akin to the likeness of God. Taking up the notion of Irenaeus, we get the hang of what it means to be like God because we have caught the vision, albeit partially. It is here that the Eucharist turns our attention to growth in the sense of depth and familiarity with the environment of heaven.

This contribution has sought to find space in a range of approaches to Church growth for a Christian anthropology in which imagination and all its potential creates the environment in which human flourishing happens. The conviction is that we are made in such a way as to need that environment. To have it denied us will result in distortion and societal dislocation.

This is not a charter for a do-nothing discipleship which waits for God mysteriously to do it all. The work of salvation is there in God's very making of us, as Irenaeus intuited. Our urgent task is to enable the people of this generation to imagine that to be so. At the conclusion of *The Vision of God*, Kenneth Kirk observed that like can only be seen by like. This again picks up a point made by Irenaeus. The problem with exploring Church growth is that the maintenance of an institution such as the Church of England through the increase of its numbers or the intensity of its activities distracts from the task of being Christian.

Increasingly, we might need to do less and pray more, thereby learning to let God give the increase. That is the direction in which Kirk points his reader and I repeat his wise advice as a conclusion to this contribution, with the reminder that the capacity to study God is given to all by virtue of our creation:

> It is therefore only by studying the nature of God as revealed in Jesus – by plunging into the depths of that nature till alien souls find themselves at home there in the end, and thought moves naturally upon lines akin to those discernible in the thought and speech of Jesus – that we can effectively prepare ourselves for the glory that is to be.[31]

[31] K. Kirk, *The Vision of God* (London: Longmans, 1932): 467.

Chapter 7

The Prodigal Spirit and Church Growth

Graham Tomlin

We are used to the regular, predictable, weary refrain that the church is dying. Pretty well every article on the church and its relevance to modern life in today's media is littered with phrases such as 'empty' pews', 'sparse attendance', church decline'. This story is often reinforced by voices within the church itself. In 1998 Jack Spong, Bishop of Newark in the USA, published a book entitled *Why the Church must Change or Die* and books with that kind of title appear every now and again.

Now it may be that, seen from the perspective of declining denominations or congregations in western Europe or the USA, such titles resonate loudly. However, elsewhere, they would simply raise quizzical looks. At least numerically, it is difficult to see the need for the 'change or die' scenario when sitting in the Winners' Chapel, in Otta, Nigeria, where the inside seating capacity is 50,000 and the outside overflow capacity 250,000, or in Hillsong in Sydney, where around 20,000 gather each week. According to Peter Brierley, in 2009, the seven largest churches in England were the following (although many of these have grown in more recent years):[1]

10,000	Kingsway International Christian Centre, Hackney
5,500	Kensington Temple, West London
5,000	Hillsong in Central London
4,000	Ruach Ministries, Brixton
2,500	House of Praise, Woolwich
2,500	St Thomas Crookes, Sheffield
2,490	Holy Trinity, Brompton, West London
2,200	Jesus House for All Nations, Brent

[1] Available at http://www.lausanneworldpulse.com/perspectives.php/1109?pg=all accessed 7 January 2015.

In London, Hillsong now has four services with over 9,000 people through the doors each Sunday, and Holy Trinity, Brompton (HTB) nearer 5,000. The black majority and immigrant churches together amounted to 27 per cent of Christian places of worship in London in 2012 and 24 per cent of churchgoers.

In terms of church growth, these are impressive numbers. And of course the key factor that they have in common here is that most of these churches are either Pentecostal or Charismatic in character or origin. Peter Brierley points out how, in London, 'Church attendance has grown from just over 620,000 in 2005 to 720,000 in 2012, a 16% increase. While these numbers are across all denominations, the growth is especially seen in the Black Majority Churches (Pentecostals) and the various immigrant churches.' The same trend is borne out by statistics on age. Whereas the average Methodist or URC church member in London is 56, the average Anglican or Roman Catholic is 45 and Baptists, Independents and Orthodox are on average 42, the average age of a Pentecostal or new church member is 33.

Globally the scenario is similar. In 2009 there were round 600 million Pentecostals worldwide, the largest global denomination after the Roman Catholic Church. There are now 175 million Pentecostals in Latin America alone, with an annual growth rate of 8 per cent. Pentecostalism worldwide is said to be expanding by 19 million per year. As Philip Jenkins put it in *The Next Christendom* (2002):

> Pentecostal expansion across the Southern Hemisphere has been so astonishing as to justify claims of a new reformation ... Within a few decades [Pentecostal and Charismatic] denominations will represent a far larger segment of global Christianity, and just conceivably a majority ... Since there were only a handful of Pentecostals in 1900, and several hundred million today, is it not reasonable to identify this as perhaps the most successful social movement of the past century?[2]

When looking at Church growth, of course not all of it worldwide is Pentecostal or Charismatic in character, but much of it is. The question is why? What is the dynamic that explains this? There have been many sociological, statistical or psychological explanations, but I want to look at it *theologically*. What theological factors in Pentecostal and Charismatic churches aid the trend towards growth?

---

[2] P. Jenkins, *The Next Christendom: The Coming of Global Christianity* (New York: OUP, 2002): 8.

Invocation of the Spirit

At the heart of Pentecostal and Charismatic Christianity is the *invocation of the Spirit upon the people of Christ*, in other words, the explicit expectation of the Spirit's direct presence and power on the believer and the church. In more catholic traditions, the emphasis perhaps falls on the invocation of the Spirit on the elements in the Eucharist. In Pentecostal and Charismatic churches, the cue is taken from the day of Pentecost, when the Spirit fell upon *people*. This takes various forms, of course, Baptism in the Holy Spirit, an expectation of the direct experience of the Spirit in prayer ministry, worship, evangelism etc., but at their heart, the distinct element of Charismatic and Pentecostal Christianity is this invocation of the Spirit – believing that without the direct action of the Spirit, the church is an empty shell and, in particular, that growth of the church is impossible.

Now there is, of course, a theological tension in this theme of invocation of the Spirit, particularly in relation to the *freedom* of the Spirit. The same tension exists in discussion about Church growth – does Church growth come about as the result of human plans and activities, or as result of the direct action of the Spirit?

One of the seminal texts in the gospels on the Holy Spirit comes in the conversation between Jesus and Nicodemus in John 3, where Jesus says:

> No-one can enter the kingdom of God unless he is born of water and the Spirit. Flesh gives birth to flesh, but the Spirit gives birth to spirit. You should not be surprised at my saying, "You must be born again". The wind blows wherever it pleases. You hear its sound, but you cannot tell where it comes from or where it is going. So it is with everyone born of the Spirit. (John 3:5–8)

The Spirit jealously guards his freedom from human control. And yet, the Spirit is given freely. Jesus in Luke's gospel says: 'If you then, though you are evil, know how to give good gifts to your children, how much more will your Father in heaven give the Holy Spirit to those who ask him!' (Luke 11:13). In John, the same pledge is expressed: 'God gives the Spirit without limit' (John 3:34). The Spirit is Gift, given without reluctance. God promises to give or send his Spirit when asked. We cannot control the Spirit but that same Spirit is still promised when we ask. The Spirit is free, in the sense that he remains free from human control, yet is given freely when requested: the Spirit is free, but not random.

This tension is brought out by the story recounted in Acts 8. Some Samaritan converts had been baptised into the name of Jesus, but the Spirit had not yet come upon them. So, Peter and John are sent to Samaria, where the Spirit comes on these new disciples when the apostles lay hands on them. Watching this, Simon the magician, on his conversion, asks if he can *buy* the Holy Spirit's power from the apostles. He is rebuked in no uncertain terms, because he has sought to *own* the Spirit, to bring the Spirit under his control with his money. The tension lies in the fact that the apostles are, it seems, able to convey the Spirit through the laying on of their hands and through prayer, and yet at the same time the Spirit cannot be possessed, owned or bought with money.

The same tension is found elsewhere in the Scriptures: God's power works through the performance of the sacraments, through preaching, through the laying on of hands and through prayer (Luke 4:40; Acts 8:18; 9:17f; 2 Tim 1:6 etc.). All of these are, on one level at least, human actions subject to human decision. We decide when and whether to baptise, preach, pray, lay on hands and so on. Yet at the same time, as John 3:8 reminds us, despite all this, God retains a sovereign liberty to act independently and despite, rather than only through, human means. Human actions do not guarantee the working of the Spirit. The Spirit responds to human action, yet retains a freedom from human control. The Spirit works through us but is not controlled by us. The Spirit works through human agency, yet is not confined to or controlled by human action.

How is this tension to be properly maintained in the church's life? The answer surely is: by *invocation*. Neither individual Christians, nor the Church as a whole possess the Spirit. Asking is part of the way in which the Spirit is given. The church needs to ask, and to ask continually. The necessity of asking expresses this vital dimension of the freedom of the Spirit from human control, yet his willingness at the same time to be tied to and work through human agency.

The church has always prayed this prayer. The *Veni Creator*, one of the classic Christian prayers, invites the Spirit to fill human hearts

> Come, Holy Spirit, Creator blest
> And in our souls take up Thy rest
> Come with Thy grace and heavenly aid
> To fill the hearts which Thou hast made.

The song then asks the Spirit to anoint us with his sevenfold gifts of understanding, knowledge, wisdom, counsel, piety, fortitude, and the fear of the Lord:[3]

---

[3] This traditional list comes from Isaiah 11.1–2.

Come, Holy Ghost, our souls inspire
And lighten with celestial fire
Thou the anointing Spirit art
Who dost Thy sevenfold gifts impart.

This practice of invocation of the Spirit has helped the church avoid two equally dangerous forms of presumption: blithely taking for granted the presence of the Spirit, or acting as if the Spirit was not necessary and that we can do it all ourselves. Invocation of the Spirit can be done confidently (as Pentecostals and Charismatics do) because the Spirit is promised freely to those who ask, yet we still have to ask, because the Spirit is a Gift, not a Right. Jürgen Moltmann puts it well: 'The relation of the church to the Holy Spirit is the relation of *epiklesis*, continual invocation of the Spirit and unconditional opening for the experiences of the Spirit who confers fellowship and who makes life truly worth living.'[4] Invocation of the Spirit is something the whole church does, but perhaps Pentecostals and Charismatics do it with a little more confidence and expectation!

The Prodigal Spirit

But what happens when the Spirit is invoked? How are we to understand this theologically?

In HTB, the UK church that has perhaps most prominently built a whole church growth movement around a strong emphasis on invocation of the Spirit, there is a bronze statue by the artist Charlie Mackesy (see Figure 7.1).[5] Mackesy is fascinated by the story of the Prodigal Son and, in particular, the moment in the story when the son returns to be embraced by his father. In a number of paintings and sculptures he depicts this moment. The image works on two levels. On the first, it captures the moment in the story when the father embraces the son after his return from the far country. It vividly conveys the pathos of the embrace, the emotional power of reconciliation. On another level, particularly when viewed by a Christian onlooker, it depicts the lost sinner returning to God. Many people have found that these sculptures and paintings express very powerfully their own sense of having been welcomed back into the presence and

---

4 J. Moltmann, *The Spirit of Life: A Universal Affirmation* (London: SCM Press, 1992): 230.

5 Available at http://www.charliemackesy.com/ accessed 7 January 2015.

Figure 7.1 *The Return of the Prodigal Son* by Charlie Mackesy. Bronze Sculpture on an Oak Plinth.
Source: Photograph used by kind permission of Charlie Mackesy.

embrace of God the Father after many years in the metaphorical and spiritual wilderness: the 'son' in the image is not the Prodigal Son of Jesus' story: it is me. It conveys that sense of 'coming home', of being picked up again in the warmth of the Father's love.

Perhaps however there is also a third level on which the image works: as a window into the life of the Trinity. From this perspective, it depicts God the Father's love for God the Son. The Son in the image is lifeless, hanging limp and helpless in the Father's arms, while the Father embraces him with wide-eyed passion and a hint of agony in his face. It is a picture of the very thing that lies at the very heart of all being – the love of the Father for the Son.

Viewed as a depiction of the relationship between the Son and the Father, it focuses on the embrace by the Father of the dead Son, the Son who has given his life in the sacrifice of the cross. It is a kind of *Pietà*, this time not of Mary cradling her dead son in her arms – in a deeper theological sense, it is the Father who catches up the dead Son in his arms and in so doing brings him to life again. In the parable of the Prodigal in Luke's gospel, the line 'for this son of mine was dead and is alive again' (Luke 15:24) makes an intriguing connection to the death and resurrection of the Son.

As a window into the life of the Trinitarian relations however, it seems to lack one important dimension: the Holy Spirit. This is where we return to the second level on which the image works, where the viewer is drawn into the picture to identify with the embraced son. This begins to highlight the role of the Spirit – to draw *us* into the very heart of all being – the love between the Father and the Son. As we gaze on this picture of embrace, it is in one sense the Son being embraced by the Father, yet at the same time, it is us. We find ourselves united with the Son, knowing the intimate, powerful love of the Father for his Son. As John Calvin put it: 'the Holy Spirit is the bond by which Christ effectually unites us to himself' (Inst 3.1.1).[6] The Spirit draws us into the Son's relationship with the Father.

Three passages from the New Testament help to draw this out. The first is the baptism of Jesus, where the Father sends the Spirit onto the Son, in one of the great Trinitarian moments of the gospels. The Father's words are significant: 'You are my Son, whom I love; with you I am well pleased' (Luke 3:22). This statement immediately locates Jesus' identity at the outset of his ministry: he is not just the Son, but the *beloved* Son of the Father. Being a son or daughter of course does not guarantee being beloved: not all children know themselves as the beloved children of their parents. But this Son is identified first and foremost as the primary object of the love of the Father. The bond between the Father and the Son is one not of disapproval or disappointment or even expectation or hope: it is love. In John's gospel, no voice is heard in the baptism story, however the whole gospel might be seen as an exploration of the theme of the love of the Father for the Son. The phrase 'the Father loves the Son' is repeated several times. Jesus is first and foremost, the beloved Son of the Father.

The second passage is Romans 8:15, where we read 'You received the Spirit of sonship. And by him we cry, "Abba, Father". The Spirit himself testifies with our spirit that we are God's children.' In other words, the Holy Spirit draws us into the same relationship with the Father as Jesus himself has. We are enabled to use the same intimate term of address: *Abba*. Our relationship with the Father is determined by Jesus' relationship with the Father. Our 'sonship' is not parallel to, or separate from that of Jesus: it is only by virtue of being 'in Christ', as Paul

[6] J. Calvin, *Institutes of the Christian Religion* (Philadelphia: Westminster Press, 1960 [1559]), 3.1.1.

puts it elsewhere, that we are sons and daughters of the Father at all. Naturally, classic Christian theology would insist that there is one crucial difference between our 'sonship' and his – he is the Son by nature, and we are sons and daughters by grace, or adoption (Romans 8:15, 23; 9:4, Galatians 4:5, Ephesians 1:5). However the point is that we are not co-opted as partners but adopted as children, adopted into the same relationship with the Father as the one true Son has.

The third passage takes us further in Romans 8:15–23, where we read:

> The Spirit himself testifies with our spirit that we are God's children. Now if we are children, then we are heirs – heirs of God and co-heirs with Christ, if indeed we share in his sufferings, in order that we may also share in his glory ... The whole creation has been groaning as in the pains of childbirth right up to the present time. Not only so, but we ourselves, who have the firstfruits of the Spirit, groan inwardly as we wait eagerly for our adoption to sonship, the redemption of our bodies.

Recalling Mackesy's sculpture of the Prodigal Son, the Son held tight by the Father is the suffering Son, helpless, at the end of his resources, yet embraced and raised to life by the loving embrace of the Father. It is that very Son with whom we are united by the prodigal Spirit, who, like the Prodigal Son, Goes into the far country to draw us back to the Father and is prodigal with the divine love. This means that Christian experience will involve both a deep and intimate knowledge of the love of the Father, an overpowering, healing and affirming sense of being loved and also sharing in the suffering of the Son Jesus for the sake of his world.

Naturally we are not called to die for the sins of the world. We do not overcome death by our death. However, if we are truly to become one with Christ, that will not only mean knowing the love of the Father, it will also involve a vocation to join in some way in his sufferings for the healing of the world (Rom 8:17, Col 1:24). Our attempts to be the channels of God's salvation to the world through acts of kindness, mercy, forgiveness, alleviating poverty, washing ugly wounds, cleaning smelly drains, visiting awkward neighbours, will at times be hard, tiresome, even painful. And yet that is the shape that love takes in a fallen world. It is as Christians enter into the suffering of a broken world, as they become one with the crucified Christ in the Spirit, 'sharing in his sufferings' that they know the fullness of the Father's love, so that they can also know his resurrection life.

This is the paradox of divine love: a true *pneumatologia crucis*. To invoke the Spirit, praying the prayer 'Come Holy Spirit' is a wonderful, but perhaps also a sombre thing to do. It is wonderful because it asks God to draw us into the same relationship of love that Jesus had with the Father. It is sombre because it is asking God to draw us into the same relationship Jesus had with the world, which led him to a cross. When the Spirit unites us with Christ, he beckons us to walk on the path blazed by the divine Son of God, through the cross to resurrection, a path that ends at the right hand of God, with Christ 'in his glory' (Romans 8:17).

We know the love of the Father for the Son and the suffering of the Son for the world, not as realities that are just objectively acknowledged, but as something subjectively experienced through our being brought into profound personal and corporate union with Christ. Being 'in Christ' entails draws us into the ecstasy of the divine love, and the agony of engagement with a suffering and hurting creation.

This has a number of implications for our thinking about Church growth. It also helps us to give a theological account of why, with its emphasis on invocation of the Spirit, Pentecostal and Charismatic Christianity has tended to foster church growth nationally and globally.

The Holy Spirit and the Trinity

This account of the Spirit's role in the Trinity emphasises the Spirit's expansive, missionary purpose. The Spirit is sent out from the heart of God, from the Father and the Son to draw us back into the love that exists at the heart of God.

The word 'mission' comes, of course, from the Latin verb *mittere*, to send. In John's gospel, there are three movements of 'sending'. The first is the sending of the Son. Repeatedly, Jesus refers to the Father as the one who sent him. God is 'the one who sent me' (1:33), Jesus is himself 'the one whom God has sent' (3:34). He describes his task as to 'do the will of him who sent me and to finish his work' (4:34) and so on. There are, in fact, over 40 references in John's gospel to this central idea that Jesus is the one sent by God to do his will and his work. Perhaps the simplest and clearest statement of the purpose of the sending of the Son is 3:17: 'For God did not send his Son into the world to condemn the world, but to save the world through him.' The Son is sent into the world to save it.

The second movement of sending is the sending of the Holy Spirit. In John 14.26, Jesus speaks of the Holy Spirit as 'the Advocate, the Holy Spirit, whom the Father will send in my name'. 15:26 refers to 'the Advocate … whom I will send to you from the Father – the Spirit of truth who goes out from the Father'. 16:7 has Jesus saying 'Unless I go away, the Advocate will not come to you; but if I go, I will send him to you.' There is, of course, an ongoing point of dispute between eastern and western theology as to whether the Spirit is sent through the Father and the Son (as the western tradition holds and as the first half of 15:26 implies) or through the Father alone (as eastern Christians believe and as the second half of John 15:26 suggests). However we conceive this, it remains clear that the sending of the Son and the Spirit by the Father are the two primary acts of mission in the New Testament.

There is a distinction to be made here between 'begetting/proceeding' and 'sending'. Christian theology holds that the Son and the Spirit do not come into being because the world needs saving. The 'begetting' of the Son and the 'procession' of the Spirit from the Father (to use later creedal language) is not a temporal but an eternal act of God: in technical language, it is part of the immanent, not the economic Trinity. God is Father, Son and Holy Spirit before he creates the world in time, even before time itself.

The 'sending' of the Son and the Spirit into the world, however, as John's gospel describes it, is a temporal act, or at least an act in which God intersects with time and history: an act in the economic, rather than the immanent Trinity.[7] However, although there is this distinction, the two are continuous with each other. Even before creation, there is this outward, centrifugal movement in God. He is not the Aristotelian 'Unmoved Mover' who is complete in static self-absorption but he is movement outwards: The Son is begotten and the Spirit proceeds eternally from the Father and this 'sending' of the Son and the Spirit into the world is but a continuation or extension of that same divine movement. The two can be conceptually distinguished, but are in fact part of the same divine, centrifugal movement outwards.

This has some important things to say to us as we think about mission, evangelism and Church growth. Theologically speaking, mission and the consequent growth of the church begins with the begetting of the Son and the procession of the Spirit from the Father. It starts with the Trinitarian life of God before it ever involves the creation, let alone the human part of that creation.

---

[7] S. Holmes, 'Trinitarian Missiology: Towards a Theology of God as Missionary', *International Journal of Systematic Theology*, 8.1 (2006): 72–90, argues that the 'sending' is itself part of the inner Trinitarian life. To my mind, this runs into difficulties when we think of the birth of Christ in time – the events of Christmas and Pentecost – and the intersection of the divine life with time. It seems to me better to preserve the point Holmes makes by retaining the distinction between begetting/proceeding and sending, but seeing an essential continuity between them.

We have discovered a doctrine of mission and, so far, humanity has not even come into the picture. There is at the very heart of God this movement outwards, the eternal *begetting* of the Son, and the eternal *procession* of the Spirit which then issues in the *sending* of Son and Spirit into the world, to draw it back into the love between the Father and the Son. This movement outwards is not a secondary activity of God but is part of his very being.

The movement outwards that we see in the eternal begetting of the Son and the procession of the Spirit is carried on into the sending of the Son and Spirit into the world. It is part of the same impulse, an expression of the divine nature. The Incarnation and the sending of the Spirit at Pentecost is not a secondary activity of God, a subsequent thought or action that he resolves to put into place once the world has gone wrong: it is an expression of the very nature and inner being of God himself: it also, incidentally bears out Karl Rahner's famous dictum that 'the "economic" Trinity is the "immanent" Trinity and the "immanent" Trinity is the "economic" Trinity'.[8] The gospel reveals the very heart of God.

Mission is part of God's nature even if there were no creation at all, even if that creation had not fallen. God existed as Trinitarian love before the fall, before even creation itself. It is part of the being of God, not just an activity of God. We can describe God as missionary in his very being. It is not just that God has a mission, but that God is missionary. The difference is important. If God has a mission, then mission is in some sense secondary to his nature. His being is one thing (which excludes mission), and his activity is another (which includes it). It the former were the case, it would be theoretically possible for the church to reflect the being of God without being itself missionary. However, if God is missionary in his very nature, it is impossible for an un-missionary church, a church that does not want to take part in God's mission to the world, to effectively bear witness to him.

This perhaps helps us to see theologically why Pentecostal and Charismatic churches, churches that constantly invoke the Spirit, tend often to grow. To invoke the presence of the Spirit on the people of Christ is to be caught up in this missionary movement of God towards his world. In 1908, J. Roswell Flower, one of the early leaders of the Assemblies of God wrote:

> the Baptism of the Holy Ghost fills our souls with the love of God for lost humanity, and makes us much more willing to leave home, friends and all to work in his vineyard ... when the Holy Spirit comes into our hearts, the missionary

[8] K. Rahner, *The Trinity* (London: Burns and Oates, 1970): 22.

> Spirit comes with it. They are inseparable as the missionary spirit is but one of the fruits of the Holy Spirit.[9]

Now we can perhaps begin to see why.

The Holy Spirit and the Mission of God

If the Trinitarian God is by his very nature missionary, then what is that mission? And in particular, what part does the Spirit play in that mission? The purpose of God is described in the book of Ephesians as 'his plan for the fullness of time, to gather up all things in Christ, things in heaven and things on earth' (Eph 1:10). Elsewhere this is described as the re-creation of all things: 'we wait for new heavens and a new earth, where righteousness dwells' (2 Peter 3:13).

This renewal of all things is explicitly linked to the work of the Spirit. Gen 1:2 has the Spirit brooding over the formless waters as the world is created and Psalm 104:30 makes the link more explicit: 'When you send your Spirit, they are created, and you renew the face of the earth.' The Holy Spirit is involved in the creative act of God as much as the Son. This connection between creation and pneumatology is developed particularly in patristic theology. Irenaeus writes: 'What could the visible fruit of the invisible Spirit be, if not to make flesh mature and receptive of imperishability ... the Holy Spirit is sent to the entire universe, and since creation, has been transforming it, carrying it towards the final resurrection.'[10] Basil the Great writes of the Spirit's operation on created things: 'He waters them with his life-giving breath and helps them reach their proper fulfilment. He perfects all other things.'[11] As Colin Gunton put it: 'the Spirit is the agent by whom God enables things to become that which they are created to be'.[12] Furthermore, the Spirit also heals creation from its bondage to decay, bringing life and vigour to what is dying or dead. The classic Scriptural picture here is Ezekiel's valley of the dry bones, where God's breath or Spirit, brings them together and to life.

---

[9] M. Dempster et al. (eds), *The Globalization of Pentecostalism: A Religion Made to Travel* (Oxford: Regnum, 1999): 36f.

[10] Irenaeus, *Against Heresies* 12.3, in R. Grant (ed.), *Irenaeus of Lyons* (London: Routledge, 1997): 166.

[11] St Basil, *On the Holy Spirit* (Crestwood, New York: St Vladimir's Press, 1980): 43.

[12] C. Gunton, '"The Spirit Moved over the Face of the Waters": The Holy Spirit and the Created Order', in D. Wright (ed.), *Spirit of Truth and Power: Studies in Christian Doctrine and Experience* (Edinburgh: Rutherford House, 2007): 70.

In other words, the Spirit brings transformation. As created things are drawn deeper into the divine love, they are transformed, because divine love is the most powerful force in the universe. The Spirit enables created things to become what they were always meant to be. We sometimes think of the 'Holy Ghost' as the odd bit of Christianity, the spooky, slightly weird part that good sensible Anglicans, for example, avoid like the plague. Yet this Patristic theology of the Spirit, glimpsed in Irenaeus and Basil tells us that the work of the Spirit is to makes things and people normal. It is to make us fully human, as fully human as Jesus himself.

There are two dimensions to this. The first is that the Spirit matures us, bringing out the distinct nature of all created things, enabling them to 'reach their proper fulfilment' as St Basil put it.[13] Creation was always intended to grow, to develop, to evolve, and the Spirit is the one who elicits that true character that lies within, developing it into the full likeness to God that we see in Christ.

The second dimension however is that of healing. The creation is not just in need of maturing, but since the fall, is also in need of healing from its brokenness and distance from God. It is as a man filled with the Spirit that Jesus heals the sick and raises the dead. Pentecostal and Charismatic churches tend to adopt an implicit Spirit Christology that suggests that all human beings are intended to do the same (although perhaps the reason it does not happen very often is that God cannot quite trust us with that power – who knows what we would do with it?).

The Spirit brings transformation, both drawing out human potential and healing the damaged tissues of emotional or physical hurt. This of course is an important dynamic of church growth. Especially in the two-thirds of the world where health care is scarce and poverty rife, a community that prays expectantly for the sick and occasionally sees actual healing is deeply attractive. In the more cynical west, the promise of personal growth and genuine change, fuelled by invocation of the Spirit and a determination to see such transformation in the church can also be a strong means of adding people to the life of local churches.

The Holy Spirit and the Mission of the Church

The work of the Holy Spirit is to bring all of creation, fully restored and healed, to its fulfilment. It is to enable creation to be fully caught up in the embrace of the Father and the Son. Yet the Spirit does not do this work in creation alone

[13] St Basil, *Holy Spirit*: 43.

or directly. Alongside the Spirit, humanity plays a distinct role in the creation stories in the development and maturing of creation. As human beings are created at the climax of creation, they are called to 'work it, and take care of it' (Gen. 2:15). Humanity is called to work with the grain of the Spirit in the divine plan to bring creation to its fulfilment, through activities such as work, art, technology, creation care and the scientific enterprise of understanding, naming and harnessing the powers of the world. It is also the human calling, as we have seen, to be involved in the healing of creation. We are not just healed and matured through the Spirit, we are also enlisted to work with the Spirit in the divine economy.

We have thought about the sending of the Son and the Spirit in John's Gospel. There is, however, a third movement of 'sending' in John's gospel, one which is different from but related to the other two: the sending of the church. As Jesus speaks to his Father, he prays: 'as you sent me into the world, I have sent them into the world' (17:18), and at the end of the gospel he announces to his disciples: 'Peace be with you! As the Father has sent me, I am sending you' (20:21).

Now this 'sending' of the church is not in any sense parallel to the other two. The church is sent not from or by the Father but by Jesus himself. Whereas the Son and the Spirit are clearly sent by the Father, in John's gospel, the church is sent into the world by Jesus. The church does not strictly speaking proceed from the Father – only the Son and the Spirit are described in those terms, which is why of course we do not think of the church as part of the Trinity!

The church is sent by Jesus, yet created and constituted by the Holy Spirit. The church, of course, is born not on Christmas Day, Good Friday, or even Easter Day but on the day of Pentecost. It is when the Spirit comes that the church is born.

The church's calling is precisely to recall humanity to *its* true calling, to care for and nurture creation. The Holy Spirit draws humanity back into the love between Father and Son, the place where healing and restoration happens so that human beings, reconciled to God, can fully play their divinely ordained role of caring for creation in God's name, as the divine image is restored in them, in fellowship with the Father, growing in likeness to the Son.

Where does this happen? Where are human beings to be reconciled to their Creator, drawn into the love that exists at the heart of God, healed, restored, forgiven and enabled to fulfil their divine calling to care for and develop the creation in God's name? In the church. That same church which Cyprian, Augustine and Calvin all called our Mother, who nurtures us, heals our hurts, enables us to grow into our full humanity.

That is why church growth matters. Healthy well-functioning churches are places where people can be restored and become agents of change and renewal within the world beyond the church. The reason we need churches to grow is not to pay the bills, or to feel good about ourselves. It is to enable humanity, in tune with the Spirit of God, to fulfil its divine calling to care for and nurture the world which God has created.

The kind of pneumatology this article has developed perhaps raises two questions for Pentecostal and Charismatic churches:

1. Do they have a sufficient *pneumatologia crucis* to allow the Spirit to do its full work of drawing us into the relationship of the Son to the world, as well as his relationship to the Father? Or is there such a stress on triumph, prosperity and blessing that this vital aspect of the Spirit's work is ignored? Prosperity teaching has in recent years become very widespread, particularly in Pentecostal churches. It has a natural appeal in less affluent parts of the world and, to its credit, builds on the holistic nature of the best of Pentecostal worship and spirituality – God's blessings are not purely 'spiritual' and other-worldly. However, if the Spirit's work is at least in part to draw us into Christ's sufferings for the world, if the Spirit and the cross are closely united in this way, is such prosperity teaching actually a denial of a proper pneumatology?
2. Is there a sufficient emphasis on the development of character, the slow growth through the Spirit into the image of the Son, in fellowship with the Father, to enable broken people to become part of the solution, rather than part of the problem of a fallen world? Or is the emphasis on dramatic, instantly experienced change so strong that the longer-term changes in deep structures of behaviour and attitude are sidelined? Some Christian traditions have emphasised virtue and character development to the exclusion of the Spirit-filled life. Only the touch of the Spirit gives the motivation to love God and the desire for restoration of the divine image in the first place. However, at the same time, such experiences of the presence and power of God do not negate the need for the longer-term spiritual disciplines through which habits and outlooks are formed, and a spirituality that truly aims at inner and outer transformation will require both.

Pentecostal and Charismatic churches can teach other traditions a great deal about church growth. Perhaps, above all, they remind the rest of the church that invocation of the Spirit, in whatever way it is done, has to form part of a church that expects to grow. Not every church has to pray for the Spirit's presence and work in exactly the same way as Charismatics and Pentecostals do, but unless they find a way to invite the Spirit to draw us into the heart of God, to enable us to fulfil our divine calling, then our churches will struggle to grow, and the story of decline may continue. However, if such invocation becomes a part of the dynamic of the whole church, then we might expect the kind of growth that always follows the movement of the Spirit of God in human life and history. A church without the Spirit is no church at all. Or in the words of the most recent Patriarch of Antioch, Ignatios IV:

> Without the Spirit, God is far away, Christ belongs to the past, the gospel is a dead letter, the church is a mere organisation, mission is turned into propaganda. But in the Spirit, God is near, the risen Christ is present with us here and how, the gospel is the power of life, the church signifies Trinitarian communion, mission is an expression of Pentecost.

PART IV: Church Growth: The Historical Setting

Chapter 8

Church Growth in the Early Church

Ivor J. Davidson

Followers of Jesus Christ were 'few in the beginning'.[1] According to Acts 1:15, 120 or so of them gathered in Jerusalem around the year 33. By the mid- to late fourth century, the picture looked very different. By then, it is possible that a majority of people in the Roman world formally called themselves Christian. There had long been flourishing Christian communities far beyond that world as well, in swathes of the Middle East, Asia, Africa and northern Europe. Christians in general had long since ceased to think of themselves as their Jewish forebears had done and there had been a painful (and tragic) severance of a great deal of Christian consciousness from its roots in Israel's faith. Expansion had brought cultural and ethnic change, intellectual and organisational development and political revolution undreamt of by the small band of brothers and sisters who kept company in Palestine in the early 30s. It was – and is – a remarkable story.

Geographical Expansion

In terms of geography, Christianity had spread quickly from the first, fanning out from Palestine across most of the major cities of the eastern Mediterranean, Asia Minor, Greece, Macedonia and Rome before the end of the first century, and almost certainly establishing holds in several areas of North Africa and Egypt. The apostle Paul had expressed a desire to head as far west as Spain (Rom. 15:23–29). According to later tradition he did so; we cannot know if this is true, but there were certainly Christians in Gaul, if not Spain, by the second century. In Edessa (modern Urfa), the capital of the northern Mesopotamian kingdom of Osrhoene, Syriac Christianity was flourishing by the late second century. By the early third, the churches in the Persian-Sassanid Empire may

[1] Origen, *Against Celsus* 3.10. NB This chapter includes several short quotations from classical authors which are widely known. The translations used here are my own, based on the original Greek or Latin, rather than any specific modern edition.

have had 20 bishops. Christian apologists could boast of the one true faith of 'the church [singular], dispersed throughout the world to the ends of the earth',[2] and of the power of the gospel to conquer peoples inaccessible to the might of Roman legions.[3]

Many Christians conventionally think of the earliest missionary activity as the work of the Twelve, those whom Jesus himself had first sent out in the days of his earthly ministry, then commissioned in risen power to be his apostles. But the word 'apostle' was also used widely of other figures – Paul, of course, and some of Paul's companions, such as Barnabas; leaders such as James, the Lord's brother, and various other itinerant preachers. Paul's pioneering endeavours are presented in the Acts of the Apostles as a series of great missionary journeys, sparked by his own encounter with the risen Christ: the gospel first proclaimed in Jerusalem arrests Paul on his murderous quest to destroy the faith, transforms him, then is carried by him, in the Spirit's power, across a great sweep of the ancient world. As in Jerusalem, so among the Gentiles: the Lord adds to the numbers of believers 'those being saved' (Acts 2:47).

We must keep in mind that the story told by Luke, striking as it is, is told with particular ends in view. Paul's approach to mission to the Gentiles was enormously controversial within the early Jesus movement. It was also by no means the only, or the first, great missionary work; others had taken the message of Jesus to Antioch, Rome, Ephesus and elsewhere before Paul and, in many places, Paul relied upon networks and opportunities already well in place. In reality also, Paul's activities as depicted in Acts are rather far removed from later images of the earnest travelling evangelist. Paul and his companions did not rush breathlessly from place to place, quickly sowing the seeds of a basic message before moving on; in some instances he did stay only a short while, but in others, such as Corinth and Ephesus, he settled down for extended periods, teaching and consolidating the faith of local believers. His usual missionary forum was not the market place, but the home (or some other settled base, such as the 'lecture-hall of Tyrannus' in Ephesus: Acts 19:9).

Other figures, variously called 'apostles', 'teachers', 'prophets' and 'evangelists', operated well into the second century. Their roles varied somewhat, with some staying attached to specific locations while others engaged in itinerant ministry. Again, it is quite hard to be sure how much they prosecuted what we might think of as primary evangelism: they were probably often more like instructors of established groups of believers. Some of them clearly did travel from place

[2] Irenaeus, *Against Heresies* 1.10.1–2.

[3] Tertullian, *Against the Jews* 7 (Tertullian's authorship is contested).

to place, often supported by local Christian charity and occupied in what was considered to be the work of the gospel. They did not all say the same thing when they purported to proclaim that gospel, however. There were from early times serious disputes about false teaching, and dire warnings about the evils of a truncated – or a supplemented – evangel. The tensions surrounding true and false messages contributed to the evolution of ministry structures, with the activities of many of the itinerant apostles, teachers and preachers constrained over the course of the second century by more settled local roles. The emergence of a monarchical episcopate, as is well known, was by no means smooth or consistent and in many contexts other models prevailed for generations. A concern to determine the boundaries of the church's message, to ensure that what was preached was consistent with the 'true faith', was certainly among the reasons for the evolution of a tighter system. In turn, the challenges which that system continued to face at many levels were heavily associated with its alleged restriction of ministry roles and potential stifling of the Spirit. The success of the New Prophecy in the later second century was only one (complex) example of the appeal of the alternative. Bishops increasingly claimed authority not only over their urban neighbourhoods but over their surrounding region and they might well clash with visitors or locals alike whose messages of spiritual power differed from their own.

Whatever the roles of its would-be leaders, though, there is little doubt that the Christian message had spread from the earliest not just through the work of 'official' servants of the gospel: it was disseminated in great measure by the activities of ordinary people, both in their everyday social contexts and as they travelled. Ancient society was often remarkably mobile, with the vast geographical expanse of imperial territory connected by road networks of a calibre that would not be bettered until the nineteenth century and plenty of opportunities for passengers to book passage on commercial ships. People moved around for all kinds of reasons – as traders and artisans, as soldiers and slaves, as economic migrants and refugees. Their faith travelled with them, 'gossiped' in everyday forms. Christian communities came to be remarkably well connected from early on, with most believers in the first century living no more than a few days' travel from one of the church's major hubs.

Not all Christians will have felt the forceful compulsion – the 'necessity' (1 Cor. 9:16) – which drove Paul's proclamation and many will not have travelled as their teachers did, primarily 'for the sake of the gospel' or 'the word'. It is easy to overstate the likely zeal of early Christians, to suppose that all of them without exception were earnestly driven along by a passion to tell others about Jesus and had a consistently clear vision of the imperatives of mission to the world around them. Almost certainly it was not so and, in terms of later understandings of evangelism at least, there is often a surprising absence of urgency in Christian exhortations to disseminate the gospel in the first few centuries. Nevertheless, there was clearly within Christian belief itself a basic drive to share the faith with others for their good. A desire for numerical expansion was natural to the logic of Christian confession.[4]

Part of the impetus for passing on the good news of Jesus in the first place was the expectation that the end of all things was approaching. The delay to the *parousia* in turn necessitated moral exposition of its own (e.g., 2 Pet. 3:3–18) but even after the passing of the initial generations the message of the evangel continued to be set in the context of looking forward to the final advent of Christ as the vindicated one and judge of history. Whether his coming was imminent or not, it would surely happen; in the meantime, his established role as victor over death was decisive for the whole world.

By the middle of the third century, the churches were sufficiently extensive in Roman society that insecure imperial authority was concerned to stamp upon their power and tackle head-on their obnoxious insistence on religious exclusivism. Yet, despite various waves of persecution, Christians remained an intractable presence. Far from being reduced by the external pressures – and the fierce internal debates which these in turn precipitated about the nature of the true church, or the status of those (probable) thousands of baptised believers who had 'lapsed' from their faith when the heat was on – they seemed to benefit from them. The troubles of the later third century actually served to increase the church's growth.

In the early fourth century came the true watershed. The conversion of Constantine, and its most immediate consequence, the so-called 'Edict of Milan' in 313, ended persecution of Christians and granted all inhabitants of the Roman world freedom of religious expression. Official state patronage followed: legitimised as a public body with formal status, the church enjoyed legal rights, massive financial patronage and the means to construct official public buildings for worship on an unprecedented scale. Nothing would ever be quite the same again. The Constantinian revolution in no sense 'Christianised' the Roman Empire, nor, certainly, did political sponsorship bring only good to the churches, but it altered the status of the faith in a way that was truly decisive.

[4] See R. Hvalvik, 'In Word and Deed: The Expansion of the Church in the pre-Constantinian Era', in J. Ådna and H. Kvalbein (eds), *The Mission of the Early Church to Jews and Gentiles* (Tübingen: Mohr Siebeck, 2000): 265–87. For a much more eager account of general Christian zeal, cf. M. Green, *Evangelism in the Early Church* (London: Hodder and Stoughton, 1970).

People did not suddenly flock in their thousands to commit their lives to Christ, nor were they coerced to profess faith, but Christianity became a visible reality, and a public authority, as never before. Whatever is to be said about the sincerity of Constantine's own conversion, it is clear that from his perspective the Christian church represented a system robust enough to be enlisted as an ally in the unification of his empire.

There would be vast new challenges in this for Christian faith, including not least the dangerous potential that had been unleashed for the church itself to become, over time, an instrument of political intolerance and an oppressive force, demanding compliance with its beliefs, trading on its alliance with power in ways which would, at their worst, seriously compromise the identity of the *ecclesia* as the community of the crucified one. Whether the Constantinian revolution was a providential turning-point which facilitated an unprecedented expansion of the gospel or, by contrast, a sheer catastrophe for the church's moral and spiritual integrity, is a matter upon which Christians continue to hold widely divergent opinions. The answers are, as usual, more challenging than simple polarities propose. In any event, the age of Constantine demonstrated conclusively that Christianity was in the Roman world to stay, and the relationship of church and power in any context, Roman or otherwise, could never be the same again.

There were, of course, subsequent revivals of paganism in the imperial world, and attempts, such as those of the erstwhile believer Julian, decisively to diminish the Christians' cause in the early 360s. But, for all their severe problems and theological divisions in that period, churches were by then far too deeply embedded in their social contexts to be eroded fatally by actions of the kind which Julian took. In the later fourth century, the vigorous ecclesiastical politics of Theodosius enhanced their position further, giving them a standing which would not be reversed. His legislation pressed with increasing force on pagan religious practices and, in 391, proclaimed a formal ban on all pagan sacrifices, a closure of temples and fines for public figures who persisted in observing conventional rites in public. Further measures followed which ensured the demise of traditional religious practices.

Such actions were concerned with externals, and could not address private beliefs and values. Once again there were no mass conversions. Nevertheless, Theodosius' policies issued the death-knell to any who hoped that the ceremonial face of Roman society might even yet escape Christian dominance; though traditionalists would try again to restore the old ways, or to plead at least for tolerance, they would not win. Christianity was, in effect, the state's official religion. The emperor's speculative dream of a stable realm united around a catholic faith always would be an illusion, but the advantages afforded to the ecclesiastical guardians of that vision, coupled with the disadvantages meted out to their opponents, were decisive indeed. Whatever the effects upon them spiritually, the church entered the turbulent world of the fifth century in a significantly stronger position politically than it might otherwise have done.

The long, slow death of the Roman Empire over the course of the fifth and sixth centuries brought serious Christian fragmentation and dangers, both theological and structural. It also saw formal Christian expansion and social development in a changing West and some important new evangelistic endeavours in eastern Central Asia, Africa, and India. Christian enrolment, in this age, was considered feasible *en bloc*: the Frankish king, Clovis, and perhaps 3,000 of his soldiers were said to have become Christians all at once in gratitude for divine assistance in defeating their enemies in battle in the late 490s (the gesture, if it happened, seems to have said more about *Realpolitik* than a consecration of the heart; at any rate, Clovis' brutal and calculating regime appeared not to change much in moral terms). Whatever is to be said about Christian initiation on that scale, the evolution of a new political context demonstrated yet again that lines on maps never had been determinative. Ireland had known a Christian presence from the fourth century at least; Armenia had become the first nation officially to embrace the faith a decade before the Edict of Milan. Associations of Christianity with imperial power would die hard but, as Augustine struggled to work out in his vast *City of God* (413–26) and western Christians today are perhaps beginning to learn for themselves at a cost, the faith never has been coterminous with any contingent cultural order.

Christian accounts of the expansion of the church were of course affected from an early date by an exceedingly complex range of traditions, romantic reconstructions and retrospective efforts to underwrite particular claims to ecclesiastical authority. The apocryphal *Acts* of the apostles, produced in the second and third centuries, depict the great missionary feats of the Lord's initial emissaries, who reportedly divided the world up between them and went each to his allotted region: Thomas to Persia and India, Andrew to Greece and northern Asia Minor and so on. Other traditions connect Andrew with Georgia, James with Spain, Bartholomew with Armenia. Many of these stories are undoubtedly pious fictions, designed to embellish the sacred histories of particular localities. What we can confidently say is that the territorial reach of the Christian message was already, within a few generations of Jesus, extensive indeed. While it is clearly simplistic to suppose that the range of the work undertaken in the middle decades of the first century was anything like as vast as Christians in far-flung places later wanted to claim, there is no reason to doubt that the gospel had some success over a remarkably large area of the ancient world within a pretty short space of time.

Numbers of Christians

It is relatively easy to map the *geographical scatter* of Christian activity; to assess its *numerical density* is much harder. The business of estimating how many people professed faith at any point is highly contentious. Particularly since the seminal work of the great German church historian Adolf Harnack, *The Mission and Expansion of Christianity in the First Three Centuries*,[5] scholars have argued over the pace at which Christianity may have grown and the overall numbers this in turn might yield. In Harnack's view, statistical expansion was rapid: by the turn of the fourth century, something like 7–10 per cent of the population of the Roman empire was Christian (Edward Gibbon had put it closer to 5 per cent). Harnack himself was wary of offering a precise estimate, but his guess as to the percentage of believers in the Empire suggests there were possibly as many as six million Christians by the year 300.

There are significant hazards in such projections. Historians do not agree on how to define 'Christians', or their 'communities', or their likely social make-up, in the early centuries. They differ as to the right number of believers with which to begin calculating in the early 30s. They disagree about the probable rates of growth over time, the likelihood or otherwise of large-scale as well as more modest increases, the possible effects of *decline* as well as growth and the possible significance of political circumstances, hostile or benign. If the computation of percentages of the Roman imperial population is a central aim, there is difficulty in that as well, for there is only limited consensus as to the scale of various cities, the diffusion of rural demographics, and the size of the Empire as a whole.

The evidence upon which Harnack drew was primarily literary, and did not always take seriously enough the possible agendas, hopes and fears of its authors. Scholars are now able to supplement these literary sources (treatises, letters, sermons, acts of church gatherings and lists of clergy who attended) with invaluable testimony from archaeology and inscriptions.[6] Even putting all this material together, though, there is only partial agreement on how to reason from it. Statistical modelling, as employed by modern scholars, was of course

---

[5] A. Harnack, *The Mission and Expansion of Christianity in the First Three Centuries*, 2 vols, second edition (London: Williams and Norgate, 1908).

[6] See R.L. Mullen, *The Expansion of Christianity: A Gazeteer of its First Three Centuries*, Supplements to *Vigiliae Christianae* 69 (Leiden: Brill, 2004).

unknown to antiquity and the evidence we have of early Christian numbers cannot simply be made to fit preconceived ideas of parametric probability.

One influential set of projections was offered in the 1990s by the American sociologist, Rodney Stark.[7] Starting with the assumption of a handful of believers at the start, perhaps a figure of 1,000 by the year 40,[8] and projecting a growth rate of 40 per cent per decade as plausible on the basis of modern assessments of likely rates of religious conversion, Stark proposes that Christian numbers over the first century remained very small indeed: there were perhaps around 7,500 believers by the year 100. A century later, however, the same rate of growth would yield a Christian population of over 217,000, and another century later almost 6.3 million, or 10.5 per cent of the empire. By the year 350, Stark suggests, there may have been a Christian population of almost 34 million, or around 56.5 per cent of the Empire. After that date, the Christian growth rate must have declined, having achieved a certain critical mass of its potential converts. These numbers and others like them have been much discussed and there is no consensus as to their plausibility. A few historians wish to see the number of Christians in the year 300 as much lower, maybe only 4–5 per cent rather than 10–11 per cent of the empire as a whole; others want to revise the latter estimate upwards slightly, to around 12 per cent or so. Some who have criticised Stark's criteria end up projecting figures of a fairly similar order by other means.[9]

The truth is that we have no *data* on which there is agreement and it must simply be acknowledged that all estimates of Christian numbers and growth-rates in the Roman world involve a heavy element of conjecture. We also know far less than we would wish about the size of the Christian churches outside the Roman Empire and even their possible statistics continue to be neglected as a vitally important element in the story: most of the scholarly speculation remains focused on the Empire itself (in the process evoking the tendencies of many early Christian writers to equate 'the world' with the sphere of Roman rule). But even if – often for lack of comparable reference points in other regions – we do confine ourselves to that world, we are able to build up only a limited picture and its sketchy nature in strictly evidential terms must be kept in mind.

---

[7] R. Stark, *The Rise of Christianity* (San Francisco: Harper Collins, 1997): 7.

[8] Stark disregards the reference to 'around 5,000' believers in Acts 4:4, and the reference to 'many thousands of Jews' as followers of Christ in Acts 21:20 (Ibid: 5).

[9] See, for example, K. Hopkins, 'Christian Number and its Implications', *Journal of Early Christian Studies*, 6 (1998): 185–226; R. MacMullen, *Christianizing the Roman Empire (A.D. 100–400)* (New Haven and London: Yale University Press, 1984): 102–19; R. MacMullen, *The Second Church: Popular Christianity A.D. 200–400* (Atlanta: Society of Biblical Literature, 2009): 98–104.

What we can say with reasonable confidence is that there were several phases of quite substantial growth in *relative* terms – in the first two generations, as the faith remained within yet also began to splinter from Judaism; in at least parts of the later second century, often in contexts of controversy and external pressure as much as through conscious outreach; in the second half of the third century, when the record of pagan religious decline and Christian expansion in the Roman world seems unambiguous (albeit that it is sometimes overstated); and – of course – from the conversion of Constantine onwards, for one or two generations at any rate. It does look as if the *overall* number of Christians, however, remained very small in real terms in the first century and was not all that large prior to the third. There was at every point considerable regional diversity: when the early churches were expanding quite rapidly in one part of the world – Asia Minor, say, or around Alexandria – they were often very small indeed in others. In many places, the origins of Christian practice remain completely obscure and we simply have no idea how quickly or slowly its local expressions grew, for we cannot tell where our earliest available evidence fits into the actual story of what happened.

There was definitely *local* diversity. To take one of the more striking instances, the total numbers of professing Christians in Rome were almost certainly higher than elsewhere, given the imperial capital's status as a magnet for migrants and visitors. But there were also several different congregations within the city, each operating fairly independently, with its own leadership; controversial as the consequences of the situation inevitably are today, a clear-cut monarchical episcopate may very well not have emerged in Rome until as late as the third century. Some of the second-century churches in the city were larger than others, and there were differences in their social and ethnic stratification, with varying proportions of rich and poor, indigenous and migrant. In Rome's case, these 'fractionated' communities may in fact have coexisted fairly amicably in theological terms for quite a long time, their differences mainly confined to geographical and social factors. Only in the third century, perhaps, did controversies of doctrine and practice among the Roman believers become much more divisive, fuelled not least by the appeal of ideas from elsewhere, such as the various types of 'monarchian' theology that arrived from Asia Minor.[10] In many other places, however, different communities of Christians in the same locality reflected self-consciously different theological foundations all along,

[10] On all this, see P. Lampe, *From Paul to Valentinus: Christians at Rome in the First Two Centuries* (Minneapolis: Fortress, 2003); also A. Brent, *Hippolytus and the Roman Church in the Third Century: Communities in Tension before the Emergence of a Monarch-Bishop*, Supplements to *Vigiliae Christianae* 31 (Leiden: Brill, 1995).

and while each group would have seen *itself* as Christian it might have regarded its neighbour otherwise.

Diversity of this sort must be borne in mind when we talk of Christian growth as a general phenomenon: most historical estimates are obliged to count Christians and their communities in generously inclusive terms, embracing many whose beliefs and practices would have been highly controversial or heretical in the eyes of their contemporaries. To Irenaeus, the myths of Valentinian Gnosticism or the Marcionite differentiation of 'two Gods' (one who creates; another, higher being who redeems) were not Christian: they were blasphemy. Orthodoxy as we have come to think of it, the 'great Tradition', was of course substantially shaped through such collisions with otherness and the efforts to specify the homogeneity – or, better, the catholicity – of the church's doctrinal essentials were certainly part of a political and rhetorical process, aimed at reinforcing a particular set of claims to ecclesial authority. The upshot would, especially from the fourth century onwards, be a sharpening of the mechanisms by which deviation from the 'common' faith of 'the one church' would be adjudicated. In historical terms, however, all of the parties, orthodox and heretical, tend to be lumped together, their differences in the end a matter of power, not 'Christianness'. On that kind of generalisation, later Christian theology which sees itself as heir of a specific notion of the catholic tradition may well wish to enter its caveats.

Calculating who may have counted as Christian in terms of the apostolic gospel, or the rule of faith as defined by an Irenaeus or a Tertullian, calls for theological as well as sociological judgements. Scholars who see the identification of orthodoxy as a regrettable flattening out of an appealingly diverse range of initial Christian beliefs and practices will reach one set of conclusions about growth; those who consider the basics of confession to have been necessarily quite determinate (albeit simply stated) from the start may prefer to be more modest in their assessments of its impact at a given point. But debates about the nature, and thus the proportions, of the church were prevalent within early Christian theology itself. The possibility of false profession, the challenges of aberrant doctrine and practice, the need to 'test the spirits' (1 Jn. 4:1) are all New Testament concerns. Questions to do with apostasy, schism, true commitment to holiness, and the proper purity and unity of the church remain as regular refrains throughout patristic theology, with rigorist interpretations clashing with more inclusive ones again and again. The results ranged from advocacy of extreme forms of separationist asceticism through to earnest appeals for the church's reform. All the while, debates concerning the church's character, or the authority of its ministers, or the practice of its sacraments, were closely bound up with fundamental issues to do with the person of Christ and the Spirit, and with the nature of redemption itself. Knowing what the gospel *was*, and what, in its particularity, it entailed for the social polity established by its arrival, lay at the heart of the matter.

If it was the case for the heirs of Cyprian's logic that 'outside the church there is no salvation' (*Epistle* 73.21), that the 'catholic' church – as distinct from those whose doctrine disqualified them for such belonging – was the universal home, the 'mother', of all true children of God, it would also be the case for Augustine, *contra* the Donatists, that the visible kingdom of God on earth included both wheat and tares, good fish and bad, which only the Judge of all was competent to separate in the end. A morally mixed church was, for Augustine, a long way indeed from a theologically diverse one of the kind championed by some in modernity, but the questions of how to determine the true from the false and of what the parameters (not to say the instruments) of doctrinal as well as moral discipline should be, were naturally enduring concerns. Just as anyone familiar with the life of the church at any point in its history might expect, identifying the boundaries of the ecclesial body in the early centuries is not a straightforward matter.

The Nature of Early Christian Growth

Rather than focusing on numbers as such, I want to look a little more closely at the *nature* of early Christianity's expansion. In the end, the numerical growth of the Christian church in its early period is only meaningful in terms of what it had to offer its world and why it was that this message outbid its competitors. The Christian gospel was not simply the most successful example of a supposedly generic species called ancient religion. It represented a wholesale challenge to the assumptions of all of the religions of antiquity and provided its converts with something very different. The numerical growth of the church is not explicable save in that light: it was not that a new god came along and attracted increasing numbers of adherents; rather, the gospel brought an entirely new social and conceptual system, which evidently offered its recipients human transformation as nothing before it had done.

Let's take two closely related questions: (1) What did Christianity offer which was basic to its growth? (2) What challenges were posed by that growth, and how, very briefly, did Christian thought and praxis evolve to address them? The questions are simple in form, but vast in their range. We can only glance at a few aspects of a possible answer in each case.

What did Christianity Offer?

The Christian faith was arguably without precedent in its commitment to the necessity of *conversion*. Graeco-Roman religion remained endlessly adaptable in character, adding new deities without difficulty and espousing unabashed pluralism in practice. The same gods could have many names. The expansion of empire naturally brought with it a widening of religious experience; new cults could be taken up without any need to relinquish old ones. First-century Judaism, by contrast, was certainly exclusivist, seeing the covenant people as God's uniquely chosen instrument of future blessing to the Gentiles. Yet Judaism prior to the Christian mission did not as a whole engage in serious or systematic efforts to proselytise, preferring simply to commend its way of life to Gentile observers and showing a certain ambivalence towards those sympathisers or 'God-fearers' who attached themselves to the synagogue in some places.[11]

The Christian message, on the other hand, from the start declared the finality of Jesus. It required Jews to acknowledge that the purposes of Israel's God had, scandalously, been fulfilled once and for all in a crucified and resurrected Messiah (Acts 2:22–36). It summoned Gentiles to recognise the one true God, and turn to him from every other putative divinity (1 Thess. 1:9). It was in the exclusivity of Christian truth-claims, and with them the establishment of a whole new view of the world, that Christianity's distinctiveness lay: the Christian church was not just a typical ancient cult which succeeded more than any other; it purveyed an account of reality which challenged in both intellectual and practical ways the cultural assumptions of the ancient world.[12]

The idea of conversion as a turning away from an old way of life to a new was familiar to classical moral philosophy, but in Christian proclamation the concept was also shaped by an expressly scriptural lineage and by the traditions concerning Jesus' own preaching of repentance. To repent was to turn back to the true God, the Creator, Lord and Judge of all, from a place of estrangement, to be reconciled to him, to give one's life to him. Initiation into Christ was utterly radical: it meant 'dying' and 'rising' with him in baptism (Rom. 6:3–11; Col. 2:12–15); the process entailed not simply cleansing and forgiveness (Acts 2:38; cf. 1 Cor. 6:11; 1 Pet. 3:21) but a complete new orientation, a decisive 'putting off' of the old life and being 'clothed ... with Christ' (Gal. 3:27;

[11] See M. Goodman, *Mission and Conversion: Proselytizing in the Religious History of the Roman Empire* (Oxford: Clarendon Press, 1994): 60–90.

[12] One version of the case is set out by J.B. Rives, 'Christian Expansion and Christian Ideology', in W.V. Harris (ed.), *The Spread of Christianity in the First Four Centuries* (Leiden: Brill, 2005): 15–41.

cf. Col. 3:9–10). Seen as a human responsibility as well as a divine gift (Acts 5:31; 11:18), repentance was not merely a desirable option for the attainment of spiritual wisdom but utterly vital for one's final welfare: without it, people remained 'without hope in the world' (Eph. 2:12).

To Jewish ears, this was not a call to a new religion; it was a summons to move decisively from one understanding of Israel's faith to another. That was certainly how it was for Paul, who – for all the issues which his attitude to the Law presented for his dissenting fellow-Jews who also believed in Jesus – never ceased to think of himself as Jewish. The proposed transition was challenging indeed, as the sharp disputes about the terms of inclusion within the covenant community made clear. The escalating rhetoric of expressly *anti*-Jewish Christian polemic in the later first and early second centuries made the issues more heated still, as increasingly strident supersessionist attitudes to Judaism faced Jewish Christian traditions which continued to prize their Jewish identity highly. The call to Jews to turn to Jesus as the Messiah could be submerged by a denunciatory rhetoric in which resistance was a sign of divine condemnation, or by arguments that those who continued to question the Pauline approach were trying to occupy a dangerous half-way house – neither conventionally Jewish any longer, nor truly Christian either.

For Gentiles, the matter of conversion was complicated in different ways. Typical pagan hearers of the Christian message had few if any of the reference points of their Jewish counterparts. They would not naturally have thought of themselves as existing in any sort of spiritual bondage, or in jeopardy of final condemnation for their moral failures. The notion of post-mortem accountability of which Christian evangelists spoke would have been quite alien to most. Fear of death would certainly have been natural, but the idea that the answer to it lay in an executed criminal raised physically to life would have made no sense at all (cf. Acts 17:32). Even the Christians' claims about the one transcendent God were weird. An overarching monotheism, above and beyond all the gods and goddesses of traditional religion, certainly had a place in antiquity, particularly among intellectuals, and there was a certain socio-political appeal in the notion that all the peoples of the world might in the end be children of a single deity (cf. Acts 17:28). But the idea that this God *loved* human beings, willed that they should know him personally and suffered and died in human form so as to make it possible – that would have struck many pagan hearers as simply bizarre.

Yet it can hardly be true that no one felt any sort of personal need and ultimate questions of human existence remain doggedly persistent across culture, time and space. What the Christian gospel insisted was that the old gods offered no finally satisfying remedy to human needs; the one creator God was, in Jesus

Christ, the redeemer from all that oppresses, including the tyranny of religious superstition. Pagan hearers might very well not have understood conversion as Christians have often pictured it – the process by which a guilt-ridden, broken individual finds peace, liberation and joy through an experience of 'amazing grace' – but they would have understood what it was to shift from one way of living to another. In the gospel of the risen Christ many of them clearly found transforming power they had not known otherwise.

The Christian message claimed superiority to everything. Ancient society was well used to putative evidences of the miraculous and signs of exceptional spiritual powers. The signs and wonders which accompanied early Christian proclamation clearly had a significant impact on many, with gifts of foreign tongues, miraculous healings and exorcisms all taken to be evidences of the definitive outpouring of God's Spirit. Such phenomena posed a serious challenge to other would-be purveyors of wonder and to the economy of traditional cults. They were by no means claimed only in the initial period; the displays of special wonders continued to be of importance (as well as controversy) throughout the early centuries. The mid-third-century Neocaesarean bishop, Gregory 'the Wonderworker', represents one celebrated example. A former student of Origen, he was missionary bishop in Pontus in the 240s and 250s; said to have been a powerful worker of miracles, he evangelised a locality in which on his arrival, we are told, there were just 17 Christians: on his departure, there were, it's said, only 17 pagans. The reliability of the sources is disputed, not least when the numbers are so neat, and scepticism in some scholarly assessment of Gregory's legend is obvious.[13] Yet there is little reason to doubt that such feats as those with which his name became associated were seen by their champions as bearing genuine weight in evangelistic endeavour – a way of showing *les autres* that the gospel was more potent by far.

Still, while some historians treat the impressions of wonder-working by early Christian evangelists as a significant aspect of their success and even take seriously the reports of Eusebius and others that there were genuine mass conversions as a result of such phenomena, it is important to recognise how different the Christian assumptions were. The miracles claimed by and for Christians were, in their eyes, not the same at all as the sorts of displays of the miraculous found in Graeco-Roman religion. The Christians' signs and wonders belonged within a logic in which there was an utter polarity between the one – true, good – God and all other – false, malign – powers; there was the Lord on the one hand, the demons on the other. When this God worked wondrously through his servants,

[13] E.g., R. Lane Fox, *Pagans and Christians* (London: Penguin, 1986): 516–45.

it was assumed, he did something which magical powers and false gods never could, for his purposes were, in the end those of the good, redeeming creator, capable as his ersatz rivals never could be of blessing his creatures. This contrast between the status and capacity of the God of Jesus Christ and the credentials of all other powers was basic to the Christian repudiation of idolatry.

The roots lay of course in Israel's faith, but Christian rhetoric pressed the exclusivism of that inheritance in a heightened form: not only could God work wonders; he *had* worked the ultimate wonder in time and space in the raising of his Son Jesus from the dead. In light of that, basically anything was easy; all the evidences of the gospel's power, physical as well as spiritual, were but attestations of its founding miracle, which had changed everything. Christianity presented a message which both interpreted the world and declared its transformation. *This* was why, in the end, church-leaders in the later fourth and fifth centuries felt it permissible, even providentially mandated, that they should invoke the resources of political power to crush traditional religious practices: 'paganism' was simply the generic opposite of the truth; its public demise was a vital demonstration of its defeat by a message which liberated inwardly in a way the old gods never could. Whether Christians ought to have been half so keen to deploy the machinery of oppression in pursuit of their cause is, naturally, another matter;[14] the convictions which fuelled them were nonetheless clear-cut.

Within such exclusivist – indeed 'totalising'[15] – Christian claims, however, there was also an *in*clusive appeal, or what might be described as the 'universal' character of their message from a human point of view. Inclusion might come with the warning that rejection risked final judgement and that there was one church, whose message and authority must not be thwarted. Fear was an evident factor in some proclamation. But the Christian message proffered plenty of positives as well: forgiveness, acceptance, dignity and social inclusion, regardless of background, status, gender, wealth or gift. And these positives yielded results. There is little question that the early Jesus movement had a significant impact upon the needy, the vulnerable and the lowly, among slaves, menials, thieves, prostitutes and drunkards (cf. 1 Cor. 6:9–11).

At the same time, it would be quite wrong to suppose that early Christianity was overwhelmingly proletarian, made up, as its critics liked to allege, mainly of

---

[14] For a provocative account of things from the potential perspective of the victims, see R. MacMullen, *Christianity and Paganism in the Fourth to Eighth Centuries* (New Haven and London: Yale University Press, 1997).

[15] See, for example, A. Cameron, *Christianity and the Rhetoric of Empire: The Development of Christian Discourse* (Berkeley, Los Angeles and London: University of California Press, 1991).

'women, children, slaves and fools'.[16] There were wealthy house-holders, public officials and members of political, military and economic elites as well. There were the educated: not just the intellectual Paul himself, or Luke the physician, but people able to read and – more notably – write serious documents: the latter facility placed one in something like the top two per cent of Roman imperial society. To judge from the New Testament's epistles, at least some could be expected to follow densely crafted arguments on the meaning of Septuagintal scripture. Viewed from one perspective, ancient Christian literature is a product of, and partly for, a cultural elite, its proliferation in the early centuries a testimony to the growing success of the faith in appealing to intellectuals, including philosophers, writers and professional teachers.

Understanding the faith did not depend upon wealth or education, however, and the illiterate and the lowly were in principle embraced on the same terms. The self-consciously 'family' ethos of the churches, where people could, regardless of social standing, be addressed alike as 'brother' or 'sister',[17] 'all one in Christ Jesus' (Gal. 3:28), undoubtedly offered love and support to lonely, vulnerable and isolated souls, providing bonds of care which made a real difference. The house-church context of most Christian worship during the first three centuries heightened the familial environment. It also helped numerically: the conversion of the head of a house will often have brought with it the conversion of all the members of the household, including its slaves, other family members and a range of freedmen, hired workers and business associates. Within the bonds of the natural family, Christians were also exhorted to be witnesses, winning over the unpersuaded by their conduct: unbelieving husbands and wives might be drawn towards faith by the testimony of their believing spouses (1 Cor. 7:12–16; cf. 1 Pet. 3:1–6).

Though the evidence is more challenging to assess than some have supposed, the relative numbers of both women and children within the early churches were almost certainly high. The movement seems to have attracted a high proportion of women from the start, and at least some of its moral convictions were conducive to their remaining a significant presence. Christians, like Jews, disapproved of abortion, which in antiquity was frequently very dangerous for women; they were strongly opposed also to the exposure of infants, one of ancient society's main methods of population control, whose victims were far more likely to be girls than boys. Adoption of orphans came to be quite widely

[16] Origen, *Against Celsus* 3.55.

[17] On the background, see P. Trebilco, *Self-Designations and Group Identity in the New Testament* (Cambridge: CUP, 2011), esp. 16–67.

encouraged and practised from the second century. The baptism of children (not necessarily babies), which seems to have become common in at least some churches by the later second century, also served to increase the numbers of children formally included in the community of believers. There would be many tensions and controversies in regard to the place of women in particular and there was an undoubted reduction in their opportunities for formal ministry from the second century, but there would also often have been in Christian communities a degree of 'status inconsistency' which seemed appealing. For all whose roles in wider society were defined in restrictive ways, the church community could seem a refuge – an 'ark' as well as a 'body'.

Christians could impress in other ways as well. In ancient cities, the vast majority of people were housed in very poor social conditions and ill-health, disease and death were constant realities. Housing was cramped and unhygienic; privacy was minimal, violent crime rife, the destruction of poorly-built structures by fire or natural disasters common. Economic upheavals affected all but the very richest. Food shortages were frequent, life-expectancy was, for many, very short. There was no welfare state; every community contained sizeable numbers of widows, orphans, destitute, sick and needy people, dependent on charity for support. Christian churches undoubtedly had a powerful witness among such. Orphans and widows, prisoners, travellers, the hungry, the sick, the aged and the dying were helped and the poor were provided with burial. In the second century and beyond, such acts of charity could be regularly presented by Christian spokesmen, such as Justin Martyr, Athenagoras and Tertullian, as emblems of Christian identity: churches collected money weekly to spend not on their own pleasures, it was pointed out, but in support of those who were struggling. After Constantine, the proceeds of imperial favour and the donations of aristocratic converts were further used in support of the poor, and the churches' increasing institutional funds came to be administered in a much more organised form. Hospices, hospitals and other church-sponsored works of poor relief were developed in many cities, with Basil of Caesarea, Ambrose of Milan and John Chrysostom playing pioneering roles in such activities. Bishops came to serve increasingly as civic leaders, exercising a range of important social, administrative and judicial functions. Not everything which the churches did with their money was charitable, it must be said, and there was from the fourth century plenty of severe criticism of clerical greed, excess and institutional corruption, not least in regard to the wealth of the Church of Rome. Nevertheless, ecclesiastical benefactions in many cases made an immense difference to the welfare of their communities.

Taken together, these and other features of Christian witness may be seen as core constituents of the church's attitude to its mission over the early centuries. The distinctiveness of being Christian, of living the life of 'the elect', 'the holy', the followers of 'the Way', was always fundamental – and it was seen as a crucial instrument of numerical growth. Believers were to testify to the transformation of character experienced through faith in Christ (1 Pet. 2:12), to set forth the 'extraordinary' lifestyle which their gospel effected in their ordinary lives.[18] After the first century especially, it was in *this* vision that Christian mission was especially focused. The great commission of Matt. 28:18–20 actually occupies a surprisingly slender role in a great deal of patristic teaching on Christian evangelism: typically, the text is said to have been a mandate given to the first apostles, and fulfilled by them; there is little sense that it still stands as an ongoing imperative following the apostolic age. The gospel had *already* spread to the ends of the (imperial) earth, second- and third-century Christian teachers wanted to say, and thus demonstrated its power. There was a certain sense that there were peoples outside that world who had not heard but, at this stage at least, there was seemingly little urgency to reach them. Crucially, however, this did *not* mean that Christian teachers were uninterested any longer in numerical growth. It was rather that they increasingly focussed the main business of being ambassadors of Christ on the formation of Christian moral character, on the church's praxis as *different*. To see that witness close up, to live and work alongside those who professed faith, would be to learn, in practical ways, what the gospel had to offer.[19] And so it was that people surely came to faith, a very great deal of the time, through their social networks, in encounter with living examples of Christian behaviour, worship, prayer and piety and first-hand contact with the seriousness with which believers pursued their everyday spiritual and moral duties.

It is of course all too possible to romanticise the appeal of the ethic in view, to suppose that the social *mores* of early Christianity were a good deal more radical or saintly than they in fact were. Natural differences were inevitably replicated in a great many pernicious ways within early Christian communities, and there was much moral failure: as early Christian teaching abundantly attests, Christian behaviour was often all too abysmally ordinary. Sexual ethics were an endless battleground; so too were social relations generally. Notwithstanding the partial egalitarianism which their assemblies at their best offered, Christians maintained fairly conventional patterns of household relationships between

[18] *Letter to Diognetus* 5.4

[19] For a useful overview of some of the essential features of the vision, see C. Osiek, 'The Self-Defining Praxis of the Developing *Ecclesia*', in M. Mitchell and F. Young (eds), *The Cambridge History of Christianity* (vol. 1; Cambridge: CUP, 2006): 274–92.

men and women, parents and children, masters and slaves. They were from early times routinely exhorted to practise material contentment, self-denial, non-retaliation and a certain political meekness. Such principles were not supposed to mean simple quietism by any means: fealty to the Lordship of the risen Christ involved radical, and potentially costly, repudiation of Caesar. But their capacity to follow through on their calling to be 'soul' to the world's body[20] depended on whom you asked: to some eager moralists, much came down to seriousness of commitment; to Augustine against the Pelagians, there was simply a fundamental tendency to fail, which only grace could overcome. If Christians were to attest to the gospel's lifestyle, and thus proclaim its truth to the world, they could only do so with God's enabling. Mission via ethical witness was tough and faced plenty of opposition, within and without.

Alongside early Christian optimism about the assured success of the gospel, there is also, in early Christian ethics, a palpable sense of the church's vulnerability, the perduring need of divine grace if growth is to occur. As we might expect, this was especially true in the pre-Constantinian period, but it is also witnessed in different ways after the fourth century. The numerical growth of the church, Christians realised, faced challenges.

The Challenges of Growth

Opposition to the church's mission was frankly acknowledged from the beginning, and harassment from the authorities is a present reality for the recipients of several of the New Testament's documents, such as 1 Peter and Hebrews. Revelation can be read as a political message to suffering Christians, urging them to resist the idolatries and corruptions of secular authority. In dissociating themselves from the perverted political, economic and moral structures of the Roman Empire, they are highly likely to suffer persecution, but they should face these trials in the knowledge that God is sovereign, that he will yet judge the forces of evil, and reward those who are faithful. Confrontation of worldly power may mean death, but that witness itself is part of the divine strategy to usher in an alternative future, the coming of a kingdom that is universal, righteous and unending. Similar themes of hope and warning pervade a good deal of second- and third-century Christian literature. They reflect a conviction that God's plan was being fulfilled in worldly history in the expansion of the church, but that the current age was also passing and would be succeeded by a

[20] *Letter to Diognetus* 6.1.

future which God alone could bring about, in which the injustices of the present life would be set right. In the meantime, Christians could die well and they had from an early stage been exhorted to handle bereavement in a spirit different from those without hope (1 Thess. 4:13). In their courage and expectation of resurrection, there was a potent witness.

Nevertheless, whatever their virtues, the exclusivity of Christians' faith and its presence in society often meant that they were, in fact, highly *un*popular. Their rejection of the conventional gods was an offence to traditional values. When they refused to make offerings to the emperor or the usual deities, they were seen as jeopardising political stability by risking the judgement of the gods upon the communities in which they lived. They could readily seem antisocial, sticking to their own circles and distancing themselves from festivals, associations and regular events in society around them. There were occupations they could not pursue, trade guilds they could not join. While they could sometimes impress with their private virtues or their works of mercy, their separatist tendencies might well be resented by neighbours, relatives and acquaintances as expressions of sheer awkwardness, if not self-righteousness. To many, especially prior to Constantine, Christians seemed not welcoming, but secretive, huddled as they appeared to be behind closed doors, engaged in their strange activities to which not all could evidently be admitted. Christian rituals were much misunderstood. Christians seemingly ate the 'flesh' and 'drank' the blood of their Lord – they must be cannibals. They addressed each other as 'brother' and 'sister', greeted one another with a 'holy kiss', and took part in so-called 'love feasts' – they must be engaging in incest. They prayed 'in the name of Jesus' and made ritual gestures – they were into magic. They met during the hours of darkness, chanted hymns and spoke in strange tongues that sounded like gibberish – they must be up to no good.

It is of course wrong to imagine that even in the first three centuries Christians were ever routinely persecuted at every turn. While arrests, torture and martyrdoms were a deadly serious matter, with enormous emotive power (and in turn a certain role in the idealisation of Christian virtues for pagan audiences), they were for the most part localised and in response to particular political situations. When circumstances were tough for the authorities, the Christians were a convenient scapegoat. The famous exchange of letters between the Roman governor Pliny and the emperor Trajan regarding the appropriate treatment of Christians in Bithynia around 112 makes it clear that there was no *policy* of executing Christians for their refusal to participate in pagan ceremony; while it was *legitimate* to execute them if they proved obdurate – they were, without doubt, members of an illicit sect – the aim of investigating their behaviour was reformation, not extermination. If the Christians would turn from the folly of their ways, they could be brought back to normal practices of civic religion, and thus cease to be, in the eyes of the authorities, a social and political nuisance. Official policy until the middle of the third century remained essentially the same: proven participation in the faith was a capital offence, and there was local harassment, but there were no large-scale assaults of the kind which occurred later. The most celebrated martyrs in the second century – figures such as Ignatius and Polycarp, or Perpetua and Felicitas – actually became famous in part because they represented relatively rare cases.

But attacks hurt at other levels and Christian apologists also worked hard to refute the caricatures of Christian belief and practice. Their efforts were variously irenic or polemic: the rather assured efforts of a Justin to set forth the intellectual and moral virtues of the faith represented one approach; the denunciations of pagan folly and corruption by a Tatian typify another. Tertullian's perspective offered realism and triumphalism all at once: the Christian faith could be shown to be manifestly superior to secular wisdom and the morality licensed by traditional religion – but in practice Christians would be hated anyhow. Their cause, even so, was invincible, and every effort to defeat them was destined to backfire: 'The more you mow us down, the more we multiply. The blood of the Christians is seed.'[21]

When we think of early Christian celebrations of growth, we must also set them in the context of taunts from those who had once attached themselves to the church and then fallen away – those in the debit column of the historians' imaginative ledger of early Christian growth statistics. The second-century pagan satirist, Lucian of Samosata, tells of a charlatan philosopher, Peregrinus Proteus, who had once been imprisoned as a Christian leader and had done so well out of the help he received from his naïve brothers and sisters while in jail that on his release he had made his fortune and was ready to go off on his next adventure. Christians were exemplars of charity, no doubt; they were also very stupid. Similar allegations of gullibility of one sort or another, not least in the giving of alms, were plentiful, and sometimes from those who had seen things up close. Other sorts of mockeries were also on display. The one-time professing believer Julian's *Against the Galileans*, produced in 362–3, debunked Christianity as a debased form of Judaism, bogus in its claims to represent a fulfilment of Hebrew prophecy and vastly inferior to Hellenistic wisdom as a system of truth. And there were severe critics whose knowledge of the faith was, if not necessarily an insider's perspective, alarmingly well-informed on texts, rituals and practices:

[21] Tertullian, *Apology* 50.13.

the Platonist Celsus, whose powerful attack on the Christians in the 170s, probably aimed against Justin's claims, elicited Origen's extensive rejoinder a generation later; the Neoplatonist Porphyry, whose serious intellectual assault on the Christians and their scriptures in the late third century was still being condemned by church-leaders (and imperial edict) in the middle of the fifth.

If the fourth century brought an end to serious persecution, a path to cultural supremacy and some revision of apocalyptic timetables (at least temporarily), it generated other issues to do with growth. Undoubtedly there had always been degrees of attachment to the Christian way of life; the volume of hangers-on as distinct from genuine devotees would now raise particular challenges. Profession might be a way of furthering career prospects, pleasing a family-member or potential marriage-partner, a means to economic advantage, a strategy for social manoeuvring. The dangers of admitting people too lightly to baptism, allowing in potential frauds, infiltrators or trouble-makers, had led by the early second century to efforts to provide clear moral teaching to catechumens, indicating the seriousness of the Christian calling and its summons to renounce the ways of the old life – idolatry, immorality, killing, theft, deceit, inappropriate entertainment and forms of employment unfit for the soldier of Christ.

In the fourth century, the spiritual significance of catechesis was substantially heightened, to emphasise still further the solemn nature of Christian initiation. Baptismal action came to be associated more with mystery, something to be kept from the prying eyes of the unworthy. To read the catechetical teaching of a figure such as Cyril of Jerusalem,[22] or Ambrose of Milan, or John Chrysostom, is to sense his resolute desire to depict initiation into the Christian lifestyle in serious moral and spiritual terms. Initiates are to be thoroughly prepared, and those about to be 'enlightened' are not to reveal the secret things of God even to ordinary catechumens, far less to their unconverted neighbours. The spiritual meaning of baptism and the Eucharist is only to be shared subsequent to entry.

This and other changes to liturgical practice, including not least an elaboration of the majesty of the Eucharist as dramatic ritual, would signal the changes which an increasingly assertive yet also morally wary church was keen to ensure. Other eloquent expressions of an evolving vision of growth would be found elsewhere – the practice of missionary monasticism, the cultivation of clerical manners as a means to social impact, the colonisation of suburban areas with increasingly grand ecclesiastical edifices, the conversion of rural shrines to new ascetic sites, the expansion of the cult of the saints as a public forum

---

[22] See E. Ferguson, *Baptism in the Early Church: History, Theology, and Liturgy in the First Five Centuries* (Grand Rapids: Eerdmans, 2009): 473–88.

for displays of spiritual power. Much as it always had been, only in new ways, numerical growth was both dangerous and a matter to advertise. In the quest to demonstrate power lay, somewhere, an enduring sense of vulnerability in the knowledge that Christian behaviour reached out as it displayed its excellences, yet remained prone to mess things up and thus to fail to be the right kind of witness to the church's destiny. Whether catechesis remained adequate for teaching the specifics of Christian moral identity over subsequent centuries remains an open question; in practice, territorial and social progress arguably trumped spiritual imperatives far too often, and conversion became much too easy – but that is a story for another day.[23]

In Retrospect

In the world of the late modern West, the church finds itself, in increasing measure, in circumstances similar to those that prevailed before Constantine's revolution, where the role of Christian communities was often marginal, struggling and unpromising. The contemporary church functions in a setting where cultural prestige such as the fourth century brought, and Western Christianity once supposed itself to enjoy, seems remote. Whether this is a threat or an opportunity to Christian faith depends greatly on perspective. Christians today may well lament their marginality, taking it as evidence that numerical church growth is not God's purpose in their generation. Alternatively, they may, as the early church did, consider it an opportunity to hope in God's promises, his power to transform the least likely of cultural situations and to do so in ways which will yet in fact mean substantial, visible growth.

In an uncanny number of ways, the rampantly pluralist and cynical context inhabited by the twenty-first century western church is akin to the environment of the earliest Christians. We may learn much from considering their understanding of mission as, if it is anything, a holistic commitment to *being Christian*. Studied closely, this is in no wise a collapse of the gospel into facile moralism; far less is it a matter of idolatrous introspection, an insular preoccupation with the believing community's spiritual progress. Early Christian mission does not reduce Christ's saving significance to the good deeds of the church's social gospel, nor at its best does it see the church's ministry as an attempt to render an otherwise absent Christ present to the world, courtesy of human actions. It is simply about

[23] See A. Kreider, *The Change of Conversion and the Origin of Christendom* (Eugene, OR: Wipf and Stock, 2007).

taking with full seriousness the practical implications of conversion, first for ourselves, then, by God's grace, for others. Just as such, it is about recognising the all-embracing capacity of the gospel to produce *change* and trusting that it will do so as *lived*, not merely talked about, however faithfully. As Christians in the early centuries sometimes learnt the hard way, the demonstration of that power is never convertible into so much cultural capital, an item of the church's possession. The evangel's potency lies in its enactment – and that will only ever occur as the God of the gospel makes it happen.

On the face of it, the strange message of early Christianity ought not to have succeeded. To its champions, its success was not attributable to human engineering. In Pauline perspective, a response of faith to the offensive story of the crucified and risen Christ depended squarely on divine activity: hearers would come only if 'called' by God (1 Cor. 1:24). The message remained foolishness to many, yet it could also mean 'the power of God for the salvation of everyone who believes' (Rom. 1:16). A similar pattern pervades early Christian theology: images of regeneration, enlightenment, opening of the heart and resurrection from death spell out the conviction that the process was ultimately miraculous and wholly gracious in nature, in no sense a work in which human capacity played a part.

That conviction, however, co-existed with a commitment to evangelise, in the confidence that God was pleased to use such testimony for his own ends. However they defined its nature, organisation or terms of inclusion, early Christians belonged, as they saw it, to a vast, mysterious and *growing* body which transcended social, political and ethnic boundaries – the *ecclesia* of the one true God. This God brooked no rivals and would prevail in the purpose to which he had committed himself. He had determined to assemble a people for himself and had set about the work of gathering them in the gospel of his Son, proclaimed in the power of his Spirit. It was his will that they should be drawn from all the nations of the earth and that the history of the world would climax in the bringing together of 'all things in heaven and earth under one head, even Christ' (Eph. 1:10). Numerical growth lay in God's hands – and thus it was assured. The future of the church was his project. To such a vision, Christian faith in any context does well to pay attention.

Chapter 9

Verbum et exemplum docere: Bede, Cuthbert, Aidan and Mission in the Early English Church

Sr Benedicta Ward

In considering the call of the Christian to 'mission' (*evangelium*) I want to suggest that mission to the Anglo Saxons in these islands in the fifth century set a unique pattern which it is refreshing to consider. At the centre was the union for each with Christ our God, not church structure or refinement of doctrine, but in a world even more chaotic than our own, they looked to what was essential:

> Amidst the vast scene of the world's problems and tragedies you may feel that your own ministry and witness seems so small, so insignificant, so concerned with the trivial. But consider – the glory of Christianity is its claim that small things really matter, and that the small group, the very few, the one man or woman or child are of infinite worth to God. Let that be your inspiration. Consider our Lord himself: amidst a vast world with its vast empires and events and tragedies, our Lord devoted himself to a small country, to small things and to individual men and women, often giving hours of time to the few, or to the one man or woman. For the infinite worth of the one person is the key to the Christian understanding of the many. You will never be nearer to Christ than in caring for the one man, the one woman, the one child. His authority will be given to you as you do this, and his joy will be yours as well.[1]

The island of Britain had been part of the Roman Empire since 40 BC and therefore had many Christians living there, whether soldiers, settlers, or natives. But with the withdrawal of the legions in 410, it began to seem to Rome an alien place rather than a distant province. Bede called it: 'The end of time and the edge

[1] M. Ramsey, *The Christian Priest Today*, revised edition (London: SPCK, 1985): 90.

of the world.'[2] In 594, Pope Gregory the Great decided the time was ripe for a new Christian approach to the former colony of Britannia. Most of what can be known about these first days of mission to these islands is contained in Bede's *Ecclesiastical History* and the influence of Gregory shines through it all. Bede gives a version of Gregory's encounter with English slaves in the market place in Rome that has all the elements of Gregory's understanding of the venture. English boys were being sold as slaves. When Gregory met them he asked:

> "What was the name of that nation?", and was answered, that they were called Angles. "Right," said he, "for they have an Angelic face, and it becomes such to be co-heirs with the Angels in heaven. What is the name," he proceeded, "of the province from which they are brought?" They said that they were from the province called Deiri. "Truly are they *De ira*," said he, "withdrawn from wrath, and called to the mercy of Christ. What is the king of that province called?" They told him his name was Alla: and he, alluding to the name said, "Alleluia, the praise of God the Creator must be sung in those parts."

Gregory then went to the Pope, not having himself yet reached that office. He urged him to send missionaries to the English in order to share with them the Christian faith, declaring that he himself was ready to take up the task, if seen fit to do so. Bede relates that Gregory was not permitted to do so since, though the Pope was willing to grant his request, the citizens of Rome would not agree that so noble, so renowned and so learned a man could be spared from the city. Once Gregory was himself made Pope, he undertook the work he had long wanted to do, sending other preachers, whom he supported by his prayers and exhortations, urging on their preaching, that it might be fruitful.[3]

Gregory wanted not numbers, structure or refinement of doctrine but individual care for people. He saw his call to be based on taking people as they were, building on that not by destroying, but by loving and admiring what God had made. Himself one of the doctors of the church, in mission he did not begin with the complexities of doctrine but with example and prayer. For him mission was to arise out of prayer since it was to be the work of God through the preachers, not their own work. The missionaries sent by Gregory the Great to the island of Britain followed his method as Gregory outlined it in great detail in his influential book, *De Pastoralis Curia,* which was one reason why Bede

[2] Bede, *On the Song of Songs*, A. Holder and B. Ward (trans) (New York: Paulist Press, 2011): 139.

[3] Bede, *Ecclesiastical History of the English People*, B. Colgrave and R. Mynors (eds) (Oxford: OUP, 1969): 133–4.

referred to him as 'our apostle'.[4] At the centre was the union of each with Christ, which would then give a channel for redeeming love to reach others.

This method was also true of Augustine and the other monks whom Gregory sent to Kent. They came carrying symbols and singing, as was fitting for the new peoples who learned by images and music; they carried the sign of the cross and the face of Jesus and offered positive promises of 'a new kingdom'. They did not insist on preaching but settled down with the Christian Queen Bertha, to wait patiently for wider access.

> As soon as they entered the dwelling place assigned them they began to imitate the course of life practiced in the primitive church; applying themselves to frequent prayer, watching and fasting; preaching the word of life to as many as they could; despising all worldly things, as not belonging to them; receiving only their necessary food from those they taught; living themselves in all respects in conformity to what they prescribed to others, and being always ready to suffer any adversity, and even to die for that truth which they preached. In short, several believed and were baptized, admiring the simplicity of their innocent life, and the sweetness of their heavenly doctrine.[5]

On the east side of Canterbury there was a church dedicated to St. Martin, built whilst the Romans still ruled Britain, where the Queen, who was a Christian, used to pray. There they first began to meet, worship, pray, say mass, preach and baptise. The King was in due course converted to the faith of his wife and then allowed them to preach openly and to build or repair churches in all places. From this point,

> When he (the king), among the rest, induced by the unspotted life of these holy men, and their delightful promises, which, by many miracles, they proved to be most certain, believed and was baptized, greater numbers began daily to flock together to hear the word, and, forsaking their heathen rites, to associate themselves, by believing, to the unity of the church of Christ.

Bede states that the King encouraged conversions but compelled no-one to embrace Christianity and admits that the King 'only showed more affection to the believers, as to his fellow citizens in the heavenly kingdom'. But he adds that the king 'had learned from his instructors and leaders to salvation, that the

---

4 Ibid: 123.

5 Ibid: 77.

service of Christ ought to be voluntary, not by compulsion'. Not long after he gave his preachers a settled residence in Canterbury, with such possessions as they needed for their subsistence.[6]

Bede presented Augustine as teaching by word and example, with private prayer as the basis of mission – out of which could grow meeting, baptising and preaching. As monks, in this they followed the example of the first Christian hermits in Egypt but with one major difference: the hermits belonged to a world where monks could be simply men of prayer, since good works and teaching were done elsewhere. In the barbarian Saxon world, someone had to know the actual words of the gospel – '*exemplum*' but also '*verbum*' *docere*. Bede mentions numbers baptised – but is clear for him that the real mission work of teaching was by example. As the only Englishman ever to be given the title 'doctor of the church', Bede was not opposed to learning but he was sure it could be only a tool to an end. He insisted that all should know by heart the rudiments of faith in the Creed and the outline of prayer in the Our Father in English. What he deplored was any learning that was prized for its own sake, leading to the kind of arrogance which prompted Peter Pan to exclaim: 'oh, the cleverness of me!'[7]

He did not despise learning – in fact Bede in particular was steadily concerned that learning of the scriptures should be offered to all who had the kind of mind that rejoiced in this. He was especially delighted to know about the school established at Canterbury by Theodore and Hadrian. As teachers, they were well read in both sacred and secular literature. They gathered a large number of disciples and, Bede relates, 'there daily flowed from them rivers of knowledge to water the hearts of their hearers; and, together with the books of holy writ, they also taught them the arts of ecclesiastical poetry, astronomy, and arithmetic'. Bede sees it as indicative of the extent of their influence that in his own day, some of their scholars were still alive, 'as well versed in the Greek and Latin tongues as in their own, in which they were born'. For Bede such times were as good as any since the English came into Britain for the kings:

> ... being brave men and good Christians ... were a terror to all barbarous nations, and the minds of all men were bent upon the joys of the heavenly kingdom of which they had just heard; and all who desired to be instructed in sacred reading had masters at hand to teach them.[8]

[6] Ibid: 75–9.

[7] J.M. Barrie, *Peter Pan* (Sacramento, CA: Malachite Quills, 2012): 25.

[8] Ibid: 333–5.

Himself the greatest scholar of his age, Bede gave examples of the refinement of doctrine by councils but his text is more concerned with examples of the long pilgrimage for each person which began with baptism.[9] One example of the path for new converts was shown in the example he gave of Aidan and King Oswine, which showed the importance of the redemption given to any part of humanity but also the gradual learning curve for the kings. It is a story which incidentally also shows the strength of a unique union of church and state by king and bishop which has lasted until the present day.

> The king Oswine had given an extraordinarily fine horse to Bishop Aidan, which he might either use in crossing rivers, or when going on a journey for any urgent necessity, though his custom was travel on foot. A short time after this, a poor man met Aidan and asked for alms; he immediately dismounted, and ordered the horse, with all its royal trappings, to be given to the beggar; for he was very compassionate, a great friend to the poor, and like a father to the wretched.[10]

The King, rooted in a culture in which a gift was meant to emphasise the greatness of the one who gave it, was upset by Aidan's readiness to dispose of the King's gift to him. Bede relates that he said to the Bishop,

> Why did you, my lord bishop, give the poor man that royal horse, which was meant for your use? Had not I many other horses of less value, and of other sorts, which would have been good enough to give to the poor, and not to give that horse, which I had particularly chosen for yourself?

To which the Bishop replied, 'What is it you say, O king? Is that foal of a mare more dear to you than a son of God?' They went in to dinner and the Bishop sat down; but the King stood warming himself at the fire. Then suddenly, whilst he stood by the fire, he remembered what the Bishop had said to him, took off his sword and gave it to a servant and immediately fell down at the Bishop's feet, begging him to forgive him; 'From this time forward', he said, 'I will never speak any more like that, nor will I judge of what, or how much of our wealth you shall give to the sons of God'.[11] Here the Germanic custom by which a gift showed the greatness of the giver is replaced by the needs of the recipient, a practical alteration of immense significance.

---

9 Ibid: 333–4.
10 Ibid: 259.
11 Ibid.

It was not the instant of baptism which gave the gospel to a new civilisation, but with Aidan as with Gregory and Augustine, conversion was done gradually by example and by appreciation of what was already there. Aidan himself was presented by Bede as an ideal apostle, in spite of their doctrinal differences, for his comprehension of this fact of mission.[12] After a year of devastation, the Christian presence had to be re-instated in the north in a new political situation. The Irish on Iona were asked to help in this. The Irish preacher who was sent at first to the English had preached a fierce gospel, alienating and terrifying the pagans to whom he had been sent. Aidan suggested a different way of giving the good news to the hearers.

> It is reported, that when King Oswald had asked a bishop of the Irish to bring the word of faith to him and his nation, there was first sent to him a man of austere disposition, who, meeting with no success, and not being listened to by the English people, returned home, and in an assembly of the elders reported that he had not been able to do any good to the nation he had been sent to preach to, because they were uncivilized, and of a stubborn and barbarous disposition.[13]

In a great council the Irish debated what was to be done, because they wanted the nation to receive the gospel that they sought but were perplexed by the rejection of the preacher sent to them. Then Aidan, who was also present in the council, said:

> I am of opinion, brother, that you were more severe to your unlearned hearers than you ought to have been and did not at first, as is taught in the apostolic rule, give them the milk of more easy doctrine, till being by degrees nourished with the word of God, they should be capable of greater perfection, and be able to practice God's more sublime precepts.[14]

Aidan's counsel deeply impressed those present, who determined that he ought to be made a bishop and be sent to offer instruction to the very people who had appeared impervious to the preaching of his predecessor. The key quality seen as fitting Aidan for this mission was that 'he was known to be endued with great discretion, which is the mother of other virtues'. Aidan was therefore ordained and sent to their friend, King Oswald, to preach. Bede related that

---

[12] Ibid: 227–9.

[13] Ibid: 229.

[14] Ibid: 431–5.

Aidan proved to possess all the other virtues, as well as the discretion for which he was already known.[15]

For Aidan, as for Gregory, Bede and Augustine, the basis of mission was neither force nor clarification of doctrine, but loving prayer and the Anglo Saxon Cuthbert, the great saint of the north, went even further into this way and saw prayer in solitude as being in itself the mission of Christ. It was from that centre of prayer when he was first a monk at Melrose that he went alone into the mountains to meet those who had been neglected; he lived with them and wept with them where they were.[16] He did not go out of a zeal to increase numbers by force or pride, or to collect tithes, but out of compassion and care that the life of Christ should be received and lived by all. Cuthbert's life was in itself his mission to all men and he saw the whole of nature also as part of redeeming love. His solitude on Farne was a prayer for the whole of creation, which was a part of redeemed humanity. His reluctance to preach in any other way was so extreme that Archbishop Theodore had personally to force him to accept a bishopric and its pastoral duties:

> Cuthbert, advancing in his meritorious and devout intentions, went on even to the adoption of a hermit's life of solitude. When he had here served God in solitude many years, the mound which encompassed his habitation being so high, that he could from thence see nothing but heaven, to which he so ardently aspired.[17]

At that time a great Synod was assembled in the presence of King Egfrid, near the river Alne in present day Northumberland, at a place called Twyford, which means 'the two fords' in which Archbishop Theodore, presided. Cuthbert was, by the unanimous consent of all, their choice as the Bishop of the church of Lindisfarne. But they could not persuade him to leave his solitude, notwithstanding many messengers and letters sent to him. Eventually the King, with Bishop Trumwine 'and other religious and great men', including many of the brothers of the island of Lindisfarne, went over to Cuthbert's Island hermitage. Bede states that

> … they all knelt, conjured him by our Lord, and with tears and entreaties, till they drew him, also in tears, from his retreat, and forced him to the synod. Being arrived

[15] Ibid: 439.
[16] Ibid: 205–6.
[17] Ibid: 437–9.

> there, after much opposition, he was overcome by the unanimous resolution of all present, and consented to take upon himself the episcopal dignity.[18]

Bede relates that Cuthbert followed the example of the apostles and became an outstanding bishop

> … for he both protected the people committed to his charge, by constant prayer, and excited them, by most wholesome admonitions, to heavenly practices; and, which is the greatest help in teachers, he first showed in his behaviour what he taught was to be performed by others; for he was much inflamed with the fire of divine charity, modest in the virtue of patience, most diligently intent on devout prayers, and affable to all that came to him for comfort. He thought it equivalent to praying, to afford the infirm brethren the help of his exhortations, well knowing that he who said "Thou shalt love the Lord thy God," said likewise, "Thou shalt love thy neighbor as thyself." He was also remarkable for penitential abstinence, and always intent upon heavenly things, through the grace of humility: lastly, when he offered up to God the sacrifice of the saving victim, he commended his prayer to God, not with a loud voice, but with tears drawn from the bottom of his heart.[19]

For Cuthbert prayer in solitude was itself mission, he undertook more external mission reluctantly and only under obedience; he withdrew from such honours to his 'beloved solitude' as soon as possible to go back to his hermitage and die there.

In numerical terms the membership of the church as the body of Christ is of course vast, and most are on the other side of Christ with the Father. Bede's sense of a multitude that none can number is present throughout his works: he saw this time as the 'sixth age' of the world, when all the Christians who had already died were living in heaven in the seventh age, alongside and often in touch with the Christians still in the sixth age on earth, all waiting together for the eighth and ultimate age, whose time was known only to the Father. To stand where Christ stands, towards the Father, was the work of the Christians now living, with the encouragement of all who had died. It is no accident that the Martyr Alban had a central place in the early history of the English mission.[20] With people who did not read or write, the spoken word and the visible action, the

---

[18] Ibid.
[19] Ibid: 437.
[20] Ibid: 29ff.

object, the ritual, the use of the body, were all used to implant the new life in the old forms, not by destroying but re-creating.

In every age, the current culture needs to be absorbed into the culture of Christ, and that means changes to formulas and images in both directions. But the basis is always the same: to stand where Christ, the Word of God, stands towards the Father; and from this depth of prayer, God will always use the person as a reservoir, with the water of life spilling over. This is often done by staying for life in one place, so that there is always one part of the created world where God's mercy is present. At times the praying person may be sent by God to show this stillness to others that they might recognise this touch of God and be remade in His image. Others might be called to be not preachers but scholars, analysing the text of the past for the use of their own age. But all these actions are meant always to uncover the image of God within, what Manley Hopkins called, 'the immortal diamond' in all created people. The work of Christ through his body, the church, is to reveal what is already there, not to impose something new. 'Opus Dei' the central work of the monk, is not the work we do for God but the work God does through us: the work *of* God, not *for* God. For these early English Christians in our island the work God does in each Christian was the true mission. As Michael Ramsey said in a sermon he preached on Lindisfarne:

> The supreme lesson is that our fathers came here because they knew that, if souls were to be won, there comes first the call to prayer to God ... it is the good part, the one thing needful which Mary chose. The glory of us children is our fathers: remember them: thank God for them: imitate their faith. And the mighty purpose of our God will move forward and instead of our fathers there shall be our children, princes of Christ in our own and in every land.[21]

[21] M. Ramsey, *Durham Essays and Addresses* (London: SPCK, 1936): 105.

Chapter 10

Growing the Medieval Church: Church Growth in Theory and Practice in Christendom c.1000–c.1500

Miranda Threlfall-Holmes

Introduction

This chapter discusses three key questions concerning church growth theory, and the reality of church growth, in medieval European Christendom. First, was church growth needed in medieval Europe? By the year 1000, all of mainland Europe was at least nominally Christian.[1] Paganism had been wiped out and it would have been hard indeed to find anyone who had not been baptised as an infant. Rulers were Christians and, increasingly, law and society were organised on Christian principles. Christianity was officially the compulsory religion of each emerging nation state. In this context, was the concept of church growth meaningless?

There is substantial academic debate surrounding the question of to what extent medieval Christendom was genuinely an 'age of faith', or whether Christianity had simply been superficially overlaid on an essentially pagan culture.[2] It is beyond the scope of this paper to address such debate, but it points to some of the subtleties involved when considering questions of church growth in this context. More importantly for our present purposes, there is a myth in the modern popular imagination that 'everyone went to church' in medieval times.

---

[1] S. Neill and O. Chadwick, *A History of Christian Missions*, second revised edition (London: Penguin, 1986): 85; M. Threlfall-Holmes, *The Essential History of Christianity* (London, SPCK, 2012): 28.

[2] See for example, E. Duffy, *The Stripping of the Altars: Traditional Religion in England, c.1400–c.1580*, second edition (London: Yale University Press, 2005); R. Swanson, *Religion and Devotion in Europe, c.1215–c.1515* (Cambridge: CUP, 1995); C. Richmond, 'The English Gentry and Religion, c.1500', in C. Harper-Bill (ed.), *Religious Belief and Ecclesiastical Careers in Late Medieval England* (Woodbridge: Boydell Press, 1991): 131–43.

This chapter will therefore look at the evidence for levels of church going and what scope clergy and others saw for growth in the medieval church. Accurate statistics for church membership and attendance in the medieval past are notoriously absent, but this chapter will consider what historical sources can be brought to bear on questions of church attendance and church growth.

Secondly, this chapter will then consider the medieval sources that explicitly discuss church growth. Through the words of those who were writing about this subject in the medieval past, we shall look at how church growth was conceptualised in a society where most were assumed to be at least nominally Christian. In particular, we will look in more detail at the ways in which the metaphor of 'growth' was used in medieval theology, as there are some very interesting differences here with our modern use of the concept. What did a medieval theology of church growth look like? And finally, this chapter will turn to the simple question: did it work? Was there church growth in medieval Europe?

Was Church Growth Needed in Medieval Europe?

It is often assumed in contemporary discussion about our Christian past, that everyone went to church in medieval times. Our modern concern with numbers of 'bums on pews' is often thought of as simply a twentieth and twenty-first century, or at most a post-industrialisation, phenomenon.

The contemporary debate about the relative importance of numbers and depth is of course just as applicable in the medieval period as it is now and we will return to questions of depth of Christian commitment and spirituality at the end of this chapter. But the focus of this volume is very much on the theology of numerical church growth and so this chapter will primarily concentrate on numbers attending church and medieval concerns with and theologies of numerical church growth. We will also look briefly at the other metric that often concerns us now – giving – as a potential further numerical indicator of levels of discipleship.

The fact that such concerns and theologies existed is itself a big clue that it is too simplistic to assume that 'everyone went to church'. Unfortunately, accurate statistical information about medieval church going is almost entirely non-existent. Registers of attendance were not yet kept and dioceses did not request and collate attendance figures or statistics for mission in the medieval period. However, we can glean enough information from letters, churchwardens' accounts, bishops' registers, archaeology and occasional court proceedings to make some deductions.

Church Attendance

It becomes clear very quickly from such sources that – then as now – church membership was a slippery thing to define. The first indicator is of course baptism rates. Nominally, 100 per cent of the population of medieval Europe were Christian and were supposed to be baptised as such in infancy. In the absence of baptismal registers we can't be entirely sure that this happened, but all the evidence is that it did and indeed that baptism was very popular. There were very few instances in the ecclesiastical court records of lay people being cited for failing to bring their infants for baptism, and those few that exist seem to have been the results of misunderstandings. Indeed, the majority of such complaints were brought by lay people complaining about clergy failing to baptise, rather than the other way round.[3]

Other than baptism, however, very little was formally required of lay people in the early medieval period. This began to change in the twelfth and thirteenth centuries, with the Fourth Lateran Council of 1215 typifying a new emphasis on both pastoral care and what we would now call developing discipleship. In England, for example, Robert Grosseteste, Bishop of Lincoln in the mid thirteenth century (1235–53) began to exhort the laity to learn at least the ten commandments and the seven deadly sins and to have a basic understanding of the seven sacraments.[4] Tanner and Watson suggest that the general reluctance of the church authorities to legislate for minimum requirements for laity, whether of understanding or church attendance, sprang from an overwhelmingly pastoral concern not to leave anyone behind or exclude anyone from salvation.[5]

After the Fourth Lateran Council, Church attendance at one's parish church and, as a minimum, the reception of communion at Christmas and Easter were in theory compulsory, but this of course begs more questions. Did people actually go? And even if they were there, to what extent were they in attendance as members of a worshipping community, and to what extent simply as a social and legal obligation, in the worst caricature chatting to neighbours and ignoring the liturgy going on up there in the chancel? The evidence is mixed. Non-attendance seems to have been fairly common, with only the most persistent offenders challenged in the courts.[6] For example, nine laypeople were charged with non-attendance at their parish church on Sundays and Feast days

---

3 N. Tanner and S. Watson, 'Least of the Laity: The Minimum Requirements for a Medieval Christian', *Journal of Medieval History*, 32 (2006): 404.

4 Ibid: 401.

5 Ibid: 401–3.

6 Ibid: 409.

in Norwich in 1492, whilst a further three were charged with having their pubs open during Sunday worship and another woman, it was said, 'observes an evil custom with various people from neighbouring households, who sit with her and drink during the time of service'.[7] A similar pattern was found in Salisbury and Lincoln dioceses, and it seems likely that people were only prosecuted when they were open and notorious offenders, or where there were other complicating factors.[8] In Flanders, for example, diocesan regulations stated that the names of those who failed to make their confession and receive communion at Easter should be collected and they were to be brought before the provincial council if they persistently failed for a period of 10 years.[9]

In late medieval Durham, however, Margaret Harvey identified no evidence of persistent non-attendance and found that clergy and archdeacons were proactive and assiduous in following up, prosecuting and indeed punishing examples of non-attendance at compulsory services.[10] For example, two weeks after Easter in 1492, two parishioners from St Margaret's parish, Joanna Pierson and Agnes Johnson, appeared before the Prior to explain why they had not received communion in St Margaret's on Easter Day.[11] Joanna said she had been in Newcastle, where she had received at St. Nicholas church, and was given a day to return with proof. Agnes claimed that she had received communion at St Oswald's church in Durham. She was also required to prove it, but in addition was given 3 floggings around the chapel for absenting herself from her parish church without permission. When she failed to bring proof, she was flogged three times around each church in punishment. It seems possible that this harshness was due to St Margaret's having only recently become an independent parish from St Oswald's, and the intention was to make an example of parishioners who persisted in refusing to transfer their loyalties.

This factor complicates matters: for it was not enough simply to attend church to fulfil the letter of the law. Rather, the legal requirement was to attend your own parish church, and clergy often jealously guarded their rights in this regard. Indeed, they seem sometimes to have been much quicker to complain about parishioners choosing to attend a different church, than about those who did not attend at all, or only occasionally. Such cases suggest a relatively high

[7] N. Tanner, *The Church in Late Medieval Norwich, 1370–1532* (Toronto: Pontifical Institute of Mediaeval Studies, 1984): 9, 167–71.

[8] Tanner and Watson, 'Requirements': 409.

[9] Ibid: 408.

[10] M. Harvey, *Lay Religious Life in Late Medieval Durham* (Woodbridge: Boydell Press, 2006): 32, 198.

[11] Ibid: 32–3.

degree of voluntary religion, that is people making a positive decision to attend a particular church or chapel, beyond mere convention or social expectation. The bishops' registers from fourteenth century Barcelona, for example, contain repeated demands that parishioners should attend their parish church regularly, implying that this was a continued concern.[12] In some instances the Barcelona priests complained about their parishioners choosing to go elsewhere and in others the Bishop issued licences for people to receive at home, almost all to noble women on grounds of age or temporary illness (perhaps including pregnancy). In some cases, questions of social status were also clearly at stake. Margaret Paston, for example, in late fifteenth century Norfolk, requested permission from her bishop to establish a private chapel in her home. This was no doubt a pious convenience, but was also a significant status symbol for this upwardly-mobile family.[13]

It was widely recognised that there were various acceptable grounds for non-attendance, beyond age and infirmity. Domestic servants might be kept from attending by their employers, for example, and those living in remote areas would necessarily attend church only occasionally. But beyond these understandable absentees, many medieval commentators complained that people hardly bothered to go to church at all, or if they did just chatted through the service, though it is hard to assess how accurate or rhetorical these assessments were. For example, in the fifteenth century Nicholas of Clamanges complained that 'few go to church and even fewer listent to the mass' on feast days; and a parish priest that 'they come not to matins thrice in a year ... they jangle, they jape, they kiss women, and hear no word of the service'.[14] Sometimes even the behaviour of the clergy at services seems to have left something to be desired: one twelfth century bishop of Worcester ruled that clergy were not to sing bawdy songs during the mass.[15]

The overall picture that emerges is one of great variation, 'a broad spectrum of responses to the medieval church, from the extravagant, intense and devout on one end, to the distracted, apathetic dismissive or hostile on the other'.[16] This is a picture we can no doubt recognise from our own, contemporary experience. However, churchgoing was considerably more engrained in the popular

[12] K. Utterback, 'Worship at the Church of your Choice? Church Attendance in Mid-fourteenth-century Barcelona', *Journal of Medieval History*, 17 (1991): 245–53.

[13] G. Pritchard, 'Religion and the Paston Family', in Richard Britnell (ed.), *Daily Life in the Late Middle Ages* (Stroud: Sutton Publishing, 1998): 74.

[14] Tanner and Watson, 'Requirements': 409–10.

[15] Ibid: 410.

[16] Ibid: 409.

imagination in the medieval period. The Paston letters, a unique survival of a family letter collection from a fifteenth century English merchant family, show clearly that religion was part of the warp and weft of everyday lives. Church attendance on Sundays is only rarely mentioned, but when it is referred to, the implication is that it was an obvious and unremarkable part of everyday life. For example, one letter refers to a subpoena being delivered at Sunday mass, the implication being that you could definitely expect the person to be there.[17] Similarly, mass and matins are often referred to in passing as markers of time – 'after Mass, I ...' – implying a regular and shared culture of attendance. Perhaps the main difference from today was that even those who didn't attend church knew which church it was that they were not attending and would often have put in a token appearance at least two or three times a year.

Church Provision

It is tempting to think that the pattern of provision of church buildings and their size and distribution, might serve as a proxy for the numbers or proportion of the population attending church. Unfortunately, however, there seems to have been very little correlation between parish church provision and population or church attendance. The parish system was largely established across Europe between 900 and 1200.[18] Over this period there was an explosion in the foundation of new churches, with parish boundaries that often mirrored manorial landholdings, gradually replacing the older system of senior minster churches until all of rural Europe was divided into parishes.[19] In Galicia, for example, the diocese of Braga had 30 churches in the late sixth century, a figure that had grown to 573 by the late eleventh century.[20]

However, the size and distribution of such churches was in many cases driven by the local lord of the manor or his equivalent and, as such, can be read much more as a statement about his status and ambition than as an indicator of churchgoing.[21] Similarly, rebuilding and enlargement programmes often owed

---

17 Pritchard, 'Religion and the Paston Family': 73.

18 J. Blair (ed.), *Minsters and Parish Churches: The Local Church in Transition, 950–1200* (Oxford: Oxford University Committee for Archaeology, 1988).

19 N. Baker and R. Holt, *Urban Growth and the Medieval Church: Gloucester and Worcester* (Ashgate: Aldershot, 2004): 239.

20 J. Campbell, 'Richard Fletcher as a Historian', in S. Barton and P. Lineham (eds), *Cross, Crescent and Conversion* (Leiden: Brill, 2008): 13.

21 Threlfall-Holmes, *Essential History*: 45.

more to the desire of a prominent parishioner to make a substantial impact on the community than to pastoral need. In Gloucester, for example, around a third of the total area enclosed by the medieval walls was taken up by churches and monastic foundations, a figure which dropped to about 18 per cent of the total built up area of the town including the suburbs, clearly disproportionate to the 'need' in terms of size or location.[22] Colchester, a fairly average town in medieval England, had a population of around 3,000 in 1330, served by three monasteries and a grand total of 12 parish churches, virtually one on every street corner.[23] Canterbury, another small town, had 22 parishes and churches by the end of the twelfth century. When one of these, Holy Cross, was rebuilt in 1379–80, its new size made no concession to the major depopulation that the town had experienced as a consequence of the Black Death in the preceding decades.[24]

Much more significant than parish church buildings as an indicator of churchgoing and devotion was the establishment of a wide range of extra-parochial chapels of ease, chantries and holy places by parishioners.[25] In Cornwall, for example, which was perhaps the best supplied county in this regard, there were 209 parishes but, in addition, there were an estimated 700 non-parochial chapels.[26] Such chapels were normally founded voluntarily by groups of lay people, either for geographical convenience in large parishes, or where changing patterns of settlement made a local place of worship desirable, or in places of historic local significance. They were maintained financially on an entirely voluntary basis by the local laity. This could be a major financial commitment, especially where a priest was employed, and of course such payments were in addition to the tithes that were legally obligatory on all parishioners, in theory at least for the upkeep of the parish church. The fact that so many lay people not only paid tithes in their parish but also voluntarily maintained additional places of worship implies a relatively high degree of voluntary religion, not merely legal conformity, in the medieval period. Again, though, there was significant local variation and presumably also a wide spectrum of levels of interest in and attendance at such chapels, as with parish churches.

---

22 Baker and Holt, *Growth*: 372.

23 R. Britnell, *Growth and Decline in Colchester, 1300–1525* (Cambridge: CUP, 1986): 16, 22.

24 T. Tatton-Brown, 'Medieval Parishes and Parish Churches in Canterbury', in T. Slater and G. Rosser (eds), *The Church in the Medieval Town* (Ashgate, Aldershot, 1998): 236, 256.

25 G. Rosser, 'Parochial Conformity and Voluntary Religion in Late-Medieval England', *Transactions of the Royal Historical Society*, Sixth Series (vol. 1; Cambridge: CUP, 1991): 173–89.

26 Ibid: 175.

Church Growth and Mission

The classic view of mission through Christian history, outlined by Hans Kung and followed by Bosch, has seen the history of Christianity in terms of six distinct and successive paradigms, each with their own distinctive approach to mission and the task of church growth.[27] In this outline, the apocalyptic primitive paradigm is succeeded historically by the Hellenistic patristic and then by the medieval Roman Catholic paradigm, covering the period from around 600 to the Reformation. Mission in this medieval Catholic paradigm is described by Bosch as being essentially about defending the borders of the Christian Empire or nation state and expanding the area covered by Christendom.[28] Certainly, overseas mission was of great interest to the medieval church. Between 1000 and 1500 the first theories of mission began to be formulated. Medieval friars made some astonishing journeys to the edge of the known world seeking converts and, towards the end of this period, the major European powers all began to look beyond Europe for new territories to exploit and missionaries went with them.[29] However, the focus of this volume is not primarily missionary endeavours overseas, but church growth at home. Bosch says nothing about the concept of mission *within* European Christendom, a very interesting omission. So let us now turn to look at what medieval theologians said about church growth.

Medieval Theologies of Church Growth

On the one hand, the basic assumption of most official church documents in the medieval period was certainly that of Christendom. That is to say, Europeans were assumed to be Christian: in most cases, the only 'growth' that was seen to be necessary was spiritual growth and growth in grace. The clearest and perhaps the most extreme example of this comes from the Council of Florence in 1439, which – in one of the few medieval Catholic official documents that actually uses the term 'growth' – discusses the role of the sacraments in bringing about growth in grace. Here, numerical growth is considered to be purely a question of

[27] D. Bosch, *Transforming Mission: Paradigm Shifts in the Theology of Mission* (New York: Orbis, 1991): 181–3.

[28] Ibid: 221, 237.

[29] Threlfall-Holmes, *Essential History*: 59–71.

procreation: 'Through confirmation we grow in grace ... by ordination the Church is governed and multiplied spiritually; by matrimony it is materially increased.'[30]

On the other hand, however, numerical concepts of church growth certainly were a concern of medieval theologians. The clearest example of this from the English context is to be found in the letters of Robert Grosseteste, the famously reforming Bishop of Lincoln in the mid thirteenth century.

In late 1244 or early 1245, Grosseteste had left his diocese on a visit to the papal curia and wrote to his archdeacons left behind in Lincolnshire.[31] In the letter, he compares their situation to the parable of the talents: 'a man who was going abroad handed over his possessions to his servants, that on his return he might receive them back increased many times through their efforts'.[32] He exhorts his archdeacons to grow the diocese in his absence and uses the metaphor of doing business with the wealth entrusted to you with the aim of making profit to refer specifically to numerical church growth.[33] The underlying theology of the letter is explicitly evangelistic. 'The Lord Jesus gave himself to save the soul of each and every person; yet only those are saved who truly believe in and love his passion. Now, as he has gone abroad, he, and I in him, have entrusted to you the responsibility of converting souls ... to faith in him and love of him ... that his death may not for them be in vain.'[34] This is not the theology and language of a church that believed everyone was a Christian already. On the contrary, Grosseteste is urgent and passionate in exhorting his archdeacons to work profitably: 'labour at it, preaching the word of life ceaselessly and indefatigably ... spread the light of your good works everywhere ... pray ceaselessly ...'[35]

The task was apparently a hard one, as it seems that Grosseteste could not even rely on all of his clergy being secure in the rudiments of their faith. His Constitutions, which had been sent to all the clergy of Lincoln diocese in 1238/9, began by urging that 'because souls are not saved without knowing the 10 commandments', all priests should know them; and all clergy should have 'at least a rudimentary understanding of the faith as contained in both the major and minor creeds'.[36] If the clergy could not be relied upon to know the creeds

---

[30] 'Decree for the Armenians', Council of Florence, 1439, available at http://legacy.fordham.edu/halsall/source/1438sacraments.asp accessed 5 January 2015.

[31] F. Mantello and J. Goering (eds), *The Letters of Robert Grosseteste, Bishop of Lincoln* (Toronto: University of Toronto Press, 2010), Letter 112: 346–9.

[32] Ibid: 346–7.

[33] Ibid: 348.

[34] Ibid: 349.

[35] Ibid: 348.

[36] Ibid, Letter 52*: 183.

and the 10 commandments, it is unsurprising that Grosseteste was concerned for the work of evangelising his diocese. Presumably because of this evangelistic concern, Robert Grosseteste had been one of the earliest supporters of the Franciscan friars when they first arrived in England in 1224 and, as Bishop of Lincoln, he actively promoted the friars' work of evangelism, both in his diocese and elsewhere.[37]

The friars themselves are the most obvious example of a concern for church growth on a large scale across medieval Europe at the height of medieval Christendom. Saint Francis famously first heard God's call in the words 'build my church', and initially embarked on a building restoration project before realising that the task was much more fundamental than that. Despite some differences in emphasis, all the various orders of friars that flourished so remarkably from the thirteenth century were explicitly founded to preach with a view to conversion: that is, for church growth.

The two main subcategories were Franciscans and Dominicans. Franciscans were particularly focused on preaching to the large numbers of unchurched peasants who were moving into rapidly growing towns in Italy, a context not seen again until Victorian industrialisation. The story is told of St Francis that soon after his conversion he consulted St Clare and others as to whether he should devote himself to a life of prayer, or also spend time preaching. The message came back, 'The Lord says, go and tell Brother Francis that he has called him to this state not to save merely his own soul, but that he may produce fruits in those of others, and that through him many souls be saved.'[38]

In the thirteenth century, as in the nineteenth, rapid urban expansion meant the disruption of historic parish connections and habits of churchgoing and domestic piety and thus the need for evangelisation of a whole generation. It is well known that St Francis invented the concept of the Christmas crib: but it is less frequently appreciated that he did so precisely because there was a pressing need for new ways to teach the story of Jesus' nativity to an ill-educated population that knew nothing of the Christian story. The work of evangelism was foundational to the friars. Chapter 12 of St Francis' 1223 Rule was devoted to 'regulating and promoting missionary activity', and for the rest of the medieval period and beyond friars were to be found preaching not only across Europe but also at the furthest reaches of the known world in eastern Europe, India, China,

[37] Ibid, e.g., Letter 34: 147–50; Letters 58 and 59: 204–8.

[38] Ugolino, 'Little Flowers of Saint Francis', available at http://www.ccel.org/ccel/ugolino/flowers.iii.xvi.html accessed 5 January 2015.

Africa and the newly discovered Americas, often well in advance of official envoys or trade delegations.[39]

In contrast to St Francis' focus on simplicity, the Dominicans were more self-consciously intellectual. The Dominican Order was founded to combat the spread of heresy through a learned and itinerant preaching ministry and to try to get the church up to date with the religious learning coming from the newly founded universities. Theology was rapidly becoming a professionalised and intellectualised academic discipline in this period and the Dominicans wanted to ensure that all the new learning was put at the service of the church, rather than being in conflict with it.

Notwithstanding these differences in emphasis, all the friars had an itinerant preaching ministry deliberately aiming to educate and convert the unchurched masses whom they identified as being at risk of heresy and damnation. Humbert of Romans (c.1200–1277), the fifth Master of the Dominican Order, wrote in his retirement a 'Treatise on the Formation of Preachers' in which he addressed the need for and the effects and aims of preaching. It is clear from this that he was not concerned simply with maintaining a Christendom *status quo*, but also with church growth. 'The church would not have made any progress in the past, nor would she be making progress now, without preaching,' he wrote.[40] Humbert made it clear that he saw the people of medieval Europe as presenting as much of a mission field as those overseas.

> There are many peple whose spirits are in their bodies like corpses in their tombs ... many who, spiritually, have nothing to live on ... many who are always eagerly on the look out for tasty things to eat ... many who go astray on all kinds of points because of their simplicity ... many who have no perception of spiritual matters but live an entirely animal life ... many who, in the darkness of this world, do not know how to hold to the right path ... [whose] piety and compunction and devotion towards God are quite dried up ... in whom charity has grown cold.[41]

Moreover, in a list of 10 'thoroughly good results of preaching' (and Humbert lists, with remarkable modern relevance, other results that are indifferent, only partly good, or positively harmful) numerical church growth is explicitly named. The first and seventh items on Humbert's list are 'the conversion of unbelievers

---

[39] D. West, 'Medieval Ideas of Apocalyptic Mission and the Early Franciscans in Mexico', *The Americas*, 45 (1989): 294; Threlfall-Holmes, *Essential History*: 68–71.

[40] Humbert of Romans, 'Treatise on the Formation of Preachers', in S. Tugwell (ed.), *Early Dominicans: Selected Writings* (New York: New York, 1982): 188.

[41] Ibid: 201.

to the faith', and 'the increase of the mystical body of Christ. Many souls are added to it through preaching'.[42]

Conversion to Penitence

Humbert of Romans' list of the good effects of preaching, however, also signals clearly to us that, as well as all these similarities with our contemporary concern for church growth, there were some major differences in how such growth was conceptualised in the medieval period. In second, third and fourth places on Humbert's list are references to the central place of the sacrament of penance in medieval theologies of conversion. The good effects of preaching include 'Secondly, the conversion of wicked men to repentance ... Thirdly, the conversion of worldly men to humility ... Fourthly, sinners going to confession'.[43]

Overall in fact, the aim of missionary work within medieval Europe and beyond was most commonly conceptualised in terms of provoking penitence. This was demonstrated, of course, by participation in the penitential discipline of the church, primarily in going to confession. In medieval saints' lives, successful ministries are most often described in terms of producing repentance, rather than conversions per se. On one occasion, for example, St Francis is described preaching in the city of Bologna, where

> ... the crowd was so great that it was with much difficulty he made his way to the market-place, which was filled with men, women, and scholars. And St Francis, on arriving there, stood upon an elevated spot, and began to preach ... and his words were like sharp arrows, which pierced through the hearts of those who listened to them. And many men and women were brought to repentance through that sermon.[44]

This makes sense in a context where the majority were already nominally Christian but it also reminds us just how central the concepts of confession and penance were to a medieval theology of the economy of salvation. The aim of preaching, teaching and churchgoing was not so much to convert unbelievers to Christianity, but to convert nominal Christians into penitents, who would

---

[42] Ibid: 275–6.

[43] Ibid: 275–6.

[44] Ugolino, 'Flowers', chapter 27, available at http://www.ccel.org/ccel/ugolino/flowers.iii.xxvii.html accessed 5 January 2015.

come to confession, do penance and generally safeguard their salvation by participating in the sacramental discipline of the church.

Fighting the Weeds: Conceptualising Church Growth in Medieval Christendom

Furthermore, in this Christendom context, when the metaphor of growth was used in theology it was used in a rather different way to our contemporary discussions of 'church growth'. The actual phrase 'church growth' was not used but the concept of growth was a common metaphor. Taking their cue from biological biblical imagery of a body or a vineyard, growth was seen as an entirely natural phenomenon. Left to itself, the nature of the world was that things would grow. So for example, the 1439 Council of Florence used the image of the body in discussing the effects of receiving communion: 'every effect of material food and drink upon the physical life, in nourishment, growth and pleasure, is wrought by the sacrament for the spiritual life'.[45] Where gardening or vineyard imagery was used, the aim was to be 'fruitful'. This terminology is used by the fourth Lateran Council of 1215, for example, and one of Robert Grosseteste's letters uses an extended analogy of a fruitful ministry in offering a living to a priest.[46]

However, this imagery was not entirely positive. Growth, of course, is natural both for wheat and for weeds. And as all gardeners know, and medieval writers familiar with the difficulties of cultivating marginal lands would have been particularly aware, weeds grow more vigorously than cultivated plants. The primary image of church 'growth' that is found in medieval theological writings uses the analogy of farming. Within the Christendom context, the task of the church is conceptualised primarily in terms of a farmer working within the fields that he has been given, constantly weeding so that the crop can grow. Growth is natural but without constant rooting out of bramble suckers, constant vigilance towards encroaching weeds, the growth that is desired will be strangled by the weeds' stronger growth.

The clearest example of this can be found in Pope Gregory IX's bull canonising St Francis, from 1228:

---

[45] Council of Florence, Session 8, 1439, available at http://www.ewtn.com/library/COUNCILS/FLORENCE.HTM#2 accessed 5 January 2015. A similar image was used in Canon 10 of the Decrees of the Fourth Lateran Council, available at www.fordham.edu/halsall/ basis/lateran4.asp. accessed 5 January 2015.

[46] Mantello and Goering, *Letters*, Letter 46: 167.

> God neither neglected the gifts of His mercy nor failed to protect uninterruptedly the vineyard planted by His hand. He sent laborers into it at the eleventh hour to cultivate it, and with their hoes and plowshares to uproot the thorns and thistles ... After the copious branches were pruned and the sucker roots with the briars were pulled out, this vineyard will produce a luscious, appetizing fruit, one capable of storage in the wine cellar of eternity, once purified in the wine-press of patience. ... Now, at the eleventh hour, he has called forth his servant, Blessed Francis, a man after His own heart ... Him the Lord sent into his vineyard to uproot the thorns and thistles.[47]

The words gardening, farming or weeding are rather too weak for the strength of the imagery used throughout this Bull and elsewhere. The task of tending the church to allow it to grow is seen as a constant battle against the encroaching briars of demonic forces, temptation, sin or, from a fourteenth century source, 'heresies and errors springing up' like perennial weeds.[48] The force and emotional impact of this image is rather more analogous to our contemporary concept of cancer: unwanted but natural growth, which might easily overwhelm the healthy and desirable growth, the fight against which is conceptualised in the popular imagination as a battle.

The primary task of the church is therefore seen as constant ploughing, or alternatively the application of medicine against disease (an image used by Humbert of Romans).[49] The aim is to prevent the unwanted growth which would otherwise naturally occur and thereby allow the growth of the wanted fruits. It is worth stressing that growth in either case is seen as naturally occurring, as simply being the nature of things: the task of the farmer, the church, is to provide the right soil, perhaps sow the seed and water it but, above all, to root out all competing growth. And as we have already noted, this task of husbandry is itself understood primarily in terms of a constant calling to repentance and the application of the penitential cycle (and, to a lesser extent, the other sacraments). Preaching, penance and the sacraments were wielded by the church as a hoe or scythe, to cut down competing growth and allow spiritual growth.

---

47 Pope Gregory IX, 'On the Canonization of St Francis of Assisi, 1228' available at http://www.franciscan-archive.org/bullarium/g9mira.html accessed 5 January 2015.

48 'Letters Patent Against the Lollards, 1384', in H. Gee and W. Hardy (eds), *Documents Illustrative of the History of the English Church* (London: Macmillan, 1896): 111.

49 Humbert, 'Preachers': 201–2.

Assessing the Medieval Experience of Church Growth

As we saw at the beginning of this chapter, statistical evidence is almost impossible to come by for the medieval period and so, by the same token, any change in numbers is impossible to estimate.

Was medieval religion 'a mile wide but inch deep'? There is a sustained academic debate about this which shows no signs of ever being resolved conclusively. However, there is considerable evidence for an explosion in lay-led religious initiatives from the middle of this period onwards which suggests, I think, that the medieval period did experience some considerable church growth.[50]

First, there was a well documented explosion in lay literacy, and in bible and prayer book ownership, from the twelfth century onwards, which is very suggestive of some growth in depth of spirituality.[51] Even before the development of printing, copy-shops working on a semi-industrial scale were able to produce a wide range of Bibles at prices that enabled the emerging middle classes to purchase their own copies. Hundreds, perhaps thousands of hand-copied Bibles survive from this period, suggesting that they were very widely owned. There was also a wide range of other spiritual literature being produced for this new literate lay market, including Bible picture books with text in the vernacular, psalters, books of hours and prayer collections.

New patterns of lay devotion and spirituality also began to emerge from the twelfth century onwards.[52] Indeed, one of the key features of church life in the high middle ages was its developing emphasis on lay religion. Theologians formulated Christian ethics and sermons aimed at different social and economic sectors of society and guilds began to develop from simple trade organisations into vibrant centres of lay-led religious activity. This period also saw the development of lay roles as churchwardens and so on: an 'increase of genuine responsibility among the laity and ... an increasing part in the appointment of minor functionaries and in the keeping of parochial records and accounts'.[53] Charitable giving also underwent considerable growth, being preached as a spiritual discipline and religious responsibility. The period from 1200–1500 was remarkable for the foundation of almshouses, hospitals, schools and colleges, some still surviving today, as well as innumerable chantries, which did

---

50 Threlfall-Holmes, *Essential History*: 49–56.

51 Ibid: 54, 56.

52 Ibid: 52–3.

53 E. Mason, 'The Role of the English Parishioner, 1100–1500', *The Journal of Ecclesiastical History*, 27 (1976): 28.

not survive the Reformation. Evidence from churchwardens' accounts suggest that a broad range of parishioners, both men and women and at all social levels, contributed financially to their parishes in the century before the Reformation in a wide variety of ways, suggesting a high degree of voluntarism.[54] If it is true, as the saying has it, that the wallet is the last thing to be converted, this would imply a reasonably high degree of success on the part of the medieval church as it worked for growth and renewal over this period.

It is arguable that over this period, broadly speaking, Christianity became something that lay people did for themselves, rather than being primarily conceptualised as done for them by clergy. It is impossible to tell how much this was due to various factors – conscious religious renewal by the friars, reforming clergy, and social and economic change. More negatively, it is possible also that the increasing awareness of other faiths that went alongside the spread and military threat of Islam and the Crusades contributed in a very ambivalent way. Certainly one consequence of the Crusades was the crystallisation of a self-consciously European Christian identity – it was in the wake of the First Crusade that the term 'Christendom' was first used – defined against Jews and Muslims with tragic consequences.[55]

Conclusion

So what can we, as budding theologians of church growth today, usefully learn from the medieval worldview? In most of our theology, the arguments and concepts that were formed in the medieval period remain foundational and it does not seem unreasonable, therefore, for us to look here for help in formulating a contemporary theology of church growth too. In doing so, there are four points that I would like to draw out.

First, an historically accurate assessment of medieval levels of churchgoing is a helpful corrective to the mythology of a golden age in which 'everyone went to church'. Contemporary discussions of the difficulties of evangelism often focus on the uniquely problematic nature of our post-modern context in a way which can gloss over the reality of the situations faced by our colleagues in previous eras. It does seem to have been the case that clergy in every generation have worried about how they could increase the levels of church attendance

[54] K. French, 'Rebuilding St Margaret's: Parish Involvement and Community Action in Late Medieval Westminster', *Journal of Social History*, 45 (2011): 148–71.

[55] Threlfall-Holmes, *Essential History*: 63, 65.

and affective Christianity amongst their flocks. An awareness of this may help to prevent counsels of despair and prompt a new realism about the task that confronts, and always has confronted, the church.

Secondly, the fully fleshed out way in which medieval theologians understood the metaphor of 'growth' is an important resource as we seek to discern a theology of church growth. Understanding the primary task as keeping down the weeds, which are constantly threatening to overwhelm the garden, resonates very accurately with the lived experience of clergy and others involved in trying to grow the church in practice. It is very easy to feel discouraged by these dynamics. A great deal of hard work is expended, yet the result is not often a great expansion of the vineyard, but simply (at best) the only-to-be-expected harvest of the vines that have been tended. In our modern understanding of work, we expect to see a product, the fruits of our labours. Emma Percy draws theological attention to the philosopher Hannah Arendt, who distinguished between three different realms of human activity: *labour*, the domestic tasks needed for everyday life; *work* or *fabrication*, where the end is a tangible product, and *action*, the work that builds up human communities.[56] We tend to conceptualise working harder as producing more. Yet the wisdom of the medieval theologians of church growth would suggest that the work of ministry might be more helpfully seen as parallel to domestic work – washing, ironing, cooking a meal and washing up – which needs to be done, but then needs to be done again, than to artisan or factory work, which produces a measurable product. This does not mean that growth does not take place, but it is more analogous to natural, organic growth – the growth of a garden, or a child – rather than to capitalist expansion and productivity.

Thirdly, and more positively, this survey of medieval church growth would suggest very strongly that intentionality is key. Throughout the history of the church, it has grown – numerically and in spiritual depth – when people have chosen to focus on that task.

Finally, there is a further historical question which arises from this evidence for medieval church growth. To what extent did this growth in lay involvement, in the depth and vibrancy of medieval Catholic religious practice over this period, inadvertently give birth to the Reformation? To extend the metaphor of growth: even if we assiduously keep the weeds under control, we can't control the shape of the growth that God gives, or whether its fruit will be to our taste.

---

[56] H. Arendt, *The Human Condition* (Chicago: University of Chicago Press, 1958; second edition, 1998), cited in E. Percy, *What Clergy Do, Especially When It Looks Like Nothing* (London: SPCK, Forthcoming 2014).

Chapter 11

Divine Allurement: Thomas Cranmer and Tudor Church Growth

Ashley Null

The heart of Tudor Protestantism was not right doctrine but right desire. Undoubtedly, Thomas Cranmer and his fellow English Reformers thought the two were closely connected. Truth about God would draw humanity homewards. Right desire could only be formed by right knowledge of both God and fallen human nature. Nevertheless, saving truth by itself was insufficient to move a self-centred humanity to return to their maker through repentance and amendment of life. The church's mission was to proclaim the unchanging message of the Gospel to each generation in ways that would move the hearts of the hearers to embrace it.

We can see this progression from apostolic teaching to transforming affections in the conversion narratives of the early English reformers Thomas Bilney and Katherine Parr. According to Bilney, he often 'felt a change' in himself 'from the right hand of the Most High God' when he read Scripture. It happened for the first time while reading Erasmus' new Latin translation of the Bible.

> I chanced upon this sentence of St. Paul (Oh most sweet and comfortable sentence to my soul!) in I Tim. 1:15: "It is a true saying and worthy of all men to be embraced, that Christ Jesus came into the world to save sinners, of whom I am the chief and principal." This one sentence, through God's instruction ... working inwardly in my heart, did so gladdened it – which before was wounded by the awareness of my sins almost to the point of desperation – that immediately I felt a marvelous inner peace, so much so that my bruised bones leapt for joy. After this, the Scripture began to be more pleasant to me than honey or the honey comb.[1]

[1] John Foxe, *Actes and Monuments* (London: John Day, 1570): 1141–3. Bilney's description of his conversion is contained in correspondence to Bishop Cuthbert Tunstall

Katherine Parr, the widow of Henry VIII, used the same emotive language to describe the result of her reading of Scripture.

> Cum to me al ye that labour, and are burdened, and I shal refresh you: what gentle, merciful, and comfortable woordes are these to all sinners? ... What a most gracious comfortable, and gentle, saying was this, with suche plesant and swete wordes, to allure his enemies to cum unto him? ... [W]hen I behold the benignitie, liberalitie, mercy, and goodnes of the lord, I am encoraged, boldened, and stirred to ask such a noble gift [as living faith] ... By this faith I am assured: and by this assurance I fele the remission of my synnes: this is it that maketh me bolde: this is it that comforteth me, this is it that quencheth all dispayre ... Thus I fele my selfe to cum, as it were in a new garment, before God, and nowe by his mercy, to be taken just and righteous ... Then began I to dwel in god by charitie, knowyng by the louyng charitie of God in the remission of my synnes, that God is charitie as S. John sayeth. So that of my fayth (whereby I came to knowe God, and wherby it pleased god euen because I trusted in him to iustifie me) sprang this excellent charitie in my heart.[2]

'I felt a supernatural change within', 'gladdened my heart', 'I felt inner peace', 'leapt for joy', 'more pleasant than honey', 'pleasant and sweet words', 'I am assured', 'I feel the remission of my sins', 'I feel myself in a new garment': to borrow a term from T.S. Eliot, the first English reformers clearly 'felt their thought'.[3]

Cranmer agreed. Consider his description of the interplay between the mental realisation of the free pardon for sins offered by the evangelical reading of Scripture and the human heart:

> But, if the profession of our faith of the remission of our own sins enter within us into the deepness of our hearts, then it must needs kindle a warm fire of love in our hearts towards God, and towards all other for the love of God – a fervent mind to seek and procure God's honour, will, and pleasure in all things – a good will and mind to help every man and to do good unto them, so far as our might, wisdom, learning, counsel, health, strength, and all other gifts which we have

during Bilney's 1527 heresy trial. Foxe has given two versions, the original Latin and an English translation. The quotations here are the author's revision of Foxe's translation in the light of the original Latin.

[2] Katherine Parr, *The Lamentation of a Sinner* (London: Edward Whitchurch, 1548), sigs B3v, B4v-B5r, B6r, B7v-B8r.

[3] T.S. Eliot, 'The Metaphyscial Poets', *Times Literary Supplement*, 20 October 1921: 669–70.

received of God, will extend – and, *in summa*, a firm intent and purpose to do all that is good, and leave all that is evil.[4]

Doctrine, rightly taught, would birth desire, but desire would enable that doctrine to be embraced and lived out in behaviour. For Cranmer, the key to increasing the spiritual vitality of the newly independent Church of England lay in transforming the affections of the English people through Protestant teaching.

Medieval English Affective Tradition

Thomas More may have mocked this 'felyng fayth' of the English Gospellers as a German import foreign to the faith and faithfulness of the English church.[5] However, the cultivation of the affections had long been deeply rooted in medieval English spirituality. As Jean Leclercq has movingly described, the pursuit of God was 'the basis for the whole program of monastic life'.[6] The culture of the cloister sought to form *athletae dei*. Consequently, like any highly motivated sportsperson, a monk was to find the power for a life of self-denial by focusing on his intense desire to gain the prize set before him. Of course, in the case of these spiritual athletes, the laurel-wreath was their souls' joyous union with God, proleptically in this life, fully in the age to come. At once deeply personal and highly affective, an on-going desire for the heavenly life was considered essential in the cloister. To foster it, monastic culture turned to the Scriptures.

However, they did not do so in a scholastic manner. Leclercq helpful distinguishes between the schoolmen's use of the Bible as 'a source of knowledge, of scientific information' aimed at the whole community whereas for monasticism Scripture was 'a means of salvation'. Every word was considered a saving gift directly from God, to be appropriated by each individual soul. Consequently, Leclercq can speak of 'a book which the finger of God writes in the heart of each monk'. If scholastic commentaries were 'addressed to the intelligence', the monastic expositions were 'addressed to the whole being', seeking 'to touch the

---

[4] J.E. Cox, ed. *Miscellaneous Writings of Thomas Cranmer* (Cambridge: Parker Society, 1846): 86.

[5] Thomas More, *The Confutation of Tyndale's Answer*, ed. by Louis A. Schuster et al., *The Complete Works of St. Thomas More* (New Haven: Yale University of Press, 1973) Vol. 8, Part II: 926.

[6] For what follows, see Jean LeClercq, *The Love of Learning and the Desire for God*, trans. Catharine Misrahi (London: SPCK, 1978), especially 90, 100, 107, 316.

heart rather than to instruct the mind'. Instead of the *sic et non* method of the schools, the cloister relied on biblical contemplation to move the heart.

Because of this emphasis on feeding the soul, the monastic approach to Scripture was sometimes referred to as *ruminatio*, spiritual mastication – an image used by Augustine.[7] The reader was encouraged to draw out as much divine nutrition as possible by dwelling on the specifics of a particular passage, chewing each sentence, bit by bit, slowly, rhythmically, repeatedly, often murmuring the words aloud as they were read. In the process, he was to assess the full weight of each individual word's contribution to the passage before him and then follow the verbal links from this passage to other places in Holy Writ so that Scripture could interpret Scripture. In the end, the reader was to ponder all the implications from both the literal meaning of the text and its spiritual associations with the rest of Christian teaching in the Bible. By such prolonged contemplation, not only would the words of Scripture be engraved on the reader's heart, but its truths would move him to long even more for union with heavenly things.

We can see the word-specific, rhythmic recitation as well as the saving, sensuously affective appropriation so characteristic of monastic contemplation in two famous medieval meditations on the name of Jesus.[8] Anselm, onetime abbot of the Benedictine monastery at Bec and then Archbishop of Canterbury, shows in his meditation why one commenter describes him as the apex of the 'Norman affective revival':[9]

> Jesus, Jesus, for the sake of your name, make me in accordance with your name. Jesus, Jesus, forget the proud one who provokes you, look instead on the wretched one who invokes you. Sweet name, delectable name, the name that comforts sinners and the name of blessed hope. For what is "Jesus" if not "Savior"?[10]

Similarly, St Bernard, Abbot of the Cistercian monastery at Clairvaux and the leading churchman of his era, was known for his use of sensuous language

[7] See, e.g., Augustine, *Enarrationes in Psalmos*, 36.3.5; cf. John A. Alford, 'Rolle's *English Psalter* and *Lectio Divina*', *Bulletin of the John Rylands Library* 77 (1995), 47–60, at p. 47.

[8] For the twelfth-century monastic affective revival, see Brian Patrick McGuire, '*C.* 1080-1215: Culture and History', in *The Cambridge Companion to Medieval English Mysticism*, eds Samuel Fanous and Vincent Gillespie (Cambridge: CUP, 2011): 29–47. For the devotion to the Holy Name, see Catherine A. Carsley, 'Devotion to the Holy Name: Late Medieval Piety in England', *Princeton University Library Chronicle* 53 (1992): 157–72.

[9] McGuire, *Cambridge Companion to Medieval English Mysticism*: 33.

[10] Carsley, 'Holy Name': 160.

'to confront his monks with a Jesus who embraces us'.[11] Over the course of 18 years, he wrote 86 sermons on the Canticles – the most frequently expounded monastic text precisely because of its highly affective language – although he got no further in the text than the beginning of the third chapter, due to his habit of following verbal links to further passages throughout the whole Scriptures.[12] Commenting on 'your Name is oil poured out' from Canticles 1:2, Bernard invokes a variety of human senses to enable his hearers to taste these words with the *palatum cordis* (palate of the heart).

> All the food of the soul is dry if not soaked with that oil; it is tasteless, if not seasoned with that salt. If you write, it has no savor for me unless I read Jesus there. If you argue or converse, it has no savor for me unless Jesus resonates there. Jesus is honey in the mouth, music to the ear, rejoicing in the heart.[13]

If the highly affective language of the English Reformers can be traced back to a monastic renaissance over four centuries earlier, the person most responsible for passing it on to them was the fourteenth-century mystic and writer, Richard Rolle (d. 1349).[14] A self-styled hermit, Rolle abandoned university studies quite quickly, preferring to devote his study of Scripture towards the stirring up of love for God in his heart and mind. According to his masterpiece the *Fire of Love*, by searching the Scriptures Rolle came to learn and deeply internalise what he considered to be the three highest stages of Christian love: heat, sweetness and song.[15] Rolle was quite clear that loving Scripture was the prerequisite for enjoying these experiences. For love for God's Word meant dwelling on it; resting in it; having it always on one's lips and in one's heart.[16] Such contemplation

---

[11] Fanous and Gillespie, *Medieval English Mysticism*: 39.

[12] Leclercq, *Love of Learning*: 106–9.

[13] Carsley, 'Holy Name': 160.

[14] For a brief introduction to his life, see Rosamund S. Allen (ed.), *Richard Rolle: The English Writings* (New York: Paulist Press, 1988): 9–32.

[15] 'Porro, ut potui in scripturis perscrutari, inveni et cognoui quidem quod summus amor Christi in tribus consistit: in *feruore*, in *canore*, et in *dulcore*', Margaret Deanesly (ed.), *The Incendium Amoris of Richard Rolle of Hampole* (Manchester: Manchester University Press, 1915): 184–5.

[16] 'Sed nunc multi sunt qui cito reiciunt verbum Dei ab ore suo et a corde, non sinentes illud ibi quiescere in se, et ideo non succenduntur calore consolacionis, sed frigidi remanent in torpore et negligencia ... Ideo enim accensus est, quia dilexit verbum tuum Domine: scilicet, meditari, et secundum illud operari.' Ibid: 203–4.

brought a 'sweetness' to the Christian's thoughts[17] and proved a great spiritual weapon with which to turn back the temptations of the Devil.[18] Those who devoted themselves to Scripture in this unceasing *lectio divina* manner would experience love's three-fold effect: 'spreading', 'knitting' and 'turning'.

> In *spreading* truly: for it spreads the beams of its goodness not only to friends and neighbours, but also to enemies and strangers. In *knitting* truly: for it makes lovers one in deed and will; and Christ and every holy soul it makes one. He truly that draws to God is one spirit, not in nature but in grace, and in onehood of will. Love has also a *turning* strength, for it turns the loving into the loved, and ingrafts him. Wherefore the heart that truly receives the fire of the Holy Ghost is burned all wholly and turns as it were into fire; and it leads it into that form that is likest to God.[19]

Naturally, Rolle described the resultant intimacy with God in the most sensuous terms.

> But no marvel that the shining soul ... is wont to have his heart's capacity fulfilled with plenteousness of sweetness; so that in this flesh made merry, as it were with angels' life, they are gladdened with songful mirth ... tasting sweetness and feeling burning he nearly dies for the greatness of love. And therefore he is fastened in the [embrace], as it were bodily, of endless love.[20]

---

[17] 'Unde et cogitaciones eorum mellite sunt in suo ministerio, quia eciam studendo et meditando in scripturis, ac eciam in scribendo uel dictando cogitant suum amatum, et a solito laudis organo non recedunt.' Ibid: 253.

[18] 'Confusio autem diaboli est quando omni temptacioni pretendimus verbum Dei.' Ibid: 235.

[19] M.M. Comper (ed.), *Fire of Love or Melody of Love and the Mending of Life or Rule of Living, translated by Richard Misyn* (London: Methuen, 1920): 80–81. Cf. 'Habet nempe amor uim diffusiuam, unitiuam et transformatiuam. Diffusiuam autem quia radios sue bonitatis non solum amicis et propinquis, sed eciam inimicis et extraneis diffundit. Unitatiuam vero quia amantes unum efficit in affectu et voluntate, et Christum et omnem sanctam animam unit. Qui enim adheret Deo, unus spiritus est, non natura sed gracia et idemptitate uolutatis. Transformatiuam eciam uim habet amor, quia amantem transformat in amatum et transfert in ipsum. Unde ignis Spiritus Sancti cor quod ueraciter capit totum incendit, et quasi in ignem conuertit, atque in illam formam redigit que Deo simillima est,' Deanesly, *Incendium Amoris*: 196.

[20] Comper, *Fire of Love*: 86–8; Cf. 'Ac nimirum innitentis anime ... cordis capacitas abundancia suauitatis solet repleri, ut eciam in hac carne letabunda quasi angelorum uite fungatur amenitate canora ... gustando dulcedinem et senciendo ardorem, pro amoris

However, note that he was careful not to neglect the ethical dimension, insisting that true love for God would lead to service 'not only to friends and neighbours, but also to enemies and strangers'. As part of his own duty to others, Rolle wrote the *Fire of Love* in order to 'stir up all people to love'.[21] In short, in the apt words of Nicholas Watson, Rolle's work was 'an exercise in affective evangelism'.[22]

Dedicated to cultivating love in his readers rather than empty scholastic learning,[23] Rolle was without doubt the most popular English devotional writer of the fifteenth century, if the sheer abundance of surviving manuscripts is any indication – over 450 with at least 70 found on the continent.[24] He was no less represented in *incunabula*. Not surprisingly, then, one of the earliest books printed in Oxford was Rolle's *Commentary on Job* in 1483.[25] Written in Latin for men and in English for women, Rolle's prodigious output in both languages helped provide literature for the 'mixed-life' tradition of the fifteenth-century. As typified by such grand ladies as Cecily, Duchess of York, and Lady Margaret Beaufort, King Henry VII's mother, this movement encouraged pious lay people to fulfil their secular responsibilities while maintaining a comprehensive devotional routine as well.[26]

Equally convinced that scholastic theology had failed to inspire the hearts of people to love God and do good, the Dutch humanist Erasmus also emphasised an affective reading of Scripture.[27] He urged theologians to study the Word of God so as to be moved by what they read: 'This is your first and only goal; perform this vow, this one thing: that you be changed, that you be seized, that

---

magnitudine multociens pene moriatur. Unde et in corporeis amplexibus eterni amoris quasi iugiter figitur,' Deanesly, *Incendium Amoris*: 200–201.

[21] '[H]ic uniuersos excito ad amorem.' Ibid: 147.

[22] Nicholas Watson, *Richard Rolle and the Invention of Authority* (Cambridge: Cambridge University Press, 1991): 123.

[23] 'Istum ergo librum offero intuendum, non philosophis, non mundi sapientibus, non magnis theologicis infinitis quescionibus implicatis, sed rudibus et indoctis, magis Deum diligere quam multa scire conantibus,' Deanesly, *Incendium Amoris*: 147.

[24] Wolfgang Riehle, *Englische Mystik des Mittelalters* (Munich: C.H. Beck, 2011): 117–18. Cf. Watson, *Rolle and Authority*: 31.

[25] Richard Rolle, *Explanationes notabiles deuotissimi viri Ricardi Hampole heremite super lectiones illas beati Iob* (Oxford: Theodoric Rood, 1483).

[26] See Hilary M. Carey, 'Devout Literate Laypeople and the Pursuit of the Mixed Life in Later Medieval England', *Journal of Religious History*, 14 (1987): 361–81.

[27] See J. Laurel Carrington, 'Desiderius Erasmus (1469–1536)', in Carter Lindberg (ed.), *The Reformation Theologians* (Oxford, 2002): 34–48; Erika Rummel, 'The Theology of Erasmus', in David Bagchi and David C. Steinmetz (eds), *The Cambridge Companion to Reformation Theology* (Cambridge, 2004): 28–38.

you weep at and be transformed into those teachings which you learn'.[28] Only then could their biblical expositions 'wring out tears' in their students and 'inflame spirits to heavenly things'.[29] With the popularity of Rolle's writings having prepared the way, Erasmus' affective *philosophia Christi* naturally found a ready welcome in England, in particular, amongst the Catholic humanists associated with Lady Margaret. Their goal of using rhetorical persuasion to move people to better live out their medieval Catholic beliefs deeply influenced theological education at Cambridge. Lady Margaret founded Christ's College. John Fisher, her confessor, was Chancellor of the University for almost 34 years and founded St John's College and two of her former servants helped found Jesus College, Cranmer's alma mater.

Although Lady Margaret had intended her support for Erasmian Humanism to inspire the English people to renew their commitment to medieval faith and morality, for some its emphasis on moving the affections became the bridge that led them to cross over to a Protestant reading of Scripture. According to Bilney, Katherine and Cranmer, only the assured free pardon associated with justification by faith brought about that 'sweetness' and 'love' in their hearts that Erasmus and the English affective tradition had stressed as the hallmark of authentic Christianity. Seen in this light, their adoption of solifidianism was not so much a repudiation of their late medieval piety, but its true affective fulfillment. They found the power to love God from the bottom of their hearts, only when they had already come to believe that he loved them enough to assure them of salvation by faith. In their view, they became 'Protestant' in order at last to be truly Catholic.

The Renewal Message of the Edwardian Regime

Not until the accession of Edward VI in 1547 did Thomas Cranmer have the freedom to implement an affective Protestant programme to promote national spiritual renewal. As a government-led, top-down movement, the first step was

[28] 'Hic primus et unicus tibi sit scopus, hoc votum, hoc unum age, ut muteris, ut rapiaris, ut affleris, ut transformeris in ea quae discis,' Erasmus, *Opera omnia Desiderii Erasmi Roterodami* (ed.), J. Leclerc (Leiden, 1703–6), V: col. 77B; Marjorie O'Rourke Boyle, *Erasmus on Language and Method in Theology* (Toronto, 1977): 73.

[29] 'At praecipuus Theologorum scopus est, sapienter enarrare Divinas litteras: de fide, non de frivolis questionibus rationem reddere: de pietate graviter atque efficaciter disserere: lacrymas excutere, ad coelestia inflammare animos,' Erasmus, *Opera omnia*, cols 83F-84A; O'Rourke Boyle, *Erasmus on Language*: 73.

officially endorsing and promoting the true nature of the Gospel, i.e., salvation by grace alone through faith alone from Scripture alone. Hence, the regime's first new ecclesiastical formulary was *Certayne Sermons or Homelies,* published barely six months into the new reign on 31 July 1547.[30] Popularly known as the *Book of Homilies*, this collection of 12 sermons in English was designed to be both a manifesto of the regime's theological agenda and the means of its revolutionary implementation. The formulary established an official epitome of scriptural teaching on the way of salvation which publicly established the regime's doctrinal plumb line. As required reading in parish churches *in seriatim* every Sunday, in repetition throughout the year, the sermons were also intended to harness the persuasive power of the local pulpit to convert the hearts of the English people to embrace the new religious orientation. So important was hearing these homilies to the regime's plans for societal reformation, that the Second Act of Uniformity (1552) made church attendance compulsory.[31]

As an affective theologian, at the heart of Cranmer's preaching programme was rumination on the true Word of God in order to cultivate a right desire for God. The very first homily was on Scripture which established biblical knowledge as the foundation of every Christian's relationship with God. Scripture was God's chosen medium to tell human beings the truth about the world around them and the struggles within them: 'In these bokes we may learne to know our selfes, how vile and miserable we be, and also to know God, how good he is of hymself and how he communicateth his goodnes unto us and to al creatures.'[32] Equally important, however, the Bible was also the means through which God worked supernaturally to turn people's hearts to himself and the doing of his will: '[The words of Holy Scripture] have power to converte [our souls] through Gods promise, and thei be effectual through Gods assistence'. On the one hand, this divine working brought about inner joy. As 'a constant and a perpetuall instrument of salvacion', the Bible 'comforteth, maketh glad, chereth and cherisheth our consciences'; 'it is more sweter then hony or hony combe'.[33] On the other, those who devoted themselves to 'continual readyng and meditacion of God's Woorde' would discover that 'the great affeccion to the

[30] See Ashley Null, 'Official Tudor Homilies', in *Oxford Handbook of the Early Modern Sermon* (eds), Peter McCullough, Hugh Adlington and Emma Rhatigan (Oxford: Oxford University Press, 2011): 348–65, at 352–7.

[31] J.R. Tanner, *Tudor Constitutional Documents, A.D. 1485–1603* (Cambridge: Cambridge University Press, 1922): 117–18.

[32] Ronald B. Bond, *Certain Sermons or Homilies (1547) and A Homily against Disobedience and Wilful Rebellion (1570)* (Toronto: University of Toronto Press, 1987): 62.

[33] Ibid: 62.

transitory thynges of this worlde shal be minished in hym, and the greate desire of heavenly thynges that bee therein promised of God shall increase in hym'. Because of God's supernatural agency 'that thyng whiche by perpetuall use of reading of Holy Scripture and diligent searchyng of the same is deply printed and graven in the harte at length turneth almoste into nature'.[34] Hence, 'the hearing and kepyng of [Scripture] maketh us blessed, sanctifieth us and maketh us holy'. Little wonder, then, that the 'Homily on Scripture' urged that '[t]hese bokes, therefore, ought to be much in our handes, in our eyes, in our eares, in oure mouthes, but moste of all, in our hartes'.[35] The homily concluded with a final exhortation drawn directly from the monastic world:

> Lette us night and daie muse, and have meditacion and contemplacion in theim. Lette us ruminate and, as it wer, chewe the cudde, that we maie have the swete jeuse, spirituall effecte, mary, hony, kirnell, tast, comfort and consolacion of theim.[36]

Thus, combining elements of monasticism, humanism and Protestantism, here is Cranmer's source for growth in a church's spiritual vitality. Because of Scripture's power to draw fallen humanity toward godly desires, he believed that the promises of the Bible were the divine vehicle through which God's love drew his children to love him in return. Through their rumination on the words of Scripture the Holy Spirit supernaturally entered and transformed human hearts, whether through preaching, receiving the sacraments, public prayer or private devotion.[37]

Having established Scripture as the key to nurturing spiritual renewal, Cranmer turned to the major doctrinal issue which he believed fostered the reorientation of the affections, namely, justification by faith. In Lutheran fashion, the next two sermons preached Law and Gospel respectively. 'The Misery of All Mankind' described the depth of human sinfulness and humanity's inability to save themselves.[38] The 'Homily on Salvation' presented the benefits of Christ and made plain they were received by faith.[39] However, Cranmer was very careful to clarify that justifying faith was more than just intellectual

[34] Ibid: 63.

[35] Ibid: 62.

[36] Ibid: 67.

[37] J.E. Cox, *Writings and Disputations of Thomas Cranmer relative to the Sacrament of the Lord's Supper* (Cambridge: Parker Society, 1844): 70–71.

[38] Bond, *Certain Sermons*: 70–78.

[39] Ibid: 79–90.

assent to dogmatic statements. Since demons also believed the principal truths of Christianity, 'right and true Christian faith' was not only agreement with Scripture but also 'a sure trust and confidence in Gods mercifull promises to be saved from everlastynge dampnacion by Christe'. From this assurance did 'folowe a lovyng harte to obey his commaundementes'. Hence, justifiying faith was always a 'lively', or living, faith, that is, a faith which showed itself by good works.[40] For Cranmer, only the assurance made possible by solifidianism birthed in human hearts this love which brought about personal fulfilment and moral transformation. According to the homily, when the benefits of God's merciful grace were considered, unless they were 'desperate persones' with 'hartes harder than stones', people would be moved by a desire to give themselves wholly unto God and the service of their neighbours.[41] Clearly, Cranmer's writing was also 'an exercise in affective evangelism'.

Incarnating the Message in the Culture

Having established the authority of the Protestant message and made hearing it compulsory, the next stage was to begin to change the religious rhythms of the nation so as to incarnate the new doctrines within the contemporary culture. As an Erasmian humanist, Cranmer believed every presentation of a message had to be tailored to the needs of its specific audience. How else could the audience be drawn to embrace the message, unless the manner of the presentation took into account what would move that society? As a Protestant reformer, however, Cranmer believed that worship was not a work of the people to move God to draw closer to them, but rather the means by which God would move the people to draw closer to him. Hence, Cranmer wanted a liturgy that promoted the alluring power of the Gospel in a culturally relevant manner. The Latin Mass had to be replaced by a reformed English liturgy, and the worship space of churches adapted to foster the new sensibilities.[42]

In due course came the banning of parochial processions and all but one light on the high altar (1547); then images, ashes, palms, creeping to the cross as well as the elevation of the host (1548); next, stone altars (1550); and, finally, vestments, except for a surplice (1552). In their place came Scripture verses written on whitewashed walls, an English liturgy exhorting lay reception of

[40] Ibid: 86.

[41] Ibid: 87.

[42] For the history of 'purifying the realm' and then 'building the temple' under Edward VI, see Diarmaid MacCulloch, *Tudor Church Militant* (London: Allen Lane, 1999).

the Sacrament on a regular basis appended to the Latin Mass (1548); a full set of English liturgical services in the *Book of Common Prayer* which restored systematic reading of Scripture and removed any mention of both personal merit and the mass as a propitiatory sacrifice (1549); wooden tables for Communion as well as an English ordinal (1550); and, finally, a second, more clearly reformed prayer book whose words of administration made plain that Christ's eucharistic presence was spiritual in nature, a holy communion in the heart of the believer through personal faith (1552). Nothing conveyed the depth of religious change more than banning the adoration of the Sacrament and instead encouraging lay communicants to gather around a wooden table for the reception of both bread and wine. Thus, by 1552, both verbally and visually, the medieval sacrifice had been fully superseded by a community fellowship meal. Little wonder then that, looking back on this period as a Marian exile, Richard Morrison wrote, 'The greater change was never wroughte in so short space in any countreye sith the world was'.[43]

Once again, at the heart of all these changes was the alluring power of Scripture. Firstly, going even further than the fifteenth-century mixed-life movement of the elite, Cranmer made the traditional monastic rumination on Scripture the norm for every English parish. Influenced by Basil's example of encouraging workers to attend Bible expositions at daily morning and evening church services,[44] Cranmer adapted the seven offices of the monastic daily routine into two services of Morning Prayer and Evening Prayer. A new lectionary was appointed for these daily offices which read through most of the Bible in one year. The Psalter was read through monthly. As the first lesson, the remainder of the Old Testament was read over 10 months, 'except for books and chapters, which be least edifying'. For the other two months readings came from the Apocrypha. As the second lesson, the New Testament was read three times a year, except for Revelation, which was used sparingly for certain proper feasts.[45] By fitting his Word-based services around the average person's work day, Cranmer was consciously trying to restructure the rhythms of normal daily English life to follow the heartbeat of monastic spirituality.

---

[43] John Gough Nichols (ed.), *Literary Remains of Edward VI* (London: J.B. Nichols and Sons, 1857): ccxxxiv.

[44] 'Horatur opifices ut cotidie sacris adsint contionibus,' Cranmer's annotation in his copy of D. Erasmus (ed.), *En amice lector thesaurum damus D. Basilium sua lingua loquentem.* (Basel: H. Froben, 1532): 18, now held in the John Rylands Library, Manchester University, Catalogue Number 18173.

[45] Joseph Ketley (ed.), *The Two Liturgies, A.D. 1549, and A.D. 1552* (Cambridge: Parker Society, 1844): 200–212.

Secondly, the language Cranmer used in composing the prayers was itself an exercise in squeezing out the 'sweet juice, spiritual effect, marrow, honey, kernel, taste, comfort and consolation' from Scripture. On the one hand, humanist writers were encouraged to be like a bee making honey 'from flowers of all the sweetest and best scents and savors which are tasted and distinguishable in the honey itself'.[46] Not surprisingly, then, it is a commonplace of Anglican liturgical studies that Cranmer's prayers stitched together countless borrowings from the whole treasury of the Bible. Indeed, what one commentary said of Rolle, applies equally to Cranmer: 'the full extent of his enormous debt to Scripture has escaped most readers simply because he was able to adapt the language of Scripture so perfectly and naturally to his own expression'.[47] On the other hand, Cranmer's luxurious prose habitually heaped up linguistic doublets: 'erred and strayed', 'devices and desires', 'acknowledge and bewail', 'sins and wickedness', 'wrath and indignation', 'do earnestly repent and be heartily sorry'; not to mention his extravagant piling on of synonyms like 'succour, help and comfort, all that be in danger, necessity, and tribulation' or 'a full, perfect and sufficient sacrifice, oblation, and satisfaction'.[48] Yet, Rowan Williams was spot on to notice something far more at work here than merely seeking an eloquence of excess through repetition and rhythm. Rather, 'a liturgical language like Cranmer's hovers over meanings like a bird that never quite nests for good – or, to sharpen the image, like a bird of prey that never stoops for a kill'.[49] Or, to sharpen the animal imagery even further, it is like a cow chewing its cud. The sheer abundance of his words is literally a mouth full, preventing readers from too quickly passing through prayer, presenting them with the opportunity to consider more fully the implications of each phrase, providing the Holy Spirit more time to write its truth on their hearts. Once the full extent of Cranmer's promotion of an affective reading of the Bible is realised, his support for the destruction of the monasteries may be seen not so much as a rejection of monastic spirituality as a determination to democratise its greatest treasure. Cranmer wanted scriptural

---

[46] Richard Fox, 'Statutes of Corpus Christi College, Oxford', in Elizabeth M. Nugent (ed.), *The Thought and Culture of the English Renaissance: An Anthology of Tudor Prose 1481–1555* (Cambridge: Cambridge University Press, 1956): 32.

[47] Alford, *Rolle's English Psalter*: 8.

[48] For the use of these phrases in the 1552 Prayer Book, see Ketley, *Liturgies of Edward VI*: 218–19, 234, 276, 279.

[49] Rowan Williams, 'The Martyrdom of Thomas Cranmer – Sermon at Service to Commemorate the 450th Anniversary', available at http://www.archbishopofcanterbury.org/articles.php/1599/the-martyrdom-of-thomas-cranmer-sermon-at-service-to-commemorate-the-450th-anniversary accessed 14 February 2015.

rumination to be the rhythmic daily norm for every English person, not just a special, holier, privileged few.

Protestant Procrustean Biblicism

Of course, although massive in themselves, not all Protestant reformers thought Cranmer's changes had gone far enough. Even with the advent of the 1552 *Book of Common Prayer*, John Knox, in particular, still pushed the King and Council for more. As a royal chaplain, he strenuously opposed Cranmer on the retention of kneeling for receiving Holy Communion, something which Knox considered an unscriptural papist tradition implying adoration. He demanded that communicants sit instead.[50] Cranmer maintained his position already outlined in the essay 'Of Ceremonies: Why some be abolished and some retained' which was first published as part of the 1549 *Book of Common Prayer*. Ceremonies should not 'be esteemed equal with God's law', hence, 'the keeping or omitting of a ceremony (in itself considered) is but a small thing: yet the wilful and contemptuous transgression and breaking of a common order and discipline is no small offence before God'.[51] Cranmer utterly rejected Knox's argument: 'Whatsoever is not commanded in the scripture, is against the scripture and utterly unlawful and ungodly ... This saying is a subversion of all order as well in religion as in common policy.'[52]

At the heart of this disagreement over liturgical practice lay a profound difference in understanding of the purpose of the Bible. The technical terms for the dispute are the *regulative* use versus the *normative* use of Scripture. For Knox and his followers, everything a person did in every aspect of life had to have a clear biblical command or rule. Otherwise, it didn't proceed from faith and, thus, was sin (Romans 14:23). And what was true of individuals was, of course, especially true for the church. Cranmer, however, made a decisive distinction between unalterable saving truth, divinely revealed in Jesus Christ and faithfully recorded in Scripture alone, and changing human traditions of the church by which the divinely established gospel message was expressed and conveyed to successive generations of Christians. The essentials of salvation, that is, matters of faith and morals, had to be founded on divine authority and, therefore, on the Word of God alone – nothing in addition to it and nothing contrary to it. Rites

[50] See Dairmaid MacCulloch, *Thomas Cranmer: A Life* (New Haven: Yale University Press, 1996): 525–9.

[51] Ketley, *Liturgies of Edward VI*: 197.

[52] MacCulloch, *Cranmer*: 526.

and ceremonies, however, as particular expressions of the Gospel for different eras and cultures, were derived from the institutional authority of the church. They must merely not contradict Scripture. The church could use or adapt other sources, like ancient traditions such as monasticism, or it could institute new liturgies more in keeping with contemporary needs, even if such practices were not explicitly detailed in Scripture. Cranmer's distinction lies behind that famous Anglican dictum 'Holy Scripture contains all things necessary for salvation': the Bible contains all things necessary for salvation (regulative on doctrine), but not a blueprint for everything in life (normative on everything else).

In essence, Knox believed that the only truly authentic human culture was found within the pages of Scripture which the church was called to manifest in the world. For Cranmer, ever the humanist, such thinking simply attempted to sacrifice the creative diversity and historic development of human cultures on a Procrustean bed of false biblical authority. He considered the Gospel message to be godly leaven, able to transform the unique culture of every nation. In the end, Cranmer won the argument with the Council by the donnish quip that if Knox really wanted the Church of England to receive Communion in the biblical manner, they would need to lie down on the ground in the chancel rather than sit at a table. While seeming perhaps merely a witty retort *ad absurdum*, Cranmer was actually pointing out that there was no such thing as only one 'biblical' way to eat food. The manner of one's eating was a thing indifferent, determined by one's culture. The famous dispute between Knox and Richard Cox in Frankfurt during the Marian Exile conveniently summarises the difference in the Knoxian and Cranmerian approach to church and culture. Cox insisted on using Cranmer's liturgy so as to 'haue the face off an English churche' in exile. Knox, however, wanted a purer worship service which would have 'the face of Christ's church'.[53]

In the end, Cranmer won the main point that kneeling to receive Communion was retained, and Knox had to be content with the 'Black Rubric' and its specific denial of a papist interpretation of the practice. The following year Cranmer sealed his victory by including his understanding of ceremonies in Article 33 of the official English statement of doctrine, The Forty-Two Articles:

---

[53] *A Brief Discourse of the Troubles Begun at Frankfort* (London: John Petheram, 1846): 37–59, especially 38, 49 and 59. The authorship of this work is disputed – see Patrick Collinson, 'The Authorship of *A Brieff Discours off the Troubles Begonne at Franckford*', *Journal of Ecclesiastical History* 9 (1958): 188–208; David Laing (ed.), *The Works of John Knox* (Edinburgh: Bannatyne Club, 1855), IV: 41–9, 55–7.

> It is not necessarie that tradicions and ceremonies bee in all places one, or vtterlie like. For at al times thei haue been diuers, and maie bee chaunged, according to the diuersitie of countries, and mennes maners, so that nothing bee ordeined against goddes worde.[54]

No doubt Cranmer was concerned that Knox's approach would not only lead to Christians looking at Scripture primarily as a book of rules – something which was anathema to Cranmer's promotion of affective biblical reading – but also eventually render the church and ever-evolving human culture deaf to one another.

Cranmer's Comfortable Words

Since cultural contexualisation of liturgy was as important to Cranmer as scriptural rumination in promoting the vitality of the church's mission, it would be fitting to conclude by turning to a prime example of their interaction – the Comfortable Words. These four verses form a Gospel commonplace which at once addresses the immediate pastoral needs of Cranmer's generation and provides an extended opportunity for the Word of God to draw human hearts heavenward. For Cranmer, the greatest spiritual need of the English people was to see Jesus as their saviour, not their judge, for only divine gracious love would inspire grateful human love. Yet, what was the ubiquitous image that visually dominated most medieval parish churches from the chancel arch? Jesus as the Lord of Doom. Of course, the rest of the church's interior would only have reinforced that message. Admitting that late medieval piety had 'a moralistic strain, which could be oppressive', Eamon Duffy comments:

> Churches contained not only the chancel-arch representation of the Day of Doom, with its threat of terrifying reckoning down to the last farthing, but wall-paintings and windows illustrating the deadly sins, the works of mercy, the Commandments, Christ wounded by sabbath-breaking, the figures of the three living and the three dead, or the related *danse macabre*.[55]

---

[54] Charles Hardwick, *A History of the Articles of Religion* (Cambridge: Deighton, Bell, 1859): 318.

[55] Eamon Duffy, *Stripping of the Altars: Traditional Religion in England 1400–1580* (New Haven: Yale University Press, 1992): 187.

With such visions of exacting retribution for each human frailty, the 'whole machinery of late medieval piety was designed to shield the soul from Christ's doomsday anger'.[56] Cranmer's scriptural response was to construct the Comfortable Words. Here is the Gospel according to Reformation Anglicanism.[57]

Come unto me, all that travail and be heavy laden, and I shall refresh you. Cranmer does not begin with sin, law, judgment or hell. He begins with the human condition, with humanity's perception of their need, their longing for relief from the wounds and weariness that human existence brings to all, in short, their longing for release and rescue.

So God loved the world, that he gave his only begotten Son, to the end that all that believe in him should not perish, but have life everlasting. Cranmer still does not yet mention sin, law, judgment or hell. Instead, having used Jesus' own words to acknowledge the depth of human longing for good news, Cranmer turns again to Jesus to establish the depth of God's own longing to respond. Moved by the love which is his very being, God the Father sent God the Son into this world to become the visible embodiment of the divine Good Shepherd. Jesus came to seek out the lost, gently freeing lambs caught in the thicket of sin. He laid down his own life so that, in the end, he could bear his wandering creatures safely back to the flock on his own wounded shoulders. In the face of such love, how could the sin-sodden hearts of the English people not find themselves drawn by their own inner longings back to their Creator?

Hear also what saint Paul sayeth. This is a true saying, and worthy of all men to be received, that Jesus Christ came into the world to save sinners. Having laid out the two sides – the longing of humanity for relief and the longing of God to rescue – Cranmer circles back to the human condition, but now at a higher level. On the one hand, humanity's situation is no longer described in subjective terms of felt needs but rather as the objective consequence of violating divine law. Humanity suffers from spiritual fatigue because that is merely the most readily apparent fruit of human sinfulness. As rebels against divine order, they are cut off from God's peace now and stand under the threat of the divine wrath to come. Humanity's refreshment can only come by addressing humanity's sin. On the other hand, to do so is also clearly beyond human beings. Having been so weakened by sin's power, humanity cannot co-operate with grace to achieve their salvation. According to Cranmer, that would be the 'ready way unto desperation'.[58] I Tim. 1:15 makes plain that here is the reason Jesus came into

[56] Ibid: 309.

[57] Ketley, *Liturgies of Edward VI*: 276.

[58] Cox, *Cranmer's Miscellaneous Writings*: 94.

this world. It is Christ's mission to save sinners, not theirs. Only upon realising this distinction would the English people find release and refreshment from their spiritual fatigue.

Hear also what Saint John sayeth. If any man sin, we have an advocate with the Father, Jesus Christ the righteous, and he is the propitiation for our sins. With I John 2:1–2 Cranmer has now come full circle. In I Tim. 1:15, the Gospel truth about the human condition was seen from the human point of view, i.e., 'How can I be saved?' Now Cranmer turns to the Gospel truth about the human condition from God's perspective, i.e., 'How can God be true to both his righteous nature and his enduring love for an unrighteous humanity?' The fourth Comfortable Word concisely states that problem from heaven's point-of-view. God's justice requires 'propitiation', i.e., the fulfilling of his determination to destroy sin because of all the hurt and harm it causes. That's why the only answer to human misery is utter divine graciousness, God's taking humanity's sin upon himself, so he can destroy sin on the cross without having to destroy humanity as well. Because Christ has made the sacrifice which has removed God's wrath from humanity, he now is our advocate. Jesus himself is the one who stands by our side. He is the one who answers for us when we are accused of being sinners. In short, Scripture makes clear that Jesus is not our judge. Rather, his unmerited love is our salvation.

Like Erasmus,[59] Luther[60] and Katherine Parr,[61] Cranmer's favourite word for evangelism was 'allurement'. When a member of his circle chided him about his notorious lenience towards those who had wronged him personally, he responded:

---

[59] 'The son of man came forth minding to stir up this nation to the love of the heavenly doctrine ... that he might allure them the more with his gentleness,' Erasmus, *The First Volume of the Paraphrase of Erasmus upon the New Testament* (London: Edward Whitchurch, 1548): fols. 38r, 68v.

[60] 'How very kindly and lovingly does the Lord allure all hearts to himself, and in this way he stirs them to believe in him,' Martin Luther, *D. Martin Luthers Werke: Kritische Gesammtausgabe* (eds), J.K.F. Knaake, G. Kawerau, et al. (Weimar: Hermann Bohlaus Nachfolger, 1883–), 8: 359, 5-6. Cf. 'Thus, when the shepherd finds the lost sheep again, he has no intention of pushing it away in anger once more or throwing it to a hungry wolf. Rather, all his care and concern is directed to alluring it with every possible kindness. Treating it with the utmost tenderness, he takes the lamb upon his own back, lifting it up and carrying it, until he brings the animal all the way home again.' Ibid: 36, 290, 38–291, 17.

[61] 'Cum to me al ye that labour, and are burdened, and I shal refresh you: what gentle, merciful, and comfortable woordes are these to all sinners? ... What a most gracious comfortable, and gentle, saying was this, with suche plesant and swete wordes, to allure his enemies to cum unto him?' Katherine Parr, *The Lamentation of a Sinner* (London: Edward Whitchurch, 1548), sig. B3v.

> What will ye have a man do to hym that ys not yet come to knowledge of the trueth of the gospell ... ? Shall we perhapps, in his jorney comyng towards us, by severitie and cruell behaviour overthrowe hym, and as it were in his viage stoppe hym? I take not this the wey to alleure men to enbrace the doctrine of the gospell. And if it be a true rule of our Saviour Christe to do good for evill, than lett suche as are not yet come to favour our religion lerne to folowe the doctrine of the gospell by our example in using them frendlie and charitable.[62]

Clearly, Cranmer thought that the inherent drawing power of divine free forgiveness was the root of all evangelism. Consequently, in his revisions for the 1552 *Book of Common Prayer*, he decided to insert the Comfortable Words immediately before the *Sursum corda*. Thus, he put his twin means of moving human affections heavenward – scriptural rumination and cultural contextualisation – at the very heart of Tudor worship. The mission, vitality and expansion of the church today would be well served by doing likewise for own time.

[62] John Gough Nichols (ed.), *Narratives of the Days of the Reformation* (London: Camden Society, First Series, 77, 1859): 246–7.

Chapter 12

New Affections: Church Growth in Britain, 1750–1970

Dominic Erdozain

Scholarship on the decline and revival of Christianity has always been a moral affair – a taking of sides. It has been common to divide the field between 'optimists' and 'pessimists', with the suggestion that historians, sensitive to locality and complexity, will tend to be optimists, while sociologists and social theorists, looking at the bigger picture, will tend to be pessimists.[1] Historians dig out encouraging vignettes; social theorists step back and announce the dismal 'trend'. Social theorists sum up. Historians heckle. You might expect theologians and church leaders to take the historical side of the debate, but the pattern has been otherwise, as several scholars have noted.[2] Buying their historical analysis wholesale, at the social theory counter, they have been all-too-willing to accept the terrible judgements of figures such as Kant, Marx or Max Weber. They have often seemed to labour under a fear that the challenges of modernity are the death pangs of Christianity itself, treating the prophecies of such intellectual giants as facts. In the 1960s, a bold, integrated theory of secularisation emerged, combining theoretical and empirical analysis to assert that religion was finally dying. The end was nigh. Even though the 'secularisation thesis' was an enormous piece of guesswork, resting on the weak assumption that the world follows where Europe leads, it became a kind of orthodoxy for social theorists and acquired the status of a social fact for a number of theologians.

In his autobiography, *Steps along Hope Street*, David Sheppard explored the challenges of urban mission in an era of doubt and demoralisation. He recalled the advice that he received from his predecessor as he took over as Bishop of Woolwich in 1969: 'Bishop John Robinson said he did not think there would be any visible church in the inner-city in 10 years' time!' Meanwhile, his diocesan bishop, Mervyn Stockwood, advised him that congregations 'are likely to be

1 C. Brown, 'Did Urbanization Secularize Britain?', *Urban History*, 15.1 (1988): 1.

2 See for example Brown's discussion of 'clerical worry'. Ibid: 2.

small'. The Church had to 'face the facts'.[3] Sheppard wrote of a 'chronic collapse of confidence' in these years, a dismal certainty of diminishing returns among some of the church's highest officers, adding that, 'even if it were not true, they acted as if it were'. Reflecting on a malaise that also affected his social ministry, he wrote: 'Christians too often think "the others" are stronger, and lack the confidence to see how much we can bring about change if we stand together.'[4]

When David Watson took up his first incumbency in York in 1965 he received a visit from two members of the hardly inspiring 'Redundant Churches Uses Committee', who informed him that his church of a dozen or so regulars would not survive and that he could have a year's grace before being moved on. The writing was on the wall. Watson feared that his spluttered optimism came across as arrogance as he begged to differ.[5] A narrative of decay had become the church's operating principle. Secularisation, argues Jeffrey Cox, has always been an 'invocatory' concept, rather than a rigorously analytical term.[6] It tells you how things are and how they are going to be. It forms a backdrop to myriad discussions of religious life and identity – and a highly coercive one. In recent years we have seen 'secularisation' invoked by Pope Benedict as a broad explanation for the Catholic sex abuse scandal[7] and strongly asserted by an Anglican clergyman in the *Guardian* as the essential context for any discussion of gay rights.[8] As I write, in November 2013, a *Daily Telegraph* headline proclaims the grave warning of an ex-archbishop that the 'Church of England "will be extinct in one generation"'.[9] Time and again, the 'facts' of decline are used to steer the ship – or not, as the case may be.

---

[3] D. Sheppard, *Steps Along Hope Street: My Life in Cricket, the Church and the Inner City* (London: Hodder & Stoughton, 2002): 121.

[4] Sheppard, *Hope Street*: 140.

[5] D. Watson, *I Believe in the Church* (London: Hodder and Stoughton, 1978): 16–17.

[6] J. Cox, 'Towards Eliminating the Concept of Secularisation: A Progress Report', in C. Brown and M. Snape (eds), *Secularisation in the Christian World: Essays in Honour of Hugh McLeod* (Farnham: Ashgate, 2010).

[7] 'Full Text of the Pope's Letter to the Catholics of Ireland on Child Sex Abuse', *The Guardian*, 20 March 2010, available at http://www.guardian.co.uk/world/2010/mar/20/full-text-popes-letter-ireland accessed 12 September 2013.

[8] G. Fraser, 'The Church of England Says It Is against Gay Marriage. Not in My Name', *The Guardian*, 12 June 2012, available at http://www.guardian.co.uk/commentisfree/belief/2012/ jun/12/church-of-england-gay-marriage accessed 12 September 2013.

[9] B. Riley-Smith, 'Church of England "Will Be Extinct in One Generation", Warns Ex-Archbishop', *Telegraph.co.uk*, 18 November 2013, sec. religion, available at http://www.telegraph.co.uk/news/religion/10457520/Church-of-England-will-be-extinct-in-one-generation-warns-ex-archbishop.html accessed 12 September 2013.

What fascinates me about these examples is the power of an implicit theory to mould attitudes and define Christian behaviour. Secularisation functions as a theology of doom. People believe it. The goading analysis of 'death' and 'endgame' enters the Christian psyche. Experts with often-limited feel for the religious cultures they study are somehow allowed to set the agenda, the problem going beyond the numbing tyranny of statistics to an insidious language of disintegration and decay. Church historians have sometimes followed suit, writing of religious revival as if it were an exception to a fixed rule of decline, patronising it with terms like 'survival' or 'resilience' and perhaps forgetting that the church has never operated in conditions of optimal sympathy. The propaganda of secularisation theory, dripping with scientific authority, exerted an immense influence on scholars and practitioners alike.[10] When you read the secularisation literature of the 1960s, you instantly feel that someone is preaching to you, even gloating. Peter Berger's book of 1967, *The Sacred Canopy,* is a clear example of that, joking about Christians and Marxists huddling together to console one another about modernity not working out for them.[11] You soon discover that this is not science. But the power of a tradition is that it is handed on and not always explored. By the time sociologists like Berger were repenting of their earlier dogmatism with such penitent works as the *Desecularization of the World* (1999) much of the damage had been done. As David Martin, one of the leading exponents of secularisation theory, later reflected: sociologists were often surprised how literally their prognostications of doom were accepted and internalised by church leaders. Martin had not 'anticipated how enthusiastically the churches would collude in their own demise' – rolling over to appease the new secular culture.[12] This was not a scientific process unfolding. It was a self-fulfilling prophecy: a narrative of doom becoming a theology of panic.

The examples of Sheppard and Watson are important not only for exposing a supine theology of resignation, a modern listlessness reminiscent of what medieval theologians called 'accidie'. They also demonstrate the power of faith to interrupt the belittling narratives of modernity. Watson was trenchant in

[10] J. Cox, 'Towards Eliminating the Concept of Secularisation: A Progress Report'; J. Cox, 'Provincializing Christendom: The Case of Great Britain', *Church History: Studies in Christianity and Culture*, 75.1 (2006): 120–30; J. Cox, *The English Churches in a Secular Society: Lambeth 1870–1930* (New York: OUP, 1982).

[11] P. Berger, *The Sacred Canopy: Elements of a Sociological Theory of Religion* (New York: Anchor Books, 1990): 110.

[12] S. Bruce, 'Secularisation in the UK and the USA', in C. Brown and M. Snape (eds), *Secularisation in the Christian World: Essays in Honour of Hugh McLeod* (Farnham: Ashgate, 2010): 207.

his criticism of Christians in the media who circulated damaging caricatures of Christianity as a 'bourgeois cult', and of theologians who pass on 'academic' fashions to the church as the reality that has to be faced. Turkeys don't vote for Christmas. You are what you read. If you are willing to let your critics define your destiny, you are in the wrong business.[13] In a similar spirit, I want to present a more optimistic account of the Christian ecology of modern Britain. I will argue that modernity has been more religious in terms of both church growth and the diffusion of Christian values in the culture than traditional accounts allow. And while there has been decline, and a loss of cultural ground, I suggest, with the French historian Jean Delumeau, that there are theological benefits. In particular, I share with him the view that the Christianity that has flourished in the modern period has been characterised by qualities that were not always on show in the so-called 'confessional age'. Christianity has become 'voluntary'. It has had to court a hearing. And it has done so by re-examining its baggage in ways that have been theologically constructive.

Broadly speaking, love has eclipsed fear in the theological firmament, while a despised material world has come to be seen as more than a divine afterthought.[14] On this reading, modernity is more Christian than the deleterious cocktail of 'Manichaeism, magic and fear' that passed for pre-Enlightenment Christendom.[15] It may be that the secularisation narrative is more than merely flawed, as a large body of scholars would now admit. It may be that our entire instinctive picture of a Christian 'past' and a secular 'present' is the wrong way up. I would not go as far as Delumeau in saying that pre-modern religion was largely pagan in its cringing psychology of fear and appeasement, its rank instrumentalism, but I share his scepticism about the penetration of Christianity at the truly popular level. It may be better to think of the modern era in terms of Christianisation rather than de-Christianisation. The idea that a modern evangelism of attenuated judgment and relational sympathy can be dismissed as 'Christianity lite' must be especially resisted. This argument, as dear to some schools of theology as it is to secularisation theorists who often delight in the notion of contemporary religion as a synonym for culture,[16] exaggerates the vitality of the religious past and ignores the degree to which the soft pedalling of modern evangelism is a

---

13 Watson, *I Believe in the Church*: 15–16.

14 J. Delumeau, *Sin and Fear: The Emergence of a Western Guilt Culture, 13th–18th Centuries* (New York: St. Martin's Press, 1990); J. Delumeau, *Catholicism between Luther and Voltaire: A New View of the Counter-Reformation* (London: Burns & Oates, 1977).

15 Delumeau, *Catholicism between Luther and Voltaire*: 230–31.

16 S. Bruce, *Secularization: In Defence of an Unfashionable Theory* (Oxford: OUP, 2011).

necessary and robust response to theologies of authority and coercion. And while acquiescence in modern culture and leisure have long represented a staple of the secularisation narrative – the discovery that Christians dance is a particular favourite of sociologists eager to establish the superficiality of revival – it is important that the opposite case is made: a religious culture urging the primacy of love and the goodness of creation may be more than the pale imitation of glories past that so many commentators have suggested.[17]

The phenomenon of church decline is real but certainly not new. Rather than interpreting every statistical crisis as the final onset of secularisation, it is helpful to recognise that levels of Christian affiliation and commitment have fluctuated dramatically over time. In addition to the theological and spiritual problems attending a system of enforced orthodoxy that held good in Britain until the eighteenth century and in parts of Europe well into the twentieth, we have to recognise that our forebears were not as pious as traditional narratives suggest. This is another reason to resist the panic button. In historical terms, the modern 'crisis' may not be worthy of the name. The classic tool of secularisation theory has been what one scholar has termed 'the handy historical tripod', which places one leg in the 'Christian' middle ages, one leg in the nineteenth century and one, somewhat shorter leg in the present. The damning contrast is then objectified into a theory of inevitable and inexorable decline: the statistics can't lie. The trouble is that they do. The decline of churchgoing in the twentieth century was not the terminus of a 1,500-year Christian era. It was the waning of the Victorian Christian boom, a time of unprecedented religious vigour in public and private life. As Jeffrey Cox has written, the turn from Victorian spiritual athleticism to twentieth century couch-potato-dom was not so much secularisation as a return to eighteenth century norms. The religious census of 1851, indicating 59 church attendances for every 100 people, caught the Victorian revival at its peak. This was an exceptional period of religious vitality. Studies of the eighteenth century have shown that between 1738 and 1811 the number of Anglican communicants was consistently low – at about five per cent of the total population – and that there 'were deep-seated and long-term causes for this malaise'.[18] A famous study of popular religion in the early nineteenth

---

[17] For some comparisons between theological critiques of modern religion and secularisation theory see D. Erdozain, '"Cause Is Not Quite What It Used to Be": The Return of Secularisation', *English Historical Review* CXXVII.525 (2012): 377–400.

[18] K. Hylson-Smith, *The Churches in England from Elizabeth I to Elizabeth II.: Vol. II, 1689–1833* (London: SCM Press, 1997): 82–3.

century argued that paganism was dominant and Christianity 'recessive'.[19] The evangelical revival was, in many cases, a process of 'primary' Christianisation and, while its intensity did not last long into the twentieth century, we have to see it for what it was – an exceptional interruption of a wider pattern of disengagement. Real religious intensity, argued William James in his influential *The Varieties of Religious Experience,* has always been a rare phenomenon – the province of spiritual athletes.[20] It is dangerous to take a period like the Victorian religious 'boom', or the English Civil War, as some sort of standard to define the present. And it is misleading to characterise the waning of such intensity as some sort of onrush of secularisation.

Cox always regretted the fact that his publisher would not agree to calling his book on twentieth century religion 'Sleeping in on Sundays'. There was no widespread revolt against Christianity among the middle and working classes in the early twentieth century, but a developing unease and distaste.[21] People found other things to do on Sundays: 'digging the garden, visiting relatives, or snoozing over the *News of the World*'.[22] Simon Green's research on West Yorkshire and Hugh McLeod's recent work on the so-called religious crisis of the 1960s has offered a similar picture. People did not stop going to church because they no longer believed, they just stopped going to church.[23] And far from the alarmist conclusions of the crisis literature, McLeod suggests that the real significance of the 1960s was the end of Christendom, that long dance with power that started with Constantine in the fourth century.[24] And, given the emergence of new Christian forms from the shadows of Christendom in this period, the language of 'death' is grossly overstated. As another scholar has recently argued, Christian revival in the late twentieth century is too substantial to be dismissed as a trivial countertrend: 'It is unsatisfactory simply to regard signs of continuing religious vitality as isolationist exceptions that prove the rule.' Many of these so-called exceptions, such as the 'growing charismatic churches of the 1970s and 80s', actually 'reflected the surrounding culture' that was supposedly their

[19] J. Obelkevich, *Religion and Rural Society, South Lindsey, 1825–1875* (Oxford: Clarendon Press, 1976).

[20] W. James, *The Varieties of Religious Experience* (London: Harvard University Press, 1985).

[21] Cox, *The English Churches in a Secular Society.*

[22] H. McLeod, *Religion and the Working Class in Nineteenth-Century Britain* (London: Macmillan, 1984): 66.

[23] S. Green, *Religion in the Age of Decline: Organisation and Experience in Industrial Yorkshire, 1870–1920* (Cambridge: CUP, 2003).

[24] H. McLeod, *The Religious Crisis of the 1960s* (Oxford: OUP, 2007).

nemesis, not least in their music.[25] Wider studies of the 1960s have similarly questioned the 'cataclysm' thesis, suggesting more organic and gradual change and anything but a flood of secularism or defiant paganism.[26] The sexual revolution, argues Sandbrook, took place in the newspapers, not in bedrooms. The 'swinging sixties' was a strictly metropolitan affair and the miniskirt took a long time to reach places like Hull. The more serious point is that we have to be wary of language of 'revolution' and 'crisis' which may bear little relation to the reality of cultural change. Callum Brown's influential book on *The Death of Christian Britain* rests its case on the power of 'discursive change' – the breakdown of 'discourses' of religion and femininity.[27] But, as I have argued elsewhere, his linguistic approach exaggerates the religious potency of 'Christian Britain' in the period before the crisis and overstates the power of the so-called 'sexual revolution' of the 1960s.[28] The secularisation literature has pounced on the language of crisis and statistical decline to build a picture of finality that the sources will not justify.[29] The secularisation literature implied a drama of resistance that never quite materialised. Pockets of aggressive *secularism* – real and dynamic in their way – should not be confused with a dominant secularity. As a student of mine commented on the 'new atheism' literature some years ago: 'you don't beat a dead horse'. Secularism itself is a kind of testimony to the failure of secularisation theory. Religion is attacked because it has refused to dissolve into the late-modern ether.

Like the onset of industrialism that was initially feared to herald Christianity's demise, late-modern pluralism has failed to operate as a decisive solvent of faith. Although countries such as Canada and European nations dominated by a single, confessional church, have suffered dramatically since the 1960s,[30] Britain's situation is far more positive. To compare either the statistics or the

---

[25] J. Wolffe, 'Religion and "Secularization"', in J. Strange and F. Carnevali (eds), *Twentieth-Century Britain: Economic, Cultural and Social Change*, second edition (Harlow: Pearson/Longman, 2007): 336.

[26] D. Sandbrook, *White Heat: A History of Britain in the Swinging Sixties* (London: Little Brown, 2006).

[27] C. Brown, *The Death of Christian Britain: Understanding Secularisation 1800–2000* (London: Routledge, 2000).

[28] See the introduction in D. Erdozain, *The Problem of Pleasure: Sport, Recreation and the Crisis of Victorian Religion* (Woodbridge: Boydell, 2010).

[29] A point well made in J. Morris, 'The Strange Death of Christian Britain: Another Look at the Secularization Debate', *The Historical Journal*, 46.4 (December 2003): 963–76.

[30] S. Bruce, 'Secularisation in the UK and the USA'; C. Sommerville, 'Happy in the State of Denmark', *Books & Culture*, 16.3 (June 2010), available at http://www.booksandculture.com/articles/2010/mayjun/happystatedenmark.html accessed 12 September 2013.

cultural resonance of Christianity in modern Britain to the experience of a country like Denmark is again to question the value of a normative language of secularisation. The contrast between Canada and the USA, where pluralism has stimulated, rather than weakened, historic patterns of revival and reinvention, is a reminder that nations develop their own spiritual ecologies. Although we can say with confidence that authoritarian confessional regimes (e.g., France) have adapted less favourably to modernity than decentralised, pluralistic ones (USA), it remains essential to explore the texture and theology of specific contexts. My objection to the sociological literature is not merely the macro analysis of decline, crudely applied across multiple cultures. It is the fact that, even when sociologists wish to emphasise revival, they tend to imply that 'modernity' itself has thrown up new religious forms as some sort of spontaneous 'process'. Structures take the place of people.[31] You can read for pages in such studies before encountering a human being, such as John Wesley or Jonathan Edwards, to mention merely the famous. And you can read entire books without a single mention of the theology involved in these 'surprising' works of modernity. Instead of regarding the evangelical revival of the eighteenth and nineteenth centuries and the charismatic movement of the late-twentieth, as throwbacks or survivals, I want to argue that they injected new life into Christendom and established hitherto neglected – even alien – Christian values. One reason why the secularisation narrative is, in my view, so out of step with reality is its failure to address ethical dimensions of religion. If pre-modern religion was, as Delumeau has extensively demonstrated, characterised by fear, persecution and hierarchy, we need to treat its Christian credentials with more caution. Correspondingly, a period of revival may be more than the recycling of old themes. If, for the sake of argument, we accept Delumeau's summary of pre-modern religion as a guilt culture dominated by 'Manichaeism, magic and fear', we can see that the Wesleyan revival addressed two of these demons head on: magic and fear. Having written on the history of Christianity and sport, however, I can affirm with depressing certainty that Manichaeism survived the evangelical revival. But this is where the late twentieth century is particularly interesting. It may be that, in the midst of all the talk of the 1960s' watershed, this was when the churches finally came to terms with the goodness of the body and creation. Cultural accommodations that one kind of scholar wishes to label secularisation may be anything but.

First the evangelical revival – as the work of Walsh, Bebbington and Hempton has shown, there was an innocence and generosity in the eighteenth

[31] P. Berger, G. Davie and E. Fokas, *Religious America, Secular Europe? A Theme and Variation* (Aldershot: Ashgate, 2008).

century revivals that did not always survive evangelicalism's transition to cultural dominance in the nineteenth century. David Bebbington has shown how the early evangelical mood of optimism and hopefulness was fertilised by Enlightenment thought, especially the psychology of John Locke. Wesley and Edwards learnt from Locke that ideas – including religious ideas – needed to be linked to experience. And experience could be trusted. The evangelical certainty of salvation, Bebbington brilliantly demonstrated, owed much to this Lockean vogue for linking knowledge to feeling or experience.[32] Bebbington's thesis that the evangelical movement was a 'child of Enlightenment' and not merely a variation on Protestant themes current since the early Reformation has been controversial. But to look at the pastoral theology of the movement is to confirm the bold thesis of 'discontinuity' – that the revival was really something new. He cites numerous examples of people converted not so much from a life of sin but from a religion of fear, the classic example being Jonathan Edwards's work in encouraging parishioners to believe that their 'quickened affections' for God were not cruel delusions but sure signs of a true faith. John Walsh's work on the origins of the revival highlighted the 'unexpected resonance' of the evangelical gospel in communities ravaged by fear and fatalism. Walsh strongly contrasts the Wesleyan emphasis on mercy with the Reformed obsession with judgement and uncertainty.[33]

I did not grasp the force of this contrast until I had read both Delumeau's *Sin and Fear* and a book by John Stachniewski called *The Persecutory Imagination,* a study of the psychological influence of Calvinism in the early modern period.[34] Stachniewski provides examples of clergy arriving in parishes to find the entire church body not merely anxious about salvation, but convinced that they were damned. He cites two academic studies on suicide, both of which described the predestinarian fear of damnation as the primary factor in the rise of the phenomenon in the seventeenth century. It is uncomfortable reading. 'Many actual suicides resulted from religious despair. Cambridge was notorious for them in the 1580s and 1590s, the period of its greatest domination by puritan

---

[32] D. Bebbington, *Evangelicalism in Modern Britain: A History from the 1730s to the 1980s* (London: Unwin Hyman, 1989).

[33] J. Walsh, '"Methodism" and the Origins of English Speaking Evangelicalism', in M. Noll, D. Bebbington, and G. Rawlyk, *Evangelicalism: Comparative Studies of Popular Protestantism in North America, the British Isles and Beyond, 1700–1990* (Oxford: OUP, 1994): 19–37.

[34] J. Stachniewski, *The Persecutory Imagination: English Puritanism and the Literature of Religious Despair* (USA: OUP, 1991).

preaching.'[35] Stachniewski quotes Richard Hooker gently introducing a sermon on the subject of doubt with the implicit acknowledgement that his listeners had been taught to interpret doubt as a sign of reprobation.[36] Puritanism, recent research has shown, was a more complex phenomenon than some of the darker accounts would imply.[37] Yet there can be no doubt that the British experience of the religious anxiety that Delumeau considered typical of the period was intensified by Calvinist theology. As a scholar as distinguished as Blair Worden has written: 'The volume of despair engendered by Puritan teaching on predestination is incalculable.'[38] The evangelical revival was not a continuation of this discourse. It was an assault. The sentiments that inspired philosophers such as Spinoza and Voltaire to repudiate Augustinian orthodoxy as a religion of fear and mental decay found direct analogues in Arminian reactions to Calvinism in England and the Netherlands.[39]

Walsh took up this theme in his analysis of the revival, showing how Reformed theology acted as an all-too-vigorous 'law' to Methodist grace. Catholic holiness literature also played a part, but it was the fatalism implicit in predestinarian theology that consistently led to despair. It is interesting that both Stachniewski and Delumeau cite Robert Burton's vast study, *The Anatomy of Melancholy,* which sought to diagnose the origins of this 'cruel' and 'epidemical disease', which 'crucifies the Soule in this life and everlastingly torments in the world to come'.[40] 'Religious melancholics' occupied a large section in the book, their condition characterised by extreme habits of self-mortification and by excessive fear of God. Burton left the question tantalisingly unresolved as to whether it was 'original sin' itself, or the *doctrine* of original sin, as then proclaimed, that had turned humankind 'the miracle of nature' into a miserable being. This, as Delumeau recognised, was profoundly ambiguous: are we miserable because of the raw logic of our nature, or because of something Pascal said?

The breathless relief of eighteenth century conversion narratives is a commentary on the transition from fear to joy. Charles Wesley roundly mocked

---

[35] Ibid: 50.

[36] Ibid: 53.

[37] J. Coffey, *John Goodwin and the Puritan Revolution: Religion and Intellectual Change in Seventeenth-Century England* (Woodbridge: Tamesis Books, 2008).

[38] Blair Worden quoted in Stachniewski, *The Persecutory Imagination*: 1.

[39] I explore this theme extensively in my forthcoming OUP book, *The Soul of Doubt: The Religious Roots of Unbelief.*

[40] J.B. Bamborough, 'Burton, Robert (1577–1640)', in *Oxford Dictionary of National Biography*, edited by H.C.G. Matthew and Brian Harrison (Oxford: OUP, 2004). Online edition edited by Lawrence Goldman, October 2009, available at http://www.oxforddnb.com accessed 27 March 2013.

Calvinist notions of a limited atonement in many of his hymns,[41] while the gaiety of the class meeting and the Love Feast was integral to the new revival culture. Walsh has shown how acutely the Wesleyan emphasis on free grace spoke to a generation terrorised by punitive holiness traditions and an ever-uncertain soteriology. He summarised the tension by saying that the culture of rigour aroused 'aspirations that it did not satisfy'. As he explained: 'There was a certain joylessness in the call to a regime of unrelenting worship, closet devotion, introspection, and asceticism; it conveyed an anxiety-inducing severity'. It is not surprising that many Christians, High Church or Reformed, were beginning 'to buckle under the psychic strain'.[42] Walsh quotes the account of one convert who spoke of the 'joy and wonder' of grasping 'the doctrines of the Saviour' and the immediate reality of forgiveness: 'This was to us all something so new, unexpected, joyful, penetrating.'[43] Meanwhile, a London Dissenter (also quoted by Walsh) explained in a letter to his pastor in 1743 that the new evangelical preaching was 'more directly adapted to my present wants than any I can hear in town'; it offered an immediate deliverance from the power of sin, while the Calvinism of the Dissenters offered only a life of constant mourning over inward depravity, which was 'like a general's commanding his soldiers to fight on towards taking … a city and at the same time telling them they must never expect to take it'. As Walsh notes, this was an emphasis that reflected the core theology of the revival. Wesley 'urged his preachers to avoid what he saw as the Puritanical overemphasis on divine wrath and to stress the joy of belief; they should hammer home the message that 'a believer walking in the light is inexpressibly great and happy'.[44] The notion that 'Holiness is happiness' has been interpreted as the fundamental principle of Wesley's theology.[45] Its pastoral potency cannot be doubted. Any reader of Jonathan Edwards on the 'religious affections' will see how intimately the so-called 'Great awakening' was linked to a spirituality of joy and mercy. As has often been remarked, Edwards's notorious sermon, '*Sinners in the Hands of an Angry God*' was unrepresentative of his genre. In stark contrast to Reformed estimates, one of Edwards' American disciples calculated that the proportion of the lost to the saved would eventually be in the ratio of 1 to 17,456 1/3.[46] To compare this outlook with the situation 20 years earlier, when Edwards' father, Timothy, was turning away anxious souls, refusing to admit

41 Bebbington, *Evangelicalism in Modern Britain*: 67.
42 Walsh, 'Methodism': 25–6.
43 Ibid: 27.
44 Ibid: 29–30.
45 Bebbington, *Evangelicalism in Modern Britain*: 60.
46 Ibid.

them to church membership until they had demonstrated all the prescribed 'stages' of conversion, is to recognise a sea-change in pastoral theology. Edwards' ruminations on the legitimacy, indeed the necessity, of the spiritual 'affections' served – in George Marsden's marvellous phrase – 'to redirect the course of Christendom'.[47] The idea that God loves people may be among the underrated forces of historical change.

One of the most emblematic sermons of the early nineteenth century was from Thomas Chalmers, entitled '*The expulsive power of a new affection*', in which he argued against cultural aggression – aimed at the 'demons' of wealth, pleasure or power and urging instead a preaching of the superior merits of Christ, the true object of human affection. It was a message increasingly ignored in subsequent decades but it demonstrates that the emphasis on love, mercy and reconciliation remained central to the evangelical revival even as it entered its phase of cultural dominance. From the 1830s, this attitude was perhaps eclipsed by a mood of aggression, stimulated by secular and theological counter-attack. Charisma was, to borrow Max Weber's phrase, 'routinised', and the revival's animating tension between 'freedom' and 'discipline' played out on the latter side. A starchy moralism and a proud orthodoxy too often became the evangelical calling cards. Yet it is striking how emphatically even a Calvinist like Spurgeon owed his success to a return to the amiability of the early revival. Spurgeon would often remark that the Bible was better than 'our orthodoxy', and his preaching conveyed a kind of reparative tone, a mood of constant and necessary reappraisal. God is approachable. He forgives. To quote his sermon on the 'Approachableness of Jesus':

> The door of his house of mercy is set wide open. Over the lintel of his palace gate is written, "For every one that asketh receiveth; and he that seeketh findeth; and to him that knocketh it shall be opened" ... You, poor trembling sinner, come to him; come to him now, for he has said, "Him that cometh to me I will in no wise cast out". Oh! if your eyes were opened to behold him, you would perceive that the glory of his person lies not in the splendour which repels, but in the majesty which divinely attracts.[48]

---

[47] G. Marsden, *Jonathan Edwards: A Life*, first edition (London: Yale University Press, 2003): 58.

[48] C.H. Spurgeon, 'The Approachableness of Jesus', A Sermon Delivered on Sunday Evening, 3 May 1868, available at http://www.spurgeon.org/lk15_1.htm accessed 12 September 2013.

Spurgeon also revived the much-troubled connection between holiness and happiness. 'No one has succeeded like him in sketching the comic side of repentance and regeneration,' gushed a glowing piece on the jovial evangelist in *Vanity Fair* in 1870. Spurgeon was a new kind of Puritan and a necessary one at a time when evangelical might was increasingly misused in the public sphere.[49] His willingness to preach in music halls, racecourses and at the notorious, Sunday-opening Crystal Palace attracted fierce criticism at the time. He grasped what a mind as subtle as F.D. Maurice's had perceived many years earlier: that to defend the Lord's Day is not always to defend the Lord. As Owen Chadwick and others have contended: you can write the story of church decline around the basic narrative of nineteenth century Sabbatarianism, hostility to pleasure and the implicit theology this conveyed.[50]

This is why, if I may fast-forward to the 1960s, the theology of the charismatic revival has such important implications for the wider church. Reading a figure like David Watson first hand, or scholarly accounts of the movement as a whole, is to be struck by the energy with which Christians of the period were trying to repent of theological suspicion of the flesh. If the evangelical revival, at its best, challenged two of Delumeau's demons – magic and fear – offering a piety at once rational and joyous, the charismatic movement appeared finally to address Manichaeism. As Bebbington has argued, use of the body in worship was the defiant symbol of the movement, followed by guitars, canary yellow suits, and a *joie de vivre* that could stretch to the consumption of ice cream on Sundays. As Wolffe and Hutchinson suggest in a new volume on *Global Evangelicalism*, the charismatic Christian of the late twentieth century was 'an evangelical who is happy about something'.[51] As a Scottish newspaper alluded to the vigorous energy of one charismatic service, this was 'a form of worship bordering on the supernatural'.[52] Yet there was also something unapologetically 'natural' about the new movement. Here was a theology that not only addressed the neglected left side of the brain but also some of the bits below. Michael Harper, one of the leaders of the movement, characterised it in terms of a reaction to a flesh-cutting dualism that stretched back to Aristotle.[53] There was a serious point to the movement's much-contested embrace of pop music and pop culture.

---

[49] J. Mill, *On Liberty* (London: John W Parker & Son, 1859).

[50] Erdozain, *The Problem of Pleasure*.

[51] M. Hutchinson and J. Wolffe, *A Short History of Global Evangelicalism* (New York: CUP, 2012): 22.

[52] Bebbington, *Evangelicalism in Modern Britain*: 227.

[53] Ibid: 240.

Such an attitude was a notable feature of David Watson's ministry at St Michael-le-Belfry in York, where he encouraged Christian involvement in the arts and was instrumental in the formation of the Riding Lights Theatre Company. An uncontroversial and much-emulated enterprise now, the Riding Lights were greeted with profound ambivalence at their launch. From sarcastic pamphlets, entitled 'And shall we dance?' to the frequent censure that a Christian theatre company is not worthy of the name if it fails to preach the gospel in every performance, the history of the company is a fascinating essay on the emergence of a theology of creation. If art is worth doing, it is worth doing well, with or without a clear, didactic payload. The irony of such criticisms, of course, is that groups like Riding Lights have grown symbiotically with the emergence of more culture-friendly evangelism, epitomised by the phenomenon of the Alpha course. I met a woman in Cambridge who told me that one of the most vivid memories of growing up in Scotland in the 1960s was the sight of the swings in the public playground chained together on the Sabbath. If the reaction to this kind of attitude was merely tactical and symbolic, it would be significant, but I am sure that it is more than that. Trends that one school of theology is inclined to denigrate as liberalisation, and sociologists to identify as secularisation, may even be better described as Christianisation.

I recently reviewed several books on secularisation for a historical journal, the material written variously by historians, sociologists, philosophers and theologians. It was a revelation to discover how closely the arguments of the secularisation gurus and the doom-laden analysis of certain theologians dovetailed. Both wanted to argue that the late-modern rapprochement between Christianity and culture as typified by the American megachurch was to all intents and purposes an expression of secularisation. Modern Christians wear make-up and dance, according to one highly influential sociologist. Case closed.[54] Another attempted to argue that Christian organisations block-booking movie theatres for their own evangelistic events was a form of 'social or everyday secularisation' – a capitulation to a dominant secular culture.[55] Meanwhile a leading theologian argued from a stance of architectural determinism that megachurches were secular spaces.[56] In *The Transformation of American Christianity,* Alan Wolfe offered similar criticism, quoting theologians to affirm

---

[54] Bruce, *Secularization*: 162.

[55] B. Turner, *Religion and Modern Society: Citizenship, Secularization and the State* (CUP, 2011): 211.

[56] J. Milbank, 'A Closer Walk on the Wild Side', in M. Warner, J. VanAntwerpen, and C. Calhoun (eds), *Varieties of Secularism in a Secular Age* (Cambridge, MA: Harvard University Press, 2010): 62.

that this kind of post-charismatic seeker-sensitive religion is a practicing of the culture, not the faith.[57] But who can say what is religious or secular in such contexts? If the film being screened in the 'secular' environment happens to be Mel Gibson's *The Passion of the Christ,* the argument for secularity appears weak. Similarly, the notion that the Alpha movement can be dismissed as a 'McDonaldisation' of Christianity, sacrificing content for access, must be treated with caution. If you want to find a master-cause for the problem of religious alienation, you are more likely to find it in a theology that could leave a Victorian child without 'the faintest idea how to "play"' than in the twentieth-century reaction.[58] Any theory that modern Christianity has lost the disciplines of an older, more rigorous piety must confront the evangelical disaster of dualism and flesh-denial as exemplified by certain strains of Victorianism. Clearly the 1960s introduced ideas and values that have created new barriers to Christian faith. But the relationship should not be expressed as simple decay. Similarly, the decline in explicit religious belief and affiliation should not be interpreted as cold, de-Christianisation. As John Stackhouse argued at a conference on secularism a few years ago, numerical decline needs to be set against a context of cultural change that has often seen Christian values incarnated even as their intellectual or political foundations have been undermined. Canada in 2009, he suggested, is in many ways a more Christian culture than it was in 1900, if by 'Christian' we consider values of equality, human rights and universal welfare. This is not to diminish the missionary challenge. It is to say that a narrative of doom is unfaithful to the spiritual chiaroscuro of modern culture.

Perhaps the greatest weakness of recent writing on secularisation is the failure to acknowledge the variety and eclecticism of modern culture, the crude assumption that everyone thinks in broadly secular ways. The chief value of Charles Taylor's enormous *A Secular Age* (2007) is the sense of open-endedness with which he characterises the modern 'conditions' of belief and unbelief. We are blown from different directions. There is no single experience of modernity. Taylor paints with a broad brush and he has little to say about the particular theologies of revival, but he helpfully conveys the shallowness of 'death of God' narratives. Religion may be just one 'option' for the late-modern citizen – but it remains a compelling one for many.[59] Taylor's remarks on the 'expressive revolution' of the 1960s, and Christianity's need to come to terms with sex

[57] A. Wolfe, *The Transformation of American Religion: How We Actually Live Our Faith* (New York: Free Press, 2003).

[58] E. Gosse, *Father and Son: A Study of Two Temperaments*, New edition (London: Penguin Classics, 1989): 138.

[59] C. Taylor, *A Secular Age* (Cambridge, MA: Belknap, 2007).

and sexuality are, to my mind, simplistic in their assumption that theology just needs to get over its vestigial scruples. The discussion is certainly undeveloped. But the general point tallies with what I have suggested about the charismatic movement: Christianity has too often operated with what one might term a 'joy deficit' – a default stance of severity and asceticism.[60] Megachurches offering fun and fellowship, perhaps bending the knee to youth and gently disdaining arbitrary theologies of judgement have to be seen in a wider historical context of reaction and repair. They cannot be seen as secularisation. Similarly, while the informal and conversational tone of such ministries has invited charges of theological attenuation and 'dumbing down', growing concerns for social action and justice must be set against any such criticism.[61]

Nostalgia, it is often said, is a permanent temptation of the Christian mind. It is easy to look back on times when the building blocks of Christian faith were as ubiquitous as church spires on the landscape, when evangelism was the reawakening of something that had never died. But any true vision of the past must account for the anxiety that lived alongside piety and acknowledge the ways in which Christian cultural presence was bought at the cost of essential constituents of the faith. Histories that trace a narrative of decline from eras in which persecution was a staple of Christian order and salvation conceived as escape from life itself are looking at the matter the wrong way round. And if we consider the degree to which churchgoing, as late as the nineteenth century, could be a matter of social obligation rather than spiritual conviction, the narrative of doom weakens further. The past was not as uniformly Christian as social memory would suggest and the modern period has been anything but secular. Church growth in the eighteenth and nineteenth centuries set the tone for British life in the Victorian period and beyond.[62] And while the figures broadly speak of decline in the twentieth century, recent work has strongly demonstrated the reality of revival.[63] Christianity is not a monolith. Some of the most dynamic expressions of religious growth – house churches and unaffiliated fellowships – are least represented in statistical returns. Historians are not equipped to advise on theologies of growth or revival, but if there is a single lesson that emerges from studying the development of religious cultures over time it is the wisdom of the parable of the leaven, the invisible grandeur of

[60] I am grateful to my friend E. Phillips for this phrase, though he uses it in a slightly different sense to refer to modern culture as a whole.

[61] 'END IT: Shine a Light on Slavery', *END IT*, available at http://enditmovement.com/ accessed 20 November 2013.

[62] Brown, *The Death of Christian Britain*.

[63] D. Goodhew, *Church Growth in Britain* (Aldershot: Ashgate, 2012).

spiritual growth. George Eliot described the influence of one of her heroines as profound and 'incalculably diffusive', though 'not widely visible' – like a river spending 'itself in channels which had no great name on the earth', a chain of small, 'unhistoric acts' which have slowly changed the world.[64] Samuel Butler wrote similarly that 'true greatness wears an invisible cloak, under cover of which it goes in and out among men without being suspected'.[65] These are, I think, deeply historical and theological sentiments, reminders that the real drama of historical change is not coterminous with public credibility or statistical muscle, reminders that influence is not synonymous with power. A true history of Christianity would have more to say about the invisible great than the visible good, and a true theology of church growth would not fret over numbers. When the outlook appears bleak, when the figures scream 'crisis', that may just be the signal to carry on.

---

64 G. Eliot, *Middlemarch* (London: Penguin, 1994): 795.

65 S. Butler, *The Way of All Flesh* (Harmondsworth: Penguin, 1966): 123.

Conclusion
Transformed, not Conformed: Towards a Theology of Church Growth

David Goodhew

> Dee dee was a member of church in Durham, England. Dee dee came up to Durham from Southend at the age of 50. She had been mentally unwell for most of her life, and had been "in the system", i.e., receiving psychiatric care for the last 40 years. When she first came to Durham, she was too socially anxious to go out at all by herself. Her confidence and self-esteem were both on rock bottom. Dee dee came to church and found faith, forgiveness and healing and was discharged from mental health services. Dee dee said that when she first started coming to church, she felt "loved". She also said that because of the love of Jesus, she felt she wanted to give that love out too. She was not well educated, could not read or write very well and in the last year of her life, she had severe physical health problems. But she led bible studies with a group of people, including homeless people. She befriended them and showed hospitality, love and friendship. She always told them about Jesus and used to say "What He did for me, He can do for you".[1]

The above words were written for Dee dee's recent funeral, an occasion at once deeply sad and yet mixed in with joy, too. Dee dee's level of education was much less than that of the readers of this book, but her understanding of Jesus and Christian community has much to teach us. Not everyone speaks as warmly of church as she did, but her comments are a reminder of the concrete blessings of Christian community. The good news of Jesus *is* good news. It offers purpose in a life that can seem random; forgiveness in a world where there is much blame and it offers hope of life beyond death in a world haunted by the fact of mortality. Whilst the value of following Jesus and being part of a Christian community is intrinsic to those practices, it is pertinent to note that such practices correlate

[1] 'Recollections of Dee dee' by Chris Gates-Jamieson, used with permission.

strongly with secular measures of 'well-being'. The leading anthropologist, Tanya Luhrmann, speaks of how:

> What one might call an avalanche of medical data has demonstrated that, for reasons still poorly understood, those who attend church and believe in God are healthier and happier and live longer that those who do not.[2]

Dee dee's individual story embodies why growing Christian churches is good. And her story finds echoes in the lives of many individuals – both now and in past centuries, both in the west and across the globe. The Christian faith holds that the good news of Jesus, whilst it has to be received as an individual, can be received *only* in a community. So, growing such communities multiplies such blessing. To keep the good news to oneself would be both mistaken and selfish. A person cannot have Christ on their own, as a kind of '"diet-plan" for the soul'.[3] The wine of Christian faith always bursts the individualist wine-skin. God loves individual human beings *and* God loves Christian congregations. So the numerical growing of congregations is a godly and essential means of mediating that love.

Dee dee's experience chimes with the heart of the Christian theology. It is striking how high a view the New Testament has both of the most humble of individual believers and of the most humble local communities of faith. This is so despite the New Testament's frequent references to the failings of New Testament churches. It is striking given the often low status of many church members and the opprobrium they frequently attracted from wider society. Yet these local communities are lauded as Christ's body, as communities of saints, as a royal priesthood and in many other deeply affirming descriptions. Consequently, as the chapters by Bonnington and Rowe show, the New Testament put a very high value of the numerical growth of such local congregations. The tendency to focus on 'kingdom' as the primary Biblical category in a way that downplays the local congregation is itself profoundly unbiblical.

McGrath's, Warner's and Tomlin's chapters have shown how not only the New Testament but core Christian doctrines possess a similarly high view of local congregations and therefore support the numerical growth of such communities. Eschatology, the doctrine of the incarnation and pneumatology are worked out in local communities of faith and believing in such doctrines requires working

[2] T. Luhrmann, *When God Talks Back: Understanding the American Evangelical Relationship with God* (New York: Vintage Books, 2012): 331.

[3] B.A. Harvey, quoted in V. Karkkainen, *An Introduction to Ecclesiology: Ecumenical, Historical and Global Perspectives* (Downers Grove: IVP 2002): 228.

to grow such communities of faith. Conversely, one inescapable aspect of much (though far from all) modern theology, which assumes local churches cannot or even should not grow, is its startlingly low view of local congregations – which are sometimes portrayed merely as a resource for other purposes, rather than good in themselves. Such theological pessimism about local congregations often flows from the influence of secular eschatology so prominent in academia and media – an eschatology which assumes local churches must decline and cannot grow – rather than the eschatology of the Christian faith.

The Christian tradition, likewise, has a deep concern for – and considerable wisdom about – the practice of church growth. As the Orthodox writer Alexsei Khomiakov states, no one is saved alone, an echo of John Wesley's comment that there is no such thing as a solitary Christian. Davidson, Ward, Threlfall-Holmes, Null and Erdozain have touched on a handful of figures within church history, largely from the western tradition. Even from this limited survey it is clear that key figures – from the early Christians to the Celtic saints to St Francis, from Thomas Cranmer to the Wesleys – focussed far more on the numerical growth of the church than is often recognised. To say this has profound consequences for all who seek to be 'Celtic', 'Franciscan', 'Anglican' or 'Methodist'. Contemporary Christianity can distort a range of Christian traditions by airbrushing out their deep commitment to the numerical growth of the local church. Conversely, proper fidelity to Christian tradition, whichever the specific tradition from which one springs, requires a readiness to recognise and emulate that tradition's attempts to grow the church numerically. Decline theology is often detached from, or distorts, church tradition.

To say all this is not to say – *at any point* – that 'bums on seats' are *all* that matter. The threefold definition of growth in the Christian life cited in the introduction – which sees such growth as encompassing numerical growth of congregations *and* growth in personal holiness *and* growth in societal transformation – is the context in which any theology of church growth needs to be formed.[4] And the chapters of this volume have crucial insights into how the pursuit of numerical growth of congregations has to be conducted within the wider context of Christian theology and living. In particular, Bonnington's, Rowe's and Davidson's chapters on the early church show how acts of mercy and the sharing of one's faith went together continuously in the first centuries of the church. There is considerable evidence across contemporary churches to

[4] Address by the Most Rev Rowan Williams to General Synod, 23 November 2010, available at http://rowanwilliams.archbishopofcanterbury.org/articles.php/919/archbishops-presidential-address-general-synod-november-2010 accessed 30 October 2013.

suggest that the same is true today. Any church which seeks numerical expansion yet ignores societal transformation has an emaciated understanding of growth in the Christian life. But the reverse is also true. Churches which seek the amelioration of their societies yet make little effort to help individuals come to faith in Christ and little or no effort to grow and proliferate congregations have a similarly stunted grasp of the gospel.

The range of authors in this volume is broad. It would be hard to find them rubbing shoulders in any other context. The authors come from the range of 'tribes' that make up the contemporary church – evangelical, catholic, liberal, charismatic. These tribes can be found as denominations but just as much within denominations. What is striking is the deep unanimity between the different scholars on the legitimacy and importance of numerical growth of the local church. Whether coming from a deeply catholic stress on sacraments to a charismatic stress on being open to the Holy Spirit, to an evangelical stress on the importance of scripture to a liberal stress on community there is a strong case for seeing numerical church growth as vital. At the same time each tradition brings particular insights that others need. For example, Sr Benedicta Ward's stress on the centrality of contemplative prayer leavens Graham Tomlin's stress on Pentecostal invocation of the Holy Spirit – and *vice versa*. The chapters in this volume sound distinctive notes but there is an underlying harmony centred around building local communities of Christian believers. Here is a modest, missional ecumenism. It gains its energy from a common focus on mission. It has no answers to the ongoing divisions over church order, ethics and theology – but it is hardly alone in lacking such answers. It offers an implicit ecumenical agenda which recognises how differently Christian traditions see many issues, but focuses on strands common to us all – such as scripture, doctrine, history, sacraments, prayer and, above all, the centrality of the local congregation as the local focus of faith.

On the cover of this volume a baptism is depicted. Baptism is at the heart of the theology of church growth. Baptism is rooted in scripture, is a junction box for Christian doctrines and has been practiced across the centuries and across a huge range of Christian traditions. It combines word and action. It links individual faith and the community of believers. And if the church is to grow, especially in the west, baptism will need to be practiced energetically in the future. It is striking that the word 'sacramental' is often used, wrongly, as a synonym for the word 'eucharistic'. Christians may disagree as to the number of sacraments, but the vast majority accept that baptism is as fully a sacrament as communion. Emphasising communion more than baptism is, thus, to be less than fully sacramental. Baptism in the late modern west is increasingly an act of subversion. It is the action of those who seek a Lord who is not the ruler of this world. Moving towards a theology of church growth means moving towards a much stronger theology and much more energetic practice of baptism.

Areas for Further Research

This volume has value as a set of pointers towards a theology of church growth. Many key aspects of theology have not been addressed. Part of the role of this conclusion is to flag further areas which might profitably be explored.

The Bible is central to the discussion of church growth and deserves much fuller discussion than has been possible here. This volume has no discussion of the Old Testament and church growth – how the first Christian communities depended on and developed the insights of the Old Testament. New Testament views on church growth need to be understood from that perspective. Whilst this volume explores the relationship of 'kingdom' and 'church', there is much more to be said on this subject. Modern discussions of 'kingdom' have substantial limitations embedded in them and the discussion of numerical church growth brings such limitations to the fore – notably a highly unbiblical tendency to split off the socio-economic consequences of discipleship from local congregations and from the individual's relationship with Christ. The common tendency to see evangelism, catechesis and social action as distinct things is hard to justify Biblically. Key places to dig further are the two books, Luke and Acts. Here is a huge slice of the New Testament, comprising a gospel shot through with kingdom language whose sequel is shot through with stress on numerical church growth. Since Luke and Acts managed to hold kingdom and church growth together, they could help us to do the same.

This volume could be taken further by wider engagement between doctrinal theology and church growth. A key task is the deeper exploration of the historical backdrop of modern theology. It is likely that many other modern western theologians, aside from those mentioned here, have internalised the secular eschatology of the age and then produced 'decline theology' consciously and unconsciously in their work. Much (though by no means all) modern theology is underpinned by a theological fatalism that has assumed that the church cannot grow, sometimes combined with an illusory picture of previous centuries as times when 'everybody went to church'. This is often supplemented by an excess of theological scrupulosity, in which seeking the numerical growth of congregations is seen as a minor, or even dubious, theme compared to other supposedly more pressing matters. This easily becomes an ecclesiology of fatalism in which it is assumed that local churches *must* decline numerically. Discerning the genesis and nature of decline theology is an urgent task for contemporary theology since it continues to warp theology and stunt congregations.

One of the many large gaps in this volume is the lack of sustained engagement with atonement. It is striking to note how offensive the cross seemed to the cultures surrounding the churches of the first centuries, how central the atoning work of Christ on the cross was to those communities and how continually it fed into the extent and nature of the church growth that they experienced. These centuries saw a parallel stress on the incarnation. A theology of church growth needs to avoid slipping into an unbiblical division of incarnation and atonement, cradle and cross – instead assisting in the work of enabling these two key theological 'pistons' to fire in concert. More widely, ecclesiology and soteriology have to interpenetrate. Ecclesiology depends on soteriology and ecclesial communities are essential to the enfleshment of soteriology. Creating a theology of church growth requires deeper conversation between soteriology and ecclesiology. Remembering why is it good to follow Jesus leads into remembering why is it good to follow Jesus in community and thus why it is good for such communities to grow.

One of the many other ways in which the early Christian centuries have much to teach the contemporary church is the way in which other aspects of theology such as ethics and liturgy and the growth of the church were interlinked. A well-rounded view of 'kingdom' leads into an avoidance of a polarised ecclesiology in which one *either* tries to behave Christianly *or* tries to draw others into a relationship with Christ – when healthy congregations instinctively do both. The early centuries of Christianity offer multiple models where such a dichotomy breaks down – as do many churches outside the contemporary west. Sharing faith in Christ and sharing the love of Christ were and are inseparable – just as melody and rhythm are inseparable in a piece of music.

There is a substantial Christian tradition of universalism which is worthy of respect – but which is also worthy of questioning. The formation of a theology of church growth raises serious questions for universalism. Whilst it is possible to hold both to a belief in universal salvation and to the value of numerical church growth, the need for such growth is seriously diminished by universalism since, with universalism, everyone is or will eventually be a member of the church. Universalism has understandable appeal for its readiness to see the God-giveness within all people but, arguably, has a quasi-colonial quality (in the way it removes human freedom to choose or not choose faith); it has a questionable basis in the Bible and Christian tradition, a questionable downplaying of the human need for redemption and sanctification and a questionable relationship with contemporary western culture (with whose hyper-consumerism it conforms, arguably, rather too closely). Concern for church growth – and for a theology of church growth – requires careful consideration of the merits and demerits of universalism, whatever perspective is taken on this issue.

Just as this volume could be taken further by wider engagement with church doctrine, so it could be taken further by wider engagement between church history and church growth. Michael Green's volume, *Evangelism in the Early Church*,[5] was written over 40 years ago and for a popular audience. It has limitations but it stands out; first, because it asks the vital question, 'how did the early churches grow?' and second, because it splices socio-economic discussion with discussion of early church theology. There is a deep need for a successor to Green's volume – a successor which both emulates Green's discussion of how early churches grew and how the local church and early church theology related to one another and also engages deeply with the scholarly debates since the period in which *Evangelism in the Early Church* was first written. Such a study would be of inestimable value in any further discussion of a theology of church growth.

The first centuries of the church have a crucial importance in formulating a theology of church growth (an importance which is arguably increasing in a post-Constantinian world, which resembles the pre-Constantinian context more closely than that of Christendom). But the many other parts of church history not covered in this volume will contribute greatly towards the work of building a theology of church growth. There are many figures and movements within the Christian tradition currently valued for their insights into prayer, liturgy, works of mercy and theology whose writings and lives also have much to teach regarding the numerical growth of the church.

This volume has been written within a western context by authors based in Britain, Germany and America, mostly rooted in the historic denominations. There is no shame in this. But the volume would be markedly different – and better – had it included perspectives from beyond the western churches and more voices from beyond the historic denominations. Such perspectives would be all the more welcome since such regions and churches have more direct experience of church growth and are less encumbered by decline theology than the historic denominations of the west.

---

[5] M. Green, *Evangelism in the Early Church*, revised edition (Eastbourne: Kingsway, 2003).

Beyond a Conclusion

There are dangers in constructing a theology of numerical church growth. The statistical might or weakness of a movement is not the measure of its value in the sight of God. Growth in the Christian life is, overall, about growth of love for God *and* love for one's fellow human beings *and* the numerical growth of congregations – and yet, and yet ... Within the context of the late modern west it is a given that Christianity is rapidly on the way out. Most congregations in the west are not in danger of being swamped by church growth. Pointing out the dangers of numerical church growth to most western churches is like pointing out the dangers of obesity to the starving.

In the context of the west in the twenty-first century it makes more sense to see thinking about and working for numerical church growth as creative subversion. Many theologians, church leaders and congregations have been formed by academic and media narratives which assume that numerical church growth is both impossible and illegitimate. It is a core conviction of this volume that such a theology of decline is as theologically questionable as it is pastorally corrosive.

To assume that the church 'must' decline is to mistake the spectacles of late modern elite culture for holy writ. It is to elide a crude historical determinism with a western mindset. It is to misread the Bible, key doctrines of the Christian faith and great slabs of lived Christian experience profoundly – from the early centuries to the 'Celtic' saints to the mediaeval Franciscans, to the Reformers and to the experience of swathes of modern believers outside the west – whose vigorous and imaginative efforts to grow churches are thereby airbrushed out of history or smeared with the largely meaningless label of 'proselytism'.

This volume offers a counter-narrative to decline theology. That narrative has four basic strands: epistemology, scripture, doctrine and history. It argues that numerical church growth is epistemologically respectable and deeply rooted in scripture, doctrine and tradition. The theological importance of growing the church numerically deserves to be recognised. And the frequent side-lining or denigration of numerical church growth needs to be treated with a hermeneutic of suspicion. There are sensible reasons for concern about church growth, but such sidelining may also be based on the internalisation of elite culture and sheer fatalism. In many previous epochs, especially during the first decades and centuries of the Christian church, its numerical growth looked highly improbable and its demise highly likely. In many parts of the contemporary world Christians face major constraints and/or opposition but refuse to give up their faith and the church in many such areas is growing. Such Christians embody a narrative of resurrection, not death. The churches in the west could follow their example.

Talking about numerical church growth is theologically legitimate. And this matters hugely. A major piece of research commissioned by the Church of England emphasised that *intentionality* is crucial to church growth.[6] Churches tend to grow numerically when they *intend* to grow numerically – a conclusion echoed in this volume.[7] This begs a prior question – what fosters intentionality and what corrodes intentionality? Decline theology provides a powerful disincentive to numerical church growth. But a study of epistemology, the New Testament, Christian doctrine and Christian tradition provides strong buttresses for the intention of growing churches, a crucial precursor to numerical church growth.

If this volume's work towards a theology of church growth has value, then it has a further chapter – the acted narration of that theology in terms of congregations which grow in numerical size and proliferate in number. The task of enabling local churches to grow is a greater challenge than the writing of theology. But the writing of theology can aid the growth of local churches. Epistemology, the New Testament, Christian doctrine and the history of the church support the attempt to grow local congregations numerically, when seen within a wider framework of growth in the Christian life. Seeking such growth will require refusal to conform to culture and a readiness to transform culture. But growing Christian community always was creatively subversive.

---

6 *From Anecdote to Evidence: Findings from the Church Growth Research Programme* (Church Commissioners for England, 2014): 8–9.

7 See Threlfall-Holmes in this volume: 195.

Index